CENTRE FOR EDUCATIONAL RESEARCH AND INNOVATION

Equity in Education: Students with Disabilities, Learning Difficulties and Disadvantages

Statistics and Indicators

ORGANISATION FOR ECONOMIC CO-OPERATION AND DEVELOPMENT

ORGANISATION FOR ECONOMIC CO-OPERATION AND DEVELOPMENT

Pursuant to Article 1 of the Convention signed in Paris on 14th December 1960, and which came into force on 30th September 1961, the Organisation for Economic Co-operation and Development (OECD) shall promote policies designed:

- to achieve the highest sustainable economic growth and employment and a rising standard of living in member countries, while maintaining financial stability, and thus to contribute to the development of the world economy;
- to contribute to sound economic expansion in member as well as non-member countries in the process of economic development; and
- to contribute to the expansion of world trade on a multilateral, non-discriminatory basis in accordance with international obligations.

The original member countries of the OECD are Austria, Belgium, Canada, Denmark, France, Germany, Greece, Iceland, Ireland, Italy, Luxembourg, the Netherlands, Norway, Portugal, Spain, Sweden, Switzerland, Turkey, the United Kingdom and the United States. The following countries became members subsequently through accession at the dates indicated hereafter: Japan (28th April 1964), Finland (28th January 1969), Australia (7th June 1971), New Zealand (29th May 1973), Mexico (18th May 1994), the Czech Republic (21st December 1995), Hungary (7th May 1996), Poland (22nd November 1996), Korea (12th December 1996) and the Slovak Republic (14th December 2000). The Commission of the European Communities takes part in the work of the OECD (Article 13 of the OECD Convention).

The Centre for Educational Research and Innovation was created in June 1968 by the Council of the Organisation for Economic Co-operation and Development and all member countries of the OECD are participants.

The main objectives of the Centre are as follows:

- *analyse and develop research, innovation and key indicators in current and emerging education and learning issues, and their links to other sectors of policy;*
- *explore forward-looking coherent approaches to education and learning in the context of national and international cultural, social and economic change; and*
- *facilitate practical co-operation among member countries and, where relevant, with non-member countries, in order to seek solutions and exchange views of educational problems of common interest.*

The Centre functions within the Organisation for Economic Co-operation and Development in accordance with the decisions of the Council of the Organisation, under the authority of the Secretary-General. It is supervised by a Governing Board composed of one national expert in its field of competence from each of the countries participating in its programme of work.

Publié en français sous le titre :
Équité dans l'enseignement : Élèves présentant des déficiences, des difficultés et des désavantages sociaux

© OECD 2004

Permission to reproduce a portion of this work for non-commercial purposes or classroom use should be obtained through the Centre français d'exploitation du droit de copie (CFC), 20, rue des Grands-Augustins, 75006 Paris, France, tel. (33-1) 44 07 47 70, fax (33-1) 46 34 67 19, for every country except the United States. In the United States permission should be obtained through the Copyright Clearance Center, Customer Service, (508)750-8400, 222 Rosewood Drive, Danvers, MA 01923 USA, or CCC Online: *www.copyright.com*. All other applications for permission to reproduce or translate all or part of this book should be made to OECD Publications, 2, rue André-Pascal, 75775 Paris Cedex 16, France.

FOREWORD

In the mid-nineties the OECD's Centre for Educational Research and Innovation published a collection of data making comparisons in the field of special needs education in a few OECD countries. This work strengthened the view that a different comparative framework would need to be developed if reliable and valid comparisons were to be made. Subsequent discussions with participating member countries identified a resource based definition as the best means of facilitating international comparison. In fact this helps to overcome different national interpretations of concepts such as special educational needs which cover very different populations of students who are experiencing difficulties in accessing the curriculum.

Concurrent work at UNESCO and OECD in revising standards for classifying education systems (ISCED) updated the definition of special needs education and reformulated it to reflect policy developments. In doing so, a much wider range of students, in all types of schools were brought into the frame. In addition, the idea that extra resourcing may be needed to assist schools to help students access the curriculum more effectively was included in the new description.

In order for policy relevant comparisons to emerge, a resource based approach would require that the students included under this definition would need to be sub-divided into some form of straightforward classification scheme. Participating countries agreed on a tri-partite system in which students are divided into three cross-national categories, A, B and C. Broadly, they cover :

- students whose disabilities have clear biological origin (category A) ;

- students whose learning and behaviour difficulties are likely to have more of an acquired nature (category B) ; and

- students who have difficulties arising from disadvantages (category C).

The book presents a complete account of the development of the work and an application of this model in practice, and provides qualitative data to contextualise the quantitative information. It provides breakdowns by national category systems as well as comparisons using the cross-national framework described.

The work was partially supported by additional contributions from the US Department of Education, Office of Special Education and Rehabilitative Services (OSERS).

The book was prepared by the chief consultant to the project Colin Robson, Emeritus Professor, University of Huddersfield, and by Peter Evans and Marcella Deluca of the OECD/CERI secretariat, in close collaboration with the countries involved. The text was prepared by James Bouch. This book is published under the responsibility of the Secretary-General of the OECD.

TABLE OF CONTENTS

Executive Summary 11

Chapter 1. Introduction 15
Background 15
From Special Educational Needs to disabilities, difficulties, disadvantages, curriculum access and equity ... 16
The resources based definition 18
Operational definitions of cross-national categories 19
The electronic questionnaire 20
The nature and sources of the database for this monograph 21
Data limitations 21
Symbols for missing data 21
OECD member country codes 22

Chapter 2. Development of the Data Collection Instrument 23
Background 23
Meeting of national representatives 23
Linkage to UOE data collection exercise 24
Operational definition of special educational needs 24
Categorisation of special educational needs 24
Educational indicators 24
Initial data to be gathered 25
Scope and country involvement of the pilot visits 25
The pilot visits 25
Second meeting of national representatives 26
Field testing of the instrument 27

Chapter 3. Qualitative Data Analysis 29
Background 29
Laws 29
How are planning decisions made to ensure that students with special educational needs receive appropriate additional resources? 30
Facilitators and barriers of equity and inclusive education 31
Definition of special education for gathering statistics 33
Use of categories 34
Cross-national classification 35
Concluding comments 36

Chapter 4. Comparative Analysis of Quantitative Data Based on Categories of Disabilities, Learning Difficulties, and Disadvantages 47
Background 47
Methodology 47

Data on individual categories 48
Description by category 51
Conclusions 76
General notes 76

Chapter 5. Analysis of the Quantitative Data for Cross-national Categories A, B and C 79
Background 79
Availability of data 80
Quantitative data on cross-national category A 80
Quantitative data on cross-national category B 88
Quantitative data on cross-national category C 95
Overall comparisons across the phases of education for the three cross-national categories 100

Chapter 6. Additional Analyses of the Quantitative Data 103
Introduction 103
Special schools 103
Special classes 104
Regular classes 106
Student/staff ratios 106
Relative numbers of male and female students receiving additional resources for disabilities,
    difficulties or disadvantages 109
Age distribution of students receiving additional resources for disabilities, difficulties or disadvantages 113
Distribution of students by age 113
Students not registered within the education system 118
Final comments 118

Chapter 7. Further Discussion of Significant Issues 121
Issues arising from the analyses of the cross-national category A, B and C data 121
Cross-national category A – Students receiving additional resources for disabilities 122
Cross-national category B – Students receiving additional resources for difficulties 123
Cross-national category C – Students receiving additional resources for disadvantages 125
Gender 128
Implications of the results of the second data collection exercise for future developments 129
Final comments 131

References 133

Annex 1. *Allocation of categories of students with disabilities, difficulties, disadvantages included
    in the resources definition to cross-national categories A, B, C* 135
Annex 2. *Distribution of individual national categories into 22 general categories used to describe
    students with disabilities, difficulties and disadvantages* 159
Annex 3. *Data availability table* 161
Annex 4. *Compulsory school education* 165

List of tables
Table 3.1. Statistical classification frameworks of SEN students used by countries 37
Table 3.2. Allocation of categories of students with disabilities, difficulties, and disadvantages
    included in the resources definition to cross-national categories A, B, C 38

Table 5.1. Comparison of numbers of children with disabilities receiving additional resources in pre-primary and primary education as a percentage of all children in that phase of education 83
Table 5.2. Comparison of numbers of children with difficulties receiving additional resources in pre-primary and primary education as a percentage of all children in that phase of education 91
Table 5.3. Comparison of numbers of students with difficulties receiving additional resources in primary and lower secondary education as a percentage of all students in that phase of education .. 93
Table 5.4. Comparison of numbers of children with disadvantages receiving additional resources in pre-primary and primary education as a percentage of all children in that phase of education 98
Table 5.5. Comparison of numbers of children with disadvantages receiving additional resources in primary and lower secondary education as a percentage of all children in that phase of education .. 99

Table 6.1. Number of special schools by level of education relative to total school population 104
Table 6.2. Size of special schools by level of education 105
Table 6.3. Percentage of public special schools 105
Table 6.4. Number and size of special classes 106
Table 6.5. Number of regular classes with students receiving additional resources 107
Table 6.6. Student/teacher ratios 107
Table 6.7. Gender ratios of students receiving additional resources for disabilities 109
Table 6.8. Gender ratios of students receiving additional resources for difficulties 110
Table 6.9. Gender ratios of students receiving additional resources for disadvantages 111

List of charts
Chart 4.1. Students receiving additional resources in primary and lower secondary education by disability category and by country as a percentage of all students 49
Chart 4.2. Blind and partially sighted students in primary and lower secondary education by location as a percentage of all students 51
Chart 4.3. Proportion of partially sighted and blind students in primary and lower secondary education by location and by country 52
Chart 4.4. Total percentage of blind and partially sighted students by phases of education and by country .. 52
Chart 4.5. Deaf and partially hearing students in primary and lower secondary education by location as a percentage of all students 53
Chart 4.6. Proportion of deaf and partially hearing students in primary and lower secondary education by location and by country 54
Chart 4.7. Total percentage of deaf and partially hearing students by phases of education and by country ... 54
Chart 4.8. Students with emotional and/or behavioural difficulties in primary and lower secondary education by location as a percentage of all students 55
Chart 4.9. Proportion of pupils with emotional and/or behavioural difficulties in primary and lower secondary education by location and by country 56
Chart 4.10. Total percentage of students with emotional and/or behavioural difficulties by phases of education and by country 56
Chart 4.11. Students with physical disabilities in primary and lower secondary education by location as a percentage of all students 57
Chart 4.12. Proportion of students with physical disabilities in primary and lower secondary education by location and by country 58
Chart 4.13. Total percentage of students with physical disabilities by phases of education and by country .. 58
Chart 4.14. Students with speech and language difficulties in primary and lower secondary education by location as a percentage of all students 59
Chart 4.15. Proportion of students with speech and language difficulties in primary and lower secondary education by location and by country 60

Chart 4.16. Total percentage of students with speech and language difficulties by phases of education and by country 60
Chart 4.17. Students in hospitals in primary and lower secondary education by location as a percentage of all students 61
Chart 4.18. Proportion of students in hospitals in primary and lower secondary education by location and by country 62
Chart 4.19. Total percentage of students in hospitals by phases of education and by country 62
Chart 4.20. Students with combinatorial disabilities in primary and lower secondary education by location as a percentage of all students 63
Chart 4.21. Proportion of students with combinatorial disabilities in primary and lower secondary education by location and by country 64
Chart 4.22. Total percentage of students with combinatorial disabilities by phases of education and by country 64
Chart 4.23. Total percentage of students with autism by phases of education and by country 65
Chart 4.24. Students with severe learning difficulties in primary and lower secondary education by location as a percentage of all students 66
Chart 4.25. Proportion of students with severe learning difficulties in primary and lower secondary education by location and by country 66
Chart 4.26. Total percentage of students with severe learning difficulties by phases of education and by country 67
Chart 4.27. Students with moderate learning difficulties in primary and lower secondary education by location as a percentage of all students 67
Chart 4.28. Students with light learning difficulties in primary and lower secondary education by location as a percentage of all students 68
Chart 4.29. Proportion of pupils with light learning difficulties in primary and lower secondary education by location and by country 69
Chart 4.30. Total percentage of students with light learning difficulties by phases of education and by country 69
Chart 4.31. Students with learning disabilities in primary and lower secondary education by location as a percentage of all students 70
Chart 4.32. Proportion of pupils with learning disabilities in primary and lower secondary education by location and by country 70
Chart 4.33. Second language and mother tongue teaching students in primary and lower secondary education by location as a percentage of all students 71
Chart 4.34. Proportion of second language and mother tongue teaching students in primary and lower secondary education by location and by country 72
Chart 4.35. Total percentage of second language and mother tongue teaching students by phases of education and by country 72
Chart 4.36. Travelling students in primary and lower secondary education by location as a percentage of all students 73
Chart 4.37. Proportion of travelling students in primary and lower secondary education by location and by country 73
Chart 4.38. Total percentage of travelling students by phases of education and by country 74
Chart 4.39. Disadvantaged students in primary and lower secondary education by location as a percentage of all students 74
Chart 4.40. Proportion of disadvantaged students in primary and lower secondary education by location and by country 75
Chart 4.41. Total percentage of disadvantaged students by phases of education and by country 75

Chart 5.1. Number of students receiving additional resources over the period of compulsory education in cross-national category A as a percentage of all students in compulsory education 81
Chart 5.2. Percentages of students receiving additional resources over the period of compulsory education in cross-national category A by location 82
Chart 5.3. Number of children receiving additional resources in pre-primary education in cross-national category A as a percentage of all children in pre-primary education 82
Chart 5.4. Percentages of children receiving additional resources in pre-primary education in cross-national category A by location 83
Chart 5.5. Number of students receiving additional resources in primary education in cross-national category A as a percentage of all students in primary education 84
Chart 5.6. Percentages of students receiving additional resources in primary education in cross-national category A by location 84
Chart 5.7. Number of students receiving additional resources in lower secondary education in cross-national category A as a percentage of all students in lower secondary education 85
Chart 5.8. Percentages of students receiving additional resources in lower secondary education in cross-national category A by location 86
Chart 5.9. Number of students receiving additional resources in upper secondary education in cross-national category A as a percentage of all students in upper secondary education 87
Chart 5.10. Percentages of students receiving additional resources in upper secondary education in cross-national category A by location 88
Chart 5.11. Number of students receiving additional resources over the period of compulsory education in cross-national category B as a percentage of all students in compulsory education 89
Chart 5.12. Percentages of students receiving additional resources over the period of compulsory education in cross-national category B by location 89
Chart 5.13. Number of children receiving additional resources in pre-primary education in cross-national category B as a percentage of all children in pre-primary education 90
Chart 5.14. Percentages of children receiving additional resources in pre-primary education in cross-national category B by location... 91
Chart 5.15. Number of students receiving additional resources in primary education in cross-national category B as a percentage of all students in primary education 92
Chart 5.16. Percentages of students receiving additional resources in primary education in cross-national category B by location... 92
Chart 5.17. Number of students receiving additional resources in lower secondary education in cross-national category B as a percentage of all students in lower secondary education 93
Chart 5.18. Percentages of students receiving additional resources in lower secondary education in cross-national category B by location... 94
Chart 5.19. Number of students receiving additional resources in upper secondary education in cross-national category B as a percentage of all students in upper secondary education 95
Chart 5.20. Number of students receiving additional resources over the period of compulsory education in cross-national category C as a percentage of all students in compulsory education 96
Chart 5.21. Percentages of students receiving additional resources over the period of compulsory education in cross-national category C by location 96
Chart 5.22. Number of children receiving additional resources in pre-primary education in cross-national category C as a percentage of all children in pre-primary education 97
Chart 5.23. Number of students receiving additional resources in primary education in cross-national category C as a percentage of all students in primary education 98
Chart 5.24. Number of students receiving additional resources in lower secondary education in cross-national category C as a percentage of all students in lower secondary education 99

Chart 5.25. Number of students receiving additional resources in upper secondary education in cross-national category C as a percentage of all students in upper secondary education 100
Chart 5.26. Mean number of students receiving additional resources at different levels of education by cross-national category, as a percentage of all students in that level of education 101

Chart 6.1. Gender ratio by location and cross-national category 112
Chart 6.2. Gender ratio by phase of education and cross-national category 112
Chart 6.3. Number of students receiving additional resources in special schools as a proportion of all students by age, 1999 114
Chart 6.4. Number of students receiving additional resources in special classes as a proportion of all students by age 116
Chart 6.5. Age distribution of students not registered within the education system 118

EXECUTIVE SUMMARY

Principles of equity and a general concern for social cohesion have led to a rapidly growing interest in the education that OECD countries provide for students who without additional help will not succeed in their schooling. All OECD countries provide additional resources to help children with disabilities, learning difficulties and disadvantages to access the curriculum to benefit as fully as possible from their education. In addition, the type of school that these children are placed in is also changing. Many countries have active policies to include more and more children in regular schools rather than in segregated placement.

This monograph describes the outcomes of the second round of data gathering about students with disabilities, learning difficulties and disadvantages (DDD) that began in 1996. Since that time an electronic questionnaire (EQ) has been developed from an original "paper and pencil" version, and it has been through two iterations. The results of the first round of data collection were reported fully in OECD (2000b) based on data gathered in 1995/96. This monograph has been thoroughly revised using 1998/99 data and, although it keeps contact with the first edition, there are a number of significant changes.

First, the title is different. The original title *Special Needs Education – Statistics and Indicators* has been abandoned for *Equity in Education – Students with Disabilities, Learning Difficulties and Disadvantages*. The main reason for this is that the term "special education" carries very different meanings in different OECD countries. In some countries students from various types of disadvantaged backgrounds are included while in others they are not. And this fact has led to some confusion about the students who are covered by the monograph. The new title responds to this concern by identifying specifically the students included (those with disabilities, difficulties and disadvantages) and the intention of the statistics that are gathered and the indicators extracted (equity).

Second, the organisation of the data for the categories of disability, learning difficulty and disadvantage is different. In the previous monograph they were to a large extent collapsed together. This followed from the logic of working within the "special needs" framework used in many countries. Apart from the problems noted above, the collapsing of these categories obscures relevant policy discussion for the three groups taken separately. Thus in the present monograph, data for the three groups are presented in different sections and the policy implications are, in consequence, also presented separately.

Third, additional data are covering more ISCED levels. In the original monograph data were covering ISCED levels 1 and 2. In the present one, these have been expanded to include levels 0 and 3.

The main purpose of the work is to bring together national data sets on students who receive additional resources to assist them to access the curriculum. These data are then used to develop an internationally comparative framework to analyse educational provision for students with disabilities, learning difficulties and disadvantages and in this way to inform national and international policy-making.

The programme works through a collaboration of representatives of participating countries and the OECD/CERI secretariat. Data derived from national data gathering procedures are provided to the CERI secretariat via the electronic questionnaire. These data are collected on the basis of national categories of disabilities, learning difficulties, and disadvantages. They are included in the analysis on the criterion that countries provide additional resources to these students in recognition that without them their chances of making adequate progress through the educational system would be unnecessarily impeded. Via this mechanism, goals of equity and social justice (Rawls, 1971; Evans, 2001) can be approached.

The "resources definition" was developed mainly to provide a way of gathering data which would not be constrained by national definitions of terms like special education and which would be consistent with the approach described in the definition of special education given in the ISCED manual (UNESCO, 1997). Thus it ensures that the largest possible envelope of students is included in the data collection. In addition the "resources definition" provides a data gathering method that goes some way to meeting objections arising from analyses which use medically based categorical approaches, since it focuses on those students who are provided with additional resources to access the curriculum regardless of the nature of their difficulty. Such a definition should also speak more directly to educational policy-making.

In order to meet the different policy questions associated with students with disabilities, learning difficulties and disadvantages, the data gathered are broken down into three categories. These are called cross-national categories A, B and C. A includes those students who have clear organic difficulties and who would normally be described as having disabilities – such as students with hearing impairments or severe cognitive disabilities. B includes those students who have learning difficulties but for whom it is unclear whether their difficulties in school learning are due to organic problems or social disadvantage. Students with specific learning disabilities, *e.g.* those with dyslexia, fall into this category. Those in C have difficulties in school which are clearly a result of social disadvantage of one sort or another. Annex 1 provides a full classificatory table showing how countries have allotted their national categories into the cross-national classification A, B and C. This table also provides all definitions of the national categories where available.

In aiming to provide information relevant to educational policy-making this method and procedure provides a compromise between categorical and non-categorical approaches and keeps contact between national data sets and their transformation into A, B and C for international comparative work.

The first chapter of the monograph provides some background to the study, expands on the resources definition and defines the cross-national categories A, B and C. It then goes on to outline the use of the electronic questionnaire (EQ) and describes the data collection tables. Technical information essential to reading and understanding the monograph is provided. Chapter 2 provides an account of the development of the data collection instrument.

Chapter 3 analyses the responses given to the qualitative questions. Laws and policies are changing to remove barriers and to facilitate inclusion. Funding provision especially for students with disabilities still remains a policy issue to be fully tackled. Creating a level-playing field for funding which does not bias placement decisions is a key issue. Decentralisation of decision-making is viewed as a facilitator of inclusion but is not without its complexities. There may be conflicts with decentralisation of school management and local funding arrangements for educational and other services that may create barriers for inclusion. Cuts in spending also seem to encourage segregated provision. Partly it seems this is because special schools are protected.

A number of significant issues arose as barriers to inclusion. Assessment practices *per se* may lead to more exclusion by identifying individuals as failures. Training for inclusion was also viewed as generally unsatisfactory. Class sizes were seen as too big and the support services were generally not adequate.

Chapter 4 provides a comparative analysis on individual categories of students with disabilities, learning difficulties and disadvantages where it seems feasible to do so. Data charts and discussions are available on: blind and partially sighted students; deaf and partially hearing students; those with emotional and/or behaviour difficulties; students with physical disabilities; speech and language difficulties; those hospitalised; those with combinatorial disabilities (*i.e.* more than one, *e.g.* deaf and blind); those with autism; with severe learning difficulties; moderate learning difficulties; light learning difficulties; learning disabilities; those in programmes for second language and mother tongue teaching; for travelling students and for those from disadvantaged backgrounds (not included in the previous two categories).

For each category, comparative charts are supplied where possible. These include: proportions of students receiving additional resources in primary and lower secondary education as a percentage of all students; the percentage in primary and lower secondary education as a proportion of all students at those stages broken down by place of education (special school, special classes or regular classes); the proportions in primary and lower secondary in each category by place of education; and the proportion in each category as a percentage of all students broken down by pre-primary, primary, lower secondary and upper secondary phases.

These data tell a number of stories. First, the very great variation in prevalence proportions, especially in many of the disability categories, such as those covering sensory or physical disabilities, raises clear questions about the procedures leading to additional resources being provided for these students. It may be that some countries include students unnecessarily in their disability categories and/or it may be that some countries fail to provide additional resources for genuine cases. Diagnostic criteria may vary substantially from country to country and interact with decision-making processes on funding. The data almost universally show no consistent patterns across the different stages of education. This finding is very hard to explain on the basis of currently available data but suggests that there is a complex web of factors operating.

From the perspective of equity, one of the key issues is the placement of students since a diagnosis into a certain category labels the students and can also lead to a very different type of educational experience in contrast to other non-disabled students. This possibility appears in the charts showing the large variation between countries in the use of special schools. To a very large extent, it has to be true that the same student in country X might go to a special school while in country Y to a regular class.

Chapter 5 provides an account of the data based on the three cross-national categories A, B and C analysed separately. This is a development on the earlier monograph, and avoids difficulties associated with collapsing these three categories together with the attendant lack of clarity in identifying policy implications. Data on ISCED levels 0 to 3 are included and broken down by place of education (special schools, special classes or regular classes).

For all ISCED levels, as for the students in cross-national categories A, B and C, there are substantial differences between countries in the proportions being provided with additional resources – and not much consistency between levels in any one country. In addition there is substantial variation in the use of different locations. In general terms special schools are used mainly by cross-national category A students. There is no simple explanation for these differences: they are most likely to be a complex interaction between policy priority, school experience and the skill level of teachers and different diagnostic criteria in use in different countries.

Chapter 6 discusses the data gathered on the physical locations of education, the gender ratios, student-staff ratios and age distributions of the students in a number of national systems. The information on the physical nature of the provision made shows that the number of special schools relative to the total school population supports the data on inclusion given in Chapter 5. For instance, in Canada (NB) there are no special schools at any ISCED level whereas in the Czech Republic and the Netherlands there are over 50 per 100 000 students at the compulsory level. The schools are usually small, the median value being 64.6 students per school in compulsory education. From the limited data available it can be seen that special classes are also usually small. One class per school with ten students are typical figures for the compulsory education period. Information on regular classes is also slight. Only two countries (Canada [NB] and Italy) were able to provide it and both of these have strong inclusion programmes. In Canada (NB) 515 classes have students receiving additional resources, in Italy it is 80 431 for the period of compulsory education.

Student/staff ratios are also very favourable with a range in special schools from 2.21 to 9.24 showing no overlap with the general OECD figures for primary level, 10.6 to 30.0. In special classes the equivalent ratios are 1.42 to 11.68. These data provide a proxy for costs and indicate at least a doubling in per capita cost for special provision.

Gender differences also emerged strongly from the findings with percentage of males exceeding the percentage of females by a typical ratio of 60/40. This split is confirmed in the data broken down by age which for many countries are available for the ages 3 to 19. There is a statistically significant difference between the proportion of males in categories A and B which provides some evidence that different mechanisms are at work in the two categories. However, insufficient information is available to allow a stronger interpretation to be made.

The age data, mainly available for special schools and classes, also show the impact of schooling on placement. For most countries the data show proportions increasing to a peak and then declining probably revealing the rate at which students are transferred from one form of provision to another – usually to special provision.

Chapter 7 draws together the main findings, provides interpretation in the form of a series of questions raised by the data and identifies some policy actions. In addition it discusses a number of issues relevant for future developments including the extension of data collection especially to improve data quality.

Suggested policy actions include the need for national reviews on how students are labelled and how decisions are made about their placement. In addition, reviews could focus on whether the additional resources that are provided for schools and other services are used effectively. Why boys receive more support than girls would also warrant further consideration.

CHAPTER 1
INTRODUCTION

Background

Interest in the performance of national education systems has never been as strong as it is at present. All OECD member countries are concerned with the standards attained by students and the type of learning that all our children and young people are engaged in, as educational reforms are planned and put in place as part of a strategy for attaining equity and moving our countries into the knowledge economy.

Students with disabilities, learning difficulties and disadvantages are no exception, and programmes are being developed to assist these students to improve their skills and to be included more fully into society and work. The demographic trends are such that in the coming years, as a result of the increasing numbers of retired citizens and the decreasing birth rate, all available skills will be needed to maintain our economies.

The gathering of statistics and the development of indicators of education systems are viewed as indispensable to this endeavour, and the effort has been spearheaded by OECD in collaboration with UNESCO and the European Union. However, it has been noticeable that data on students who have difficulties in accessing the curriculum is more difficult to come by than for the rest of the student population.

In 1995, OECD published a first set of data intended to provide a comparative review of provision for students with disabilities and disadvantages in OECD countries. Although the work showed that the definitions used were so different among countries that comparisons were almost impossible to make, sufficiently large differences existed between countries to indicate the occurrence of substantial variations in provision.

This monograph follows on from this work and describes the continuation of a process which is intended to improve the quality of the database and international comparability. In this way policy making in the field of education for disabled and disadvantaged students will be better informed.

More recently, and providing additional motivation for a new initiative in this area, the instrument used for defining the nature of education statistics to be gathered internationally, the International Standard Classification of Education (ISCED), has been revised. In the original version of the classification, special education was defined as the education provided in special schools; a definition wholly out of keeping with both theory and practice obtaining in many countries, and which in itself limits interest in obtaining data in this area.

The most recent version of ISCED (ISCED 97) has attempted to put this right and provides the following definition of special education:

Special needs education – Educational intervention and support designed to address *special educational needs*. The term "special needs education" has come into use as a replacement for the term "special education". The older term was mainly understood to refer to the education of children with disabilities that takes place in special schools or institutions distinct from, and outside of, the institutions of the regular school and university system. In many countries today a large proportion of disabled children are in fact educated in institutions of the regular system. Moreover, the concept of "children with special educational needs" extends beyond those who may be included in handicapped categories to cover those who are failing in school for a wide variety of other reasons that are known to be likely to impede a child's optimal progress. Whether or not this more broadly defined group of children are in need of additional support depends on the extent to which schools are able to adapt their curriculum, teaching and organisation and/or to provide additional human or material resources so as to stimulate efficient and effective learning for these pupils. (UNESCO, 1997)

It is clear that this definition substantially changes and updates the definition of special education – particularly in terms of resources made available, and it carries with it a requirement for a rather different operationalisation for the purposes of gathering statistics.

As noted above, earlier work had identified the difficulty in comparing data in special needs education among countries. Two outstanding problems were identified. First, the term "special needs education" means different things in different countries. In some it covers only children with traditional disabilities, while in others it includes a broader range of students covering, for instance, disability, learning difficulty and disadvantage. Second, because of the wide variations in the definitions of disability and learning difficulty which are in use, the extent to which quantitative estimates for any particular category from different countries are comparable remains unclear. Furthermore, there has been in special educational circles, particular concern about the lack of educational utility of descriptive categories which are derived from medical classifications. Disability categories are viewed as having only partial implications for educational provision or for the development of teaching programmes, which inevitably have to take the whole child into account. In this way, therefore, categories based on medical descriptions are at best of only limited value to education policy-makers, who are the main audience for data gathered within the ISCED framework at OECD.

From Special Educational Needs to disabilities, difficulties, disadvantages, curriculum access and equity

It is clear that in an international setting the use of the term "special educational needs" leads to confusion because it means different things for different countries. As a result, except where necessary for historical reasons, the term is not used in this monograph. Instead the words disabilities, difficulties and disadvantages are used. These terms broadly describe the students for whom countries make additional resources available so that they can access the curriculum more effectively.

In addition, the data gathered on these students is presented separately for the three cross-national categories A, B and C (students with disabilities, difficulties and disadvantages respectively). This is because it facilitates educational policy–making. Although some features are in common there are a number of issues that do not apply across all three categories; for instance those relating to including disabled students into regular schools.

Furthermore, it was agreed that a new title was needed that would more accurately reflect the nature of the work. After many discussions the following title was affirmed: *Equity in Education – Students with Disabilities, Learning Difficulties and Disadvantages*.

Hopefully the adoption of these changes will clarify the purposes of the work.

The revised title also introduces the notion of equity since it is an important component of the work. As a result some discussion is needed around this term to explain how it fits with our data-gathering framework.

There are many discussions in the literature on equity which are too involved to enter into here (see Hutmacher *et al.*, 2001). OECD (1993) identified four basic interpretations which apply to this work presented here adapted from Demeuse *et al.* (2001).

- **Equity of access or equality of opportunity**: Do all individuals (or groups of individuals) have the same chance of progressing to a particular level in the education system?

- **Equity in terms of learning environment or equality of means**: Do all individuals enjoy equivalent learning conditions? This question is generally taken to mean: Do disadvantaged individuals or groups benefit from a learning environment equivalent to advantaged individuals or groups in terms of the level of training of their instructors and professionals attached to the scholastic infrastructures, and quantity and quality of didactic tools?

- **Equity in production or equality of achievement (or results)**: Do pupils or students all master, with the same degree of expertise, skills or knowledge designated as goals of the educational system? Most particularly, are individuals from different social backgrounds given, over the period of instruction of training, equal skills? Or do all individuals have the same chance of earning the same qualifying degrees (for example, a diploma) when they leave and can they do so, independent of their circumstances of origin? This concern about equality in achievement is founded on an ideal of corrective justice (Crahay, 2000) and is inevitably accompanied by a desire to reduce the gap between the strong and the weak in terms of academic performance from the start to the end of a pedagogic action (Bressoux, 1993).

- **Equality of realisation or exploitation of results**: Once they have left the system, do individuals or groups of individuals have the same chances of using their acquired skills to realise their individual or group goals in society and validate their skills?

In addition, however, Rawls' theory of justice is relevant and is taken up in discussions of equity concerning students with disabilities by Brighouse (2000). Rawls argues (Rawls, 1971) from the "difference principle" that institutions should be structured with a built-in bias in favour of the disadvantaged. As a result there seems little doubt that equity in education should not be based on an equal distribution of resources to all students. Some will need additional resources to help them access the curriculum and to profit from "the benefits that education provides opportunities for" (Brighouse, 2000).

OECD countries favour students with disabilities, difficulties and disadvantages in this way. They provide additional resources to help them access the curriculum and to benefit as fully as possible from education. Following the OECD interpretation of equity above, further analysis of how these resources are used and for whom and to what ends become key aspects of helping to understand whether education systems are as equitable as they should be. It is towards illuminating this goal that the data collection on students with disabilities, difficulties and disadvantages is directed. Given the very different approaches taken by member countries of the OECD it is an area which should benefit from international comparisons.

The resources based definition

The points raised above argue, then, for a new approach and following proposals from the Secretariat at OECD and in discussion with member countries it was decided to tackle the problem in the following way. In order to overcome the different definitions of special needs education that operate among countries, it was necessary to provide a means to identify and include all students for whom extra provision is made in order to help them make progress through the school curriculum.

It was decided to identify this envelope of students through a supply side approach based on resources made available. This has the advantage of being educationally based and at the same time fits with the intent of the ISCED 97 definition.

Thus, the definition of special needs education agreed is that "those with special educational needs are defined by the additional public and/or private resources provided to support their education". The use of this definition in a consistent manner calls for agreement about the term ADDITIONAL and an appreciation of the various kinds of possible RESOURCES PROVIDED which should be considered.

Thus "Additional resources" are those made available over and above the resources generally available to students[1] where no consideration is given to needs of students likely to have particular difficulties in accessing the regular curriculum.

Resources can be of many different kinds. Examples are:

- PERSONNEL RESOURCES. These include a more favourable teacher/student ratio than in a regular classroom where no allowance is being made for students with special needs; additional teachers, assistants or any other personnel (for some or all of the time); training programmes for teachers and others which equip them for work in special needs education.

- MATERIAL RESOURCES. These include aids or supports of various types (e.g. hearing aid); modifications or adaptations to classroom; specialised teaching materials.

- FINANCIAL RESOURCES. These include funding formulae which are more favourable to those with special needs (including classes where it is known or assumed that there are students with special needs); systems where money is set aside for special educational needs within the regular budget allocation; payments made in support of special needs education; and the costs of personnel and material resources.

The key question is whether these resources are made available to support their education and are provided when students have particular difficulties in accessing the regular curriculum.

One result of the resources approach is that it brings together students with learning difficulties with very different causes, and it was recognised that a group formed in this way would itself need to be further sub-divided. To achieve this, a tri-partite categorisation system was devised based on perceived causes of difficulty in accessing the regular curriculum. Countries are asked to re-classify the data into this framework based on the classification and data collection arrangements used in their own national system following the operational definitions provided.

---

1. The term "student" is used. It is to be regarded as synonymous with "pupil" or "(school) child".

Operational definitions of cross-national categories

The three categories which were agreed are called A, B, and C and are defined as follows.

Category A: Refers to educational needs of students where there is substantial normative agreement – such as blind and partially sighted, deaf and partially hearing, severe and profound mental handicap, multiple handicaps. These conditions affect students from all social classes and occupations. Typically, adequate measuring instruments and agreed criteria are available. Typically considered in medical terms to be organic disorders attributable to organic pathologies (*e.g.* in relation to sensory, motor or neurological defects).

Category B: Refers to educational needs of students who have difficulties in learning which do not appear to be directly or primarily attributable to factors which would lead to categorisation as A or C.

Category C: Refers to educational needs of students which are considered to arise primarily from socio-economic, cultural and/or linguistic factors. There is some form of disadvantage or atypical background for which education seeks to compensate.

The definition of special educational needs (SEN) given in the ISCED 97 manual and the derived resources definition have in practice presented problems for some countries. Specifically for example the association of students from ethnic minorities with those with SEN clashes with some national policy frameworks and national understanding of the concept of SEN.

Given the roots of this work it is not straightforward to easily deal with this issue. Nevertheless the statistical analysis recognises the problem and in general analyses data for A, B and C separately unless it is clear that combining the data is useful.

The issue is taken up more fully in the final chapter where policy implications are drawn out.

In the following chapters, these ideas and descriptions are elaborated upon and data gathered within this new framework are presented.

- *Chapter 2* provides an outline of the methodology used to develop the data gathering instrument.

- *Chapter 3* provides an analysis of the qualitative data.

- *Chapter 4* provides a comparative analysis of quantitative data based on individual disability categories.

- *Chapter 5* provides an analysis of quantitative data for cross-national categories A, B, C.

- *Chapter 6* provides an additional analysis of the quantitative data.

- *Chapter 7* provides discussion and conclusions.

The electronic questionnaire

An electronic questionnaire was designed to gather data on special educational needs and develop a database, methodology and technology compatible with the general education statistics work undertaken by OECD.

It was developed from the initial phase of this study where corresponding data were collected using a paper and pencil version of the questionnaire and data collection tables. Preliminary findings from that phase were incorporated into the edition of *Education at a Glance – OECD Indicators* (OECD, 1998b); further analyses were included in the version of *Education at a Glance – OECD Indicators* (see OECD, 2000a). A monograph, giving a full account of the development and the results of this work to date appeared in October 2000 (OECD, 2000b).

The questionnaire has been put together to take account of the wide variety of national systems in use which was highlighted in the initial phase. It allows for the collating of data as it is collected in different countries whether or not it falls under the resources definition and for a reclassification of these data into a simplified set of three categories which is intended to facilitate international comparisons. These categories are described as cross-national categories A, B and C and a full description of them is given above.

The electronic version of the questionnaire builds upon the experience gained in this initial phase. It is much less time-consuming to complete while following the same general approach of the earlier instrument.

It comprises:

- **Table 0** which requests information on any categories of students which are considered to fall within the resources definition and their classification into cross-national categories A, B or C.

- **Table 1** which asks for information on the starting and ending ages of various stages of education.

- **Table 2** which asks for information on number of students with special educational needs in special schools, on the institutions (public and private), numbers of classes and on the teaching staff.

- **Table 3** which asks for information on number of students with special needs in special classes, on the institutions (public and private), numbers of classes and on the teaching staff.

- **Table 4** which asks for information on number of students with special needs in regular classes, on the institutions (public and private), and numbers of classes.

- **Table 6** which asks for information on all students enrolled in special educational programmes classified by age as well as on those not registered in the education system.

In addition, information on total numbers of students in each level of education including compulsory is requested as well as gender breakdowns.

The electronic questionnaire aims to simplify data collection and already available information is pre-entered individually for each country and thereby only needs checking during completion. However, the opportunity has been taken to extend the requested coverage to include both pre-school and upper secondary education, since both of these phases of education are of considerable interest in relation to special educational needs provision and are necessary for providing a full picture of the education of these students. Other technical changes have been made to allow ultimately for data sets fully compatible with the new ISCED requirements. In particular, consideration for classification by programme content is allowed for.

The electronic questionnaire is designed so that the data requested are almost exclusively based on those already collected for other purposes, although not necessarily currently collated nationally. However, it may be feasible for central agencies in countries to provide different or additional breakdowns of statistics to those they currently produce; or to augment these data with statistics normally held only at regional or even local level.

As in the first paper and pencil version, the 1998/99 version of the electronic questionnaire also included a section to gather qualitative data and the findings are reported fully in Chapter 3.

The nature and sources of the database for this monograph

Twenty-four 1999 returns were received from the following 21 countries and provinces: Belgium (Fl.), Canada (Alb., BC, NB, SK) the Czech Republic, Finland, France, Germany, Greece, Hungary, Ireland, Italy, Japan, Luxembourg, Mexico, the Netherlands, Poland, Spain, Sweden, Switzerland, Turkey, the United Kingdom and the United States.

The data are provided by national authorities from databases already gathered in countries for administrative purposes. The work reported has benefited from close collaboration between the OECD/CERI Secretariat and country representatives and the data presented are therefore as accurate as possible.

Because it has not yet proved possible to use the programmatic definitions of the ISCED levels the terms pre-primary, primary, lower secondary and upper secondary are used as proxies for ISCED levels 0 to 3.

Data limitations

Despite increasing agreement about the cross-national definitions and growing adherence to these definitions among countries when allocating their individual country categories, there remain some divergences. Work is continuing on harmonising international reporting of these data. For example, the allocation of national categories to cross national categories A, B and C is permanently under review. Work is also continuing to provide full data sets on all national and cross-national categories. New work based on local data gathering has been initiated for this purpose.

Symbols for missing data

Five symbols are employed in the tables and graphs to denote missing data:

a   Data not applicable because the category does not apply.

m   Data not available.

m: Data partially missing.

n   Magnitude is either negligible or zero.

x   Data included in another category/column of the table.

OECD member country codes

Australia	AUS	Japan	JPN
Austria	AUT	Korea	KOR
Belgium	BEL (Fl.)	Luxembourg	LUX
Canada Alberta	CAN (Alb.)	Mexico	MEX
Canada British Columbia	CAN (BC)	Netherlands	NLD
Canada New Brunswick	CAN (NB)	New Zealand	NZL
Canada Saskatchewan	CAN (SK)	Norway	NOR
Czech Republic	CZE	Poland	POL
Denmark	DNK	Portugal	PRT
Finland	FIN	Slovak Republic	SVK
France	FRA	Spain	ESP
Germany	DEU	Sweden	SWE
Greece	GRC	Switzerland	CHE
Hungary	HUN	Turkey	TUR
Iceland	ISL	United Kingdom	UKM
Ireland	IRL	United States	USA
Italy	ITA		

CHAPTER 2
DEVELOPMENT OF THE DATA COLLECTION INSTRUMENT

Background

The data collection instrument needed to achieve the aims discussed in the previous chapter was developed in the autumn of 1996 and through 1997. Initial proposals were discussed at meetings of a small steering group consisting of OECD, UNESCO, EUROSTAT (the statistical arm of the European Community) and representation of the Directorate General of Education, Training and Youth of the European Commission (DGXXII). Broad agreement was reached on the approach to be taken. In particular it was agreed that, in the first instance, it would be highly desirable for the instrument used in this study to follow the general approach, terminology and conventions of the already existing UOE (UNESCO/OECD/EUROSTAT) data collection exercise. A very substantial amount of information about the nature and working of national educational systems has been collected yearly under the joint auspices of these three organisations.

In the then existing UOE data collection exercise, data relating to special educational needs were restricted to the number of students in special schools which gives only a partial and, in many countries, misleading and inappropriate picture of the extent of provision for students with special needs. It was agreed that by seeking to link this study conceptually to the wider UOE exercise there would be the advantage that in many countries persons responsible for collecting statistical information nationally might be involved with completing entries for this study on special needs, and hence find the task more manageable. It was also seen as a long term aim that, if this initial study demonstrated the feasibility of the approach taken, then this form of data collection about special educational needs would be incorporated into the general data collection exercise.

Meeting of national representatives

The approach agreed by the steering group formed the basis of proposals made to a meeting of country representatives and experts in October 1996. This meeting was mainly composed of representatives of OECD member countries but there was also representation from UNESCO.

The meeting achieved its objectives of agreeing the conceptual framework of the study, the initial data to be gathered, and the scope and country involvement of a set of pilot studies. These latter studies were to examine and discuss the issues raised by this type of data collection. In particular they were seen as a means of trying to establish the types of data which were likely to be readily available because they are already collected nationally, together with those types of data which while not currently collected nationally would both be of interest for the country concerned, and be collectable without major additional resource implications.

There was a clear consensus of support for the purposes of the study. The following issues were seen as important.

Linkage to UOE data collection exercise

The central concern of the study is the development of a data collection instrument, with the end product specified as a joint UNESCO/OECD/EUROSTAT recommendation to data providers to include the data collection instrument in the UOE data collection. It was seen as crucial that this central concern was kept firmly in mind throughout the study.

The omission of the special educational needs dimension from the current UOE instrument, apart from numbers of students in segregated special schools, was a clearly perceived lack and is increasingly commented on by member countries. Many legislative frameworks now relate to persons with special needs and disabilities, and more generally concerns for equity of treatment call for information which can be used to monitor progress in these fields.

Operational definition of special educational needs

At that stage, special educational needs were defined by the additional public and/or private resources committed to them to support their education. Note that this definition is not identical to that eventually adopted for the data collection exercise. While the reference here is to resources committed, the final version used refers to resources provided (recommended during the pilot visits discussed below as being simpler to operationalise).

The proposed definition was a version of that in the then current revision of the ISCED manual ("the additional intervention and support needed by children and youth with disabilities and other recognised learning difficulties"). This type of definition attempts to encompass a wide range of needs which are differentially labelled and categorised in national systems and where the provision is in different facilities including regular schools and regular classrooms.

After lengthy discussion which revealed many of the complexities linked to this kind of resource-allocation based definition, it was agreed that the working definition should be adopted for the study but that it should continue to be refined as the study progresses.

Categorisation of special educational needs

This topic also generated much discussion, in part because of the growing movement in national systems which are implementing integrated provision in regular school settings for those with special educational needs in order to avoid such categorisation. However many systems do continue to employ various forms of categorisation which could provide useful data. It will also help link this study to the previously used categories based on disability. A consensus was achieved in favour of employing a simple categorisation system in the pilot work, while recognising that there will be practical difficulties for national systems which do not categorise.

It was agreed at the meeting that a simple tri-partite scheme should be adopted covering respectively students with the most clear impairments (*e.g.* blind, deaf, physically and intellectually handicapped); those with learning difficulties; and those where their educational difficulties arise primarily from socio-economic and linguistic factors. It was accepted that major amplification and exemplification would be needed to clarify their meaning and assist in the provision of comparable information.

Educational indicators

The development of appropriate education indicators in the domain of special education was agreed as the second central thrust of the project. Possible approaches were explored and suggestions made. For example, in connection with indicating the extent to which a system treats all persons equitably, an approach might be to identify barriers in the system to such equality of treatment, whether at the simple level of physical access or in relation to flexibility of curriculum. It appeared that the goal should be the development of a small set of powerful indicators.

Initial data to be gathered

It was agreed that a prototype version of a data collection instrument to fulfil the purposes of the study, and cover the issues noted above should be developed by the consultant in discussion with the secretariat.

This would be followed by study visits to eight countries to test the viability of the instrument and to gather pilot data. The visits were planned to start before the end of 1996 and to be completed in 1997. Countries likely to be faced with different issues and problems in completing the data collection instrument (and in particular in completing it in a manner which produced reliable and valid data comparable across countries) should be chosen. It was envisaged that the data collection instrument would be developed over this set of visits in an iterative manner.

Scope and country involvement of the pilot visits

It was agreed that the countries should be selected by the secretariat, after the meeting, through discussion with representatives of the countries. Criteria for choice should include willingness to be involved, and the countries selected should reflect differing political organisational structures (*e.g.* Federal and non-Federal states), different educational structures (*e.g.* concerning extent of integration of disabled pupils), and regional variation (*e.g.* Europe, North America). While it would be desirable to include varied regional representation there appears to be such major variation within region that regionality in itself is not an appropriate variable. Representation from developing countries should also be sought.

Given the severely limited set of visits it was crucial that the choice of country participation be strongly influenced by the extent to which the host countries would be both prepared and able to devote resources to provide detailed feedback and support on the data collection exercise. There was a very encouraging response from national representatives at the October 1996 meeting, with several indicating their willingness to be involved with this pilot work.

These arrangements were then followed by a meeting of the steering group to discuss outcomes and to plan for a later meeting of country representatives which would also discuss outcomes and agree the timeframe for the gathering of a more extensive data set using the modified version of the instrument. Following collection and analysis of data and calculation of experimental indicators for publication at the end of the study there would be meetings to discuss outcomes and future developments.

The pilot visits

Eight countries, selected to reflect different political structures and educational organisation, were visited over the time-scale envisaged above. They comprised six OECD countries – Belgium (Fl.), Denmark, Hungary, the Netherlands, Switzerland and the United States, and two developing countries – Sri Lanka and Zambia. Notes on the points and issues raised by the visits were presented in the first monograph (OECD, 2000b, pp. 14-23).

Second meeting of national representatives

A further revision of the proposed data collection instrument, based upon the experience of the pilot visits, was presented to a meeting of country representatives (plus representation from DGXXII of the European Commission and from UNESCO) in November 1997. It was explained that in order to embed the work in the full UOE data collection exercise, the version of the instrument which was pilot tested was designed to provide, as far as possible, a parallel special needs version of the UOE data structure. However, it became clear from the first pre-pilot (amply confirmed on the second pilot) that it was not possible, at this stage, to provide such a version since many of the necessary data were not widely available. Thus what was included in the version presented to the meeting reflected what was seen as both possible and important and was strongly influenced by the information obtained during the course of the field visits.

The instrument was divided into two parts, a questionnaire and a set of data tables. The first part comprises a questionnaire which asks for mainly qualitative information about special educational needs. A key feature is the resources-based definition of special needs education.

There was further discussion about the implications of using this definition. The definition (in terms of additional resources made available to those with particular difficulties in accessing the regular curriculum) raises a fundamental question as to whether those students with disabilities and/or learning difficulties but for whom no additional resources are available still have special educational needs? This problem emphasises that the concept of special educational needs is not simply another euphemism for disability but one which changes the point of reference. That is, it focuses on the adaptations that the school system must make to meet the needs of the child and not on the within-child impairments. Thus, from the point of view of the education system, it is the relative additional effort it has to make to improve the quality and the outcomes for those with special educational needs within the context of providing an efficient education for all children which becomes the key policy concern, and it is these positive developments which the resource-based definition is trying to highlight.

A second key feature, which obtained very substantial support in the pilot work, is the adoption of a classification scheme which affords countries the opportunity to reinterpret their data in a way that would allow for international comparisons to be made. To achieve this, the tri-partite categorisation scheme was developed. As indicated earlier, cross-national category A refers to the educational needs of students where there is substantial normative agreement concerning the nature of the special need – such as blind and partially sighted, deaf and partially hearing. Cross-national category B refers to educational needs of students who have difficulties in learning which do not appear to be directly or primarily attributable to factors which would lead to categorisation as either A or C. And cross-national category C, which refers to educational needs of students which are considered to arise mainly from socio-economic and/or linguistic factors, *i.e.* where some sort of disadvantage is perceived to be present. It was stressed that it was up to countries to choose into which of the categories A, B or C they placed their own national categories.

The second part of the instrument comprises a set of data collection tables which asks for quantitative data in the form of readily available statistics about national educational systems in relation to special educational needs.

An extensive discussion at the meeting touched on a wide variety of issues. In general terms the complexity and difficulty of the task was well recognised and many representatives commented on its potential usefulness. The secretariat received considerable praise for the work completed. Most countries noted that despite the fact that the instrument, quite inevitably, raised problems of both a conceptual and technical nature they did not feel that these were insurmountable and that they would be able to provide relevant information and to complete some, if not all, of the data tables. The view was expressed that the instrument should be concise and that all the data provided should be useful, usable and used in the reporting of the work and the construction of indicators.

The main areas where revisions were required included additional clarification to the use of cross-national categories A, B and C; and in particular where children with behaviour difficulties, the gifted and those with multiple handicaps would fit. Further description was needed on the classification of those who act as teachers in special education since many of them are not necessarily trained as teachers. The link between institutions and categories of special needs was also seen as requiring further exploration, since they do not necessarily map onto each other in any direct way. In addition, it was noted that there are other forms of institutional provision that exist to cope with low incidence handicapping conditions which should be considered. The division of the questionnaire into primary and secondary sections was suggested along with a number of technical points concerned with avoiding overlap and repetition of data gathered. The addition of information in the areas of the social services that support schools (*e.g.* parent education programmes) was suggested.

There was considerable discussion on the type of indicators that would be useful. Indicators which would be available if the current instrument were completed comprised: numbers and proportions of those with special educational needs; the location of their education; teacher/pupil ratios; relative resourcing; and system features relating to obstacles and facilitators to integration. Other indicators were identified during discussion. These included: the expected years of schooling; equity in terms of gender and ethnic minority issues; systems indicators *e.g.* linking school organisation to behaviour problems; and partnerships.

In addition there was great interest in the development of outcome indicators particularly with reference to the contexts of education; achievement; costs; quality of education; the link to post-compulsory placement; employment; the link between inclusion and outcomes for those children without special educational needs; and the costs of policies of not integrating students with special needs.

The countries agreed to take part in a wider field testing of the questionnaire. It was agreed that this sample should include those countries present at the meeting, plus a number of others to be identified. In addition the representatives from UNESCO agreed to include up to ten other countries making a sample of approximately 30 countries in all. It was agreed that data from the year 1995/96 should as far as possible be used.

It was also agreed that the instrument should be revised in the light of the discussion and be re-circulated for completion at the beginning of 1998. The countries present would endeavour to return completed forms as soon as possible with the intention of reviewing the information and data thus obtained at a meeting in the summer of 1998.

Field testing of the instrument

The instrument was circulated to all OECD countries and to a number of developing countries. This latter part of the exercise was undertaken by UNESCO. Analysis of the responses from OECD countries forms the main empirical basis for the first monograph arising from this project (OECD, 2000b).

A report based on the first ten responses which had been received by the beginning of June 1998 was presented to a third meeting of country representatives in July 1998. An earlier presentation was made at the meeting of the INES Technical Group at The Hague, the Netherlands on 27-29 April 1998 on the Special Study in Special Educational Needs giving an indication of the approach taken and the type of data resulting from the exercise. There was a full discussion of the issues involved. Following discussion at the INES Technical Group meeting in July 1998, agreement was reached for the analysis of the first set of responses to be included in the next edition of *Education at a Glance – OECD Indicators* (OECD, 1998b, pp. 221-229). A fuller data set has also been reported in Education at a Glance (see OECD, 2000a, Indicator C6, p. 187).

It was very encouraging to note that completion of the questionnaire and data collection tables, while difficult, was regarded as feasible by representatives involved in widely differing types of educational systems ranging from largely integrated to largely segregated, and from both categorical and non-categorical-based systems. The use of a resource-based definition of special educational needs appeared to achieve a high degree of acceptance.

Subsequent meetings have confirmed this. In addition, there have been extensive discussions of the allotment of national categories to cross-national categories A, B and C. The group of national representatives have been closely involved with the development with Table 3.2 and Annex 1 to ensure international comparability and each country's allotment of their data has been agreed by consensus at a number of meetings.

Further discussion of the findings from the exercise and their implications is provided in the following chapters.

CHAPTER 3
QUALITATIVE DATA ANALYSIS

Background

Apart from gathering quantitative data, countries were asked to provide some qualitative descriptions. These comprised:

- Information on the country's definition of special education used for gathering educational statistics.

- The use of categories in gathering data in this field along with the names and definitions of the categories and whether or not they fall within the resources definition.

- Whether there were categories of students currently used for data collection which fall within the resources definition but not within the national definition of special needs.

- How the categories fit into the cross-national categorisation A, B and C.

- How planning decisions are made to ensure that students with special educational needs receive appropriate additional resources.

- Whether there is specific coverage of special educational needs in the current legislative framework and if so what it is.

- Factors considered to be facilitators of inclusion and equity; and factors acting as barriers to inclusion and equity.

Replies to these questions are synthesised in the following paragraphs based on returns from 28 OECD member countries: Austria, Belgium (Fl.), Canada (Alb., BC, NB, SK), the Czech Republic, Denmark, Finland, France, Germany, Greece, Hungary, Iceland, Ireland, Italy, Japan, Korea, Luxembourg, Mexico, the Netherlands, Norway, New Zealand, Poland, Portugal, Spain, Sweden, Switzerland, Turkey, the United Kingdom and the United States where appropriate data provided in both 1996 and 1999 are combined.

Laws

All countries surveyed have laws covering special education provision or they are in preparation or under review ensuring access to education for all students. Some are more specific than others. In the United Kingdom, for instance, a definition of learning difficulties is given in the Education Act (1976), whereas in contrast in the Czech Republic the laws are framed mainly in regard to provision for students with disabilities, difficulties, and disadvantages and the validity of Czech sign language for those with severe hearing disabilities. This latter situation is currently under review with the goal that special education will be included within the general framework of regular schools. Iceland, too, has no separate law for special education, which is covered in a sub-section. Thus it is clear that this remains an area where there has been substantial development.

The most significant change in these legal frameworks is a move towards inclusion which is being driven by an agenda comprising human rights issues, equity, parental involvement and social cohesion with the growing understanding that the concept of special educational needs implies that students' failures to make adequate progress in their learning are in large part the responsibility of the school and cannot be viewed as being caused wholly by the "disability" diagnosis.

The changes in thinking are reflected, for instance, in the Netherlands where new laws on Primary Education (WPO) and on special education (WEC) came into force in 1998. The WPO regulates primary education including the education of children attending special primary schools. According to the WPO, primary schools (including special primary schools) should offer all children appropriate instruction and an uninterrupted school career. All children should receive instruction geared to their educational needs, promoting intellectual, emotional growth and creativity and oriented to inclusion. Directly linked to this new funding system is a re-organisation of special education. The number of different special schools (now ten) will be reduced to four types of expertise centres for students with visual, communication, physical and mental disabilities and severe behaviour problems. Parallel arrangements for older students will come into force with a Secondary Education Act.

The interactive compensatory view of special educational needs has in some countries led to an expansion of the numbers of students under consideration to include those with disadvantages. In Denmark and Spain the term "special education requirements" is used and reflects the fact that many students will need a flexible approach to engender achievement. Furthermore, for instance in Mexico, it is importantly recognised that some disabled students may not have special educational needs. This follows from the observation that if certain disabilities are being skilfully handled in a school as part of the regular provision additional help to access the curriculum is not needed.

The recognition that schools must adapt themselves is being reflected in other modifications to educational delivery. Where special needs students are included class sizes are sometimes reduced. In Hungary, for example, a student with special needs counts as three non-special needs students. So a class of 16, comprising two special needs students and 14 others would be equivalent to a class of 20 all non-special needs. More recent directives describe the necessary modifications and extensions to national core curriculum. To help regular schools adapt, outreach from special schools to regular schools is encouraged as is the development of clusters of schools. The aim here is to help develop the necessary skills in the regular schools so that those with special needs can be more effectively educated there. This approach has been described more fully elsewhere, *e.g.* in Canada (NB) (OECD, 1999).

Many countries also offer an extension in age of formal education for disabled students. In New Zealand this can extend from the under fives right up to the age of 21.

The significance of parental involvement is widely recognised especially in the assessment arrangements. But more and more parents are being given the right for their disabled child to be educated in regular schools as for instance in Italy (OECD, 1999).

How are planning decisions made to ensure that students with special educational needs receive appropriate additional resources?

Fifteen countries and four Canadian Provinces (Alb., BC, NB and SK) responded to this question approaching the topic from many different viewpoints.

The majority of countries planned within the context of a national legal framework for identifying special needs students which included providing additional resources. This varied from the United States, whose complex federal system and federal laws require that states establish inter-agency agreements with agencies responsible for services for special education students, in contrast to Switzerland where there is no comprehensive uniform statutory approach.

Within these legal frameworks, special education students are identified and classified to varying degrees of complexity often via a multi-disciplinary approach, *e.g.* Luxembourg. These classifications form the basis for resource allocation. In Canada (Alb.) for instance, in 1999/2000, 9.88% of students were classified as having mild/moderate disabilities. To meet their special needs a particular sum is incorporated into the regular per capita student funding and school boards pool these resources to meet the needs of these students. In addition 2.58% of students are described as having severe disabilities, with each student receiving additional funding in addition to the regular per capita allowance. Other countries (*e.g.* Finland, the Netherlands) seem to have more complex arrangements but student classification remains the basis of subsequent statistical data gathering and planning. Resulting budgets could be determined for five year periods (*e.g.* the Netherlands) or annually (Mexico). Other countries such as Sweden appeared to have looser arrangements, frequently decentralised. In Germany, a qualitative and quantitative profile is demanded.

Countries varied considerably in the monitoring arrangements followed for ensuring that funds allotted for SEN were used appropriately. In Canada (BC), for instance, there is a reporting and auditing process to ensure compliance. Schools themselves are also reviewed, and individual education plans for special needs students are required. This centralised process looks very different from the decentralised models that are working in countries such as Norway and Sweden. These countries appear to have less strong monitoring procedures in place and in the latter country there is a well used complaints procedure for parents who feel that their child is not receiving adequate support.

Methods were not uniformly applied across the cross-national categories A, B and C. For instance when students are in special schools (usually category A) resources are often based on actual numbers but if students are from disadvantaged backgrounds (category C) then determination of resources may be made on the basis of local indicators, such as in Italy and in funding education priority zones (ZEPs) in France. In the Netherlands resources needed for students from category A in regular schools are estimated from projections.

At the classroom level countries also varied in degree of specificity. For instance in Hungary in a classroom, one special needs student counts for three regular students in the calculation of class sizes. By contrast, in Canada (NB) the Superintendent must make sure that appropriate provision is made. Several countries make arrangements for students who cannot easily attend school to receive education at home and many extend the age-range outside the normal compulsory school age limits.

Facilitators and barriers of equity and inclusive education

Countries were asked to identify characteristics of their educational systems which they believe act as either facilitators or barriers to equity and inclusive education.

Given the diversity of systems involved it is not surprising that answers covered a wide range of topics from the legal system to the practicalities of assessment.

Many countries commented on the importance that legal and policy frameworks may play in encouraging inclusion and equity and creating respect for diversity or in creating barriers. Compulsory free education for all children and youth, and mandated integration in one country, were identified as obvious facilitators. If children are not in the system they can hardly be included! One identified the opportunities provided by the EU Helios programme on the inclusion of disabled students into mainstream schools as being especially helpful in achieving changes in attitudes and practices. In the United States (Individuals with Disabilities Education Act [IDEA] and the 1973 Rehabilitation Act) serve to guarantee education and the needed services in the least restrictive environment. In Greece, general educational reform and the development of new pedagogies and the implementation of new technologies were seen as beneficial for inclusion.

The monitoring of these laws for compliance was also given importance in some countries (*e.g.* Canada [BC]). In Italy the legal change of 1977 is credited with leading to a change in society stimulating a positive acceptance of disability where the school for instance is treated as a little community. In Switzerland, decentralisation of the educational system was also cited as a factor beneficial for inclusion. France noted that the central concept of education blocks individual treatment of students and the implementation of individual programme planning. Other countries noted that policies for inclusion were not always implemented consistently.

This relatively straightforward position may, however, be contrasted with other complex effects which appear when policies are put into practice. In Austria for instance, the abolition of statements of special needs for some students, guaranteeing certain forms of provision, were found to be a barrier to effective education of disabled students since without them they were obliged to follow the regular aims of the school. In addition, regular schools provided two years less required education than special schools. In contrast in the Flemish part of Belgium, the stigmatising effects of assessment and a heavy bureaucratic approach were identified as barriers to inclusion.

The historical structure of the education and special education systems were frequently cited as a severe barrier. These had led to inflexible school organisation (tracking for instance was viewed as a barrier to inclusion), over large class sizes, the lack of relevant teaching skills and of individualised teaching programmes, prejudiced attitudes on the part of teachers and parents, poor quality or limited teacher preparation, biased funding systems, unhelpful contractual agreements involving employers and trade-unions and a lack of co-operation between relevant ministries and services.

More recent developments in some countries such as the existence of pre-schools and special classes and special schools and a continuum of placement possibilities and links between special and mainstream schools were viewed as facilitators.

Funding of special education was also identified as a key factor. The creation of a level playing field for funding which does not bias placement decisions was seen as an important facilitator. In some countries, *e.g.* Denmark, Finland, Hungary and New Zealand, funds follow students and not schools and, at least in principle, this opens the way to inclusive practices. A paradox emerged in New Zealand with regard to the decentralisation of the special educational needs grant. While central control was viewed as a barrier to inclusion, and decentralisation seen as an important way to help local authorities implement relevant inclusionary policies, decentralisation in the form of the local management of schools in New Zealand was seen as a barrier. A general lack of funds and bias in funding formulae were both perceived to be barriers. Other countries, *e.g.* Switzerland and the United States, reported inconsistencies in the way funding formulae worked at local level while for others the lack of resources and the complexity of their delivery were viewed as barriers. Cuts in spending seemed to encourage segregated provision, partly perhaps because special schools were safeguarded but also because parents, perhaps for the same reason, thought that their children would receive higher quality provision there.

That resources are needed to develop inclusion and equity cannot be denied. Mexico for instance, has modified buildings and provided free textbooks and materials aimed at special education students. Furthermore, these have been translated for the indigenous communities and scholarships provided for students living in isolated areas. In Finland, nutrition and transport are arranged and in Canada (BC) extra funds are made available for INSET and a telephone help line. The government there has also made loans available for the purchase of expensive equipment.

Outside of these points the most frequently mentioned topics were on assessment and training.

Assessment – many countries mentioned that assessment practices can both facilitate and block inclusion. In Sweden a change from a normative to a criterion based model of pupil assessment led to more students with severe learning difficulties being identified as "failing" and this increased the likelihood of special school placement. In Canada (Alb.) annual tests with well planned accommodations were reported as facilitating inclusion while at the same time they were also seen as being a way of excluding students with difficulties from the testing arrangements. The reason given for this was fear on the part of schools that including students with special needs would lower average scores. An outcome challenged by research conducted in Alberta, which found just the opposite result.

Training – In many countries, even those who have been practising inclusion for many years, lack of training and skills, were identified as main barriers. This appeared to hold at all levels of pre-service and in-service with a weakness in university level training being identified in one country, Canada (NB). The development of individual training programmes, preventive measures and early diagnosis were particularly mentioned. In Canada (SK), the degree of self-confidence of classroom teachers and school administrators was also cited in the face of growing pupil diversity and the need for more appropriate in-service-education (INSET) and skill development. Class sizes were seen as a barrier to inclusion as were the need for effective support services, *e.g.* educational psychologists, speech/language pathologists, social workers and the use of classroom aides.

Other aspects of structure were seen as barriers. These included, a shorter period of education for regular students, in contrast to that available for those with disabilities, and the structure of primary education itself. At the classroom level, class size and streaming or tracking were seen as barriers. The lack of specialists and the proper use of teachers' aides were seen as obstacles to be overcome. On the positive side, the addition of extra teachers was a facilitator presumably because they bring additional skills to the classroom, allow for joint planning and lead to a reduction in pupil teacher ratio in classes where disabled students are included.

The involvement of parents as advocates facilitated inclusion but the lack of parental involvement and knowledge were viewed as barriers.

The existence of educational priority policy and non-discriminatory equal opportunities were also important in the fight for equity and deliberately balancing the numbers of ethnic minorities in schools was seen as a positive equity measure.

Definition of special education for gathering statistics

Based on the returns from the countries who responded to this question, the definition of special education for the purposes of gathering national statistics may be grouped into four basic patterns.

Almost all countries collect data via disability categories (always remembering that the term disability itself has limited common usage across countries and in France two systems, emanating from two ministries, operate in parallel); in Canada (SK), for instance, four criteria need to be met: a) the student needs to meet the classification criteria identified in the definitions; b) the student must be being provided with an appropriate programme that meets his/her needs; c) the programme must be delivered by or the delivery must be supervised by a teacher with special education teacher qualifications acceptable to the minister; and d) the costs of the programme are equal to or greater than the recognised costs in the grants structure.

Second, there are those countries such as Greece, Ireland and Switzerland, which also include disadvantaged students. Additionally, some countries such as Switzerland include children with a Foreign First Language within these categories whilst others do not.

Third, there are those, *e.g.* Canada (Alb., BC), Mexico, Spain and Turkey, which also include gifted students.

The fourth approach used in Denmark and in the United Kingdom is to base provision on the need to respond to exceptionalities leading to perceived difficulties in the schooling process rather than defining students *per se* via a categorical approach.

The data are summarised in Table 3.1, which is provided at the end of this chapter.

Use of categories

The data show that most countries gather data by means of categories and this question invited them to provide the names of the categories and their definitions. Most countries were able to provide definitions and the outcomes are provided in full in Annex 1 which reveals the complexity of the different arrangements. In this annex the national categories have been placed into cross-national categories A, B and C according to the classifications provided by the countries themselves as requested. Definitions of the categories are also provided where available. In addition, those categories which receive additional resources but which are not part of the national special needs category system are included in the table. A detailed discussion based on national categories is provided in Chapter 4.

Fifteen of the 27 countries report having categories which receive additional resources but which lie outside their national definition of special needs. These tend to cover disadvantaged students, those from ethnic minorities and those with short term learning problems and those with specific learning difficulties. However, some countries include gifted students, those with mild behaviour problems and those with speech impairments. These categories of provision exist in other countries too, but in those countries they will be included under the general rubric of special education.

A small number of countries do not fit this classification and fit into the fourth pattern noted above. This approach deserves further comment. The Canadian Province of New Brunswick does not keep categorical data but does have categories which receive resources but are not part of the special needs framework. The United Kingdom does not gather data by categories but for the current data round were able to identify students with special needs but without statements who received extra resources. These they placed in cross-national category B. Denmark also has a non-categorical system but makes a distinction between students with more extensive special needs (being about 1% who have the most severe disabilities and who need extensive support with their learning) and those with less extensive needs (being about 12% and includes those with disadvantages) a framework which is conceptually similar to that in the United Kingdom where 2.74% of students with SEN have statements of special educational need and a further 14.41% have special educational needs but do not have statements in compulsory education. Resourcing arrangements for these two groups are different. In these three countries resources are made available for the increased costs which arise in educating students with special educational needs, but they are allotted through local decision-making structures.

Cross-national classification

Countries were asked to carry out the task of re-classifying their categories both national and resource based according to the cross-national model described in Chapter 1. Briefly, cross-national category A refers to those students whose special needs appear to stem from a clear biological impairment such as deafness or severe learning difficulty. Cross-national category C comprises those whose difficulties stem more apparently from social disadvantage of one sort or another and cross-national B covers those who fit clearly neither cross-national category A nor C.

Countries seemed to have little difficulty in using this framework and the results are summarised in Table 3.2 which shows that most categories were placed as might be expected. Annex 1 presents an elaborated version of Table 3.2 and indicates full definition of each category where available. The allotment of national categories to cross-national categories was verified at a meeting of participating countries.

Table 3.2 and Annex 1 reveal that the majority of countries use categories to classify their special needs population for the purposes of statistical data gathering. In terms of national categories, *i.e.* excluding those that additionally fall into the resources definition, they vary between two, *e.g.* the United Kingdom, and 19 in Switzerland. Between these extremes many countries use 12 or 13. Although the categories used cover broadly similar disabling conditions, in many countries actual definitions in use render comparisons difficult. For instance, in regard to students with learning difficulties as far as cross-national comparisons are concerned, it is not possible to distinguish between students who would appear under the various headings of severe learning difficulties, moderate learning difficulties, light learning difficulties and learning disabilities. Some countries gather data on students who are blind or have visual impairment separately, others group them together, and similarly for those with serious or partial hearing impairments.

Students with emotional and behavioural problems represent an interesting case. In Greece, Hungary, Italy and Turkey there is no such category. In Ireland several levels of the category are described.

In terms of the way these national categories are allotted into cross-national categories A, B and C there is general consistency with students with traditional impairments being placed in A and those from disadvantaged backgrounds in C. However, other interesting observations may be made. Students classified as having learning disabilities as well as slow learners often appear in B, *i.e.* the reasons for difficulties with school learning are unclear, being neither due to disadvantage nor a clear impairment. Those with behaviour problems usually appear under A but in Ireland, Finland, and the United States they appear under B, perhaps implying different causal understanding among countries and this may indicate the need for further refinement of the use of categories A, B and C.

This discussion of the results of the findings on national categories and the way they are allotted to the cross-national categories of A, B and C strongly supports the rationale of the present study. That is, if meaningful international comparisons are to be made, a method such as the one developed here, which includes all children receiving additional resources, and their allotment into straightforward and operationally defined categories substantially simplifies the situation and improves the possibility of making policy relevant decisions based on internationally valid comparisons.

Concluding comments

In general terms the qualitative data gathered during the study reveals the great national interest in this area as laws, policies and educational provision are adjusted to meet the needs of students who are failing in the regular system. Factors thought to be facilitators for, or barriers to equity and inclusion cover a whole range of issues which include legal frameworks, funding models, assessment arrangements, school structure, class size, individual teaching programmes, involvement of additional teachers and aides, teacher training, parental involvement and co-operation with other services. Together these make a substantial agenda for reform.

The next three chapters examine in detail the quantitative data gathered.

Table 3.1. **Statistical classification frameworks of SEN students used by countries**[1]

COUNTRIES / PATTERNS	Disability categories only	Disability categories plus disadvantaged students	Disability categories plus gifted and talented students	Essentially non categorical systems
Austria	✓			
Belgium (Fl.)	✓			
Canada (Alb.)			✓	
Canada (BC)			✓	
Canada (NB)	✓			
Canada (SK)	✓			
Czech Republic	✓			
Denmark				✓
France	✓			
Finland	✓			
Germany	✓			
Greece		✓[2]		
Hungary	✓			
Italy	✓			
Ireland		✓[2]		
Japan		✓[2]		
Korea	✓			
Luxembourg	✓			
Mexico			✓	
Netherlands	✓			
New Zealand		✓		
Norway				✓
Poland		✓		
Portugal	✓			
Spain			✓[3]	
Sweden	✓			
Switzerland		✓[2]		
Turkey			✓	
United Kingdom				✓
United States		✓		

1. This table combines both 1996 and 1999 data.
2. Includes learning difficulties linked to linguistic barriers or disadvantage associated with ethnic groupings.
3. Includes disadvantaged students.

Table 3.2. **Allocation of categories of students with disabilities, difficulties, and disadvantages included in the resources definition to cross-national categories A, B, C**

Country	Cross-National Category A	Cross-National Category B	Cross-National Category C
Belgium (Flemish Community)	1. **Minor mental handicap –** Type 1 2. **Moderate or serious mental handicap –** Type 2 4. **Pupils with a physical handicap –** Type 4 5. **Children suffering from protracted illness –** Type 5 6. **Visual handicap –** Type 6 7. **Auditory handicap –** Type 7 9. **Support at home for children who are temporarily ill**	3. **Serious emotional and/or behavioural problems –** Type 3 8. **Serious learning disabilities –** Type 8 10. **Extending care** 11. **Remedial teaching**	12. **Educational priority policy** 13. **Reception classes for pupils who do not speak Dutch** 14. **Travelling children** 15. **Children placed in a sheltered home by juvenile court** 16. **More favourable teacher/pupil ratio in the schools of the Capital region of Brussels** 17. **Additional resources for schools in some municipalities around the Capital region of Brussels and at the linguistic border between the Flemish and the Walloon regions**
Canada (Alberta)	1. **Severe mental disability** (Code 41) 3. **Severe multiple disability** (Code 43) 4. **Severe physical or medical disability** (Code 44) 5. **Deafness** (Code 45) 6. **Blindness** (Code 46) 7. **Severe communications disorder** (Code 47; ECS only) 8. **Mild mental disability** (Code 51) 9. **Moderate mental disability** (Code 52) 12. **Mild/moderate hearing disability** (Code 55)	2. **Severe emotional / behavioural disability** (Code 42) 10. **Mild/moderate emotional / behavioural disability** (Code 53) 11. **Learning disability** (Code 54) 17. **Gifted and talented** (Code 80)	

Country	Cross-National Category A	Cross-National Category B	Cross-National Category C
Canada (Alberta) (cont.)	13. **Mild/moderate visual disability** (Code 56) 14. **Mild/moderate communication disability** (Code 57) 15. **Mild/moderate physical/medical disability** (Code 58) 16. **Mild/moderate multiple disability** (Code 59)		
Canada (British Colombia)	1. **Visual impairments** 3. **Deaf/Blindness** 4. **Multiple disabilities** 5. **Hearing impairments** 6. **Autism** 8. **Moderate to severe to profound intellectual disabilities** 10. **Severe behaviour disorders** 14. **Physical disabilities or chronic health impairments**	2. **Specific learning disabilities** 7. **Mild intellectual disabilities** 9. **Mild to moderate behaviour disorders, including rehabilitation** 11. **Gifted** 12. **Learning assistance**	13. **English as a second language** 15. **Aboriginal education programme**
Canada (New Brunswick)	2. **Communicational** 3. **Intellectual** 4. **Physical** 5. **Perceptual** 6. **Multiple**	1. **Behavioural exceptionalities**	7. **Immigrant**
Canada (Saskatchewan)	1. **Intellectual disabilities** 2. **Visual impairments** 4. **Orthopaedic impairments** 5. **Chronically ill** 7. **Multiple disabilities**	3. **Social, emotional or behavioural disorder** 6. **Learning disabilities**	

Country	Cross-National Category A	Cross-National Category B	Cross-National Category C
Canada (Saskatchewan) (cont.)	8. Deaf or hard of hearing 9. Autism 10. Traumatic brain injury		
Czech Republic	1. Mentally retarded 2. Hearing handicaps 3. Sight handicaps 4. Speech handicaps 5. Physical handicaps 6. Multiple handicaps 9. Other handicaps 10. With weakened health (Kindergarten only)	7. Students in hospitals 8. Development, behaviour and learning problems	11. Socially disadvantaged children, preparatory classes in regular schools
Finland	2. Moderate mental impairment (MOMI) 3. Most severe mental impairment (SMI) 4. Hearing impairment (HI) 5. Visual impairment (VI) 6. Physical and other impairment (POHI) 8. Other impairments	1. Mild mental impairment (MIMI) 7. Emotional & social impairment (EI) 9. Speech difficulties 10. Reading and writing difficulties 11. Speech, reading and writing difficulties 12. Learning difficulties in mathematics 13. Learning difficulties in foreign languages 14. General learning difficulties 15. Emotional and social difficulties 16. Other special difficulties 18. Remedial teaching	17. Remedial teaching for immigrants

Country	Cross-National Category A	Cross-National Category B	Cross-National Category C
France	1. Severe mental handicap 2. Moderate mental handicap 3. Mild mental handicap 4. Physical handicap 5. Metabolic disorders 6. Deaf 7. Partially hearing 8. Blind 9. Partially sighted 10. Other neuropsychological disorders 11. Speech and language disorders 12. Other deficiencies 13. Multiply handicapped	15. Learning difficulties	14. Non-francophone students 16. Disadvantaged children – ZEP
Germany	2. Partially sighted or blind 3. Partially hearing or deaf 4. Speech impairment 5. Physically handicapped 6. Mentally handicapped 8. Sick 9. Multiple handicaps 11. Autism (No statistical data of the large groups available, but programmes are provided)	1. Learning disability 7. Behavioural disorders 10. Unknown, no information 12. Remedial instruction (No statistical data of the large groups available, but programmes are provided)	13. Travelling families (No statistical data of the large groups available, but programmes are provided) 14. German for speakers of other languages (No statistical data of the large groups available, but programmes are provided)
Greece	1. Visual impairments 2. Hearing impairments 3. Physical impairment 4. Mental impairments 5. Autism	6. Learning difficulties 7. Multiple impairment	8. Socio-economic/cultural educational difficulties

Country	Cross-National Category A	Cross-National Category B	Cross-National Category C
Hungary	2. Pupils with moderate degree mental retardation 3. Pupils with visual disabilities 4. Pupils with hearing disabilities 5. Pupils with motoric disabilities 6. Pupils with speech disabilities 7. Pupils with other disabilities	1. Pupils with mild degree mental retardation	8. Children of minorities 9. Disadvantaged pupils/Pupils at risk
Ireland	1. Visually impaired 2. Hearing impaired 3. Mild mental handicap 4. Moderate mental handicap 7. Physically handicapped 8. Specific speech and language disorders 9. Specific learning disability 11. Severely and profoundly mentally handicapped 12. Multiply handicapped	5. Emotionally disturbed 6. Severely emotionally disturbed 15. Pupils in need of remedial teaching	10. Classes of children of travelling families 13. Young offenders 14. Children in schools serving disadvantaged areas 16. Children of refugees
Italy	1. Visual impairment 2. Hearing impairment 3. Moderate mental handicap 4. Severe mental handicap 5. Mild physical handicap 6. Severe physical handicap 7. Multiple handicap		8. Students with foreign citizenship (No statistical data available)

Country	Cross-National Category A	Cross-National Category B	Cross-National Category C
Japan	1. Blind and partially sighted 2. Deaf and hard of hearing 3. Intellectual disabilities 4. Physically disabled 5. Health impaired 6. Speech impaired 7. Emotionally disturbed		8. Students who require Japanese instruction
Luxembourg	1. Mental characteristic 2. Emotionally disturbed children 3. Sensory characteristic 4. Motor characteristic	6. Learning difficulties	5. Social impairment
Mexico	1. Blindness 2. Partial visual disability 3. Intellectual disability 4. Auditory or hearing disability 5. Deafness or severe auditory disability 6. Motor disability 7. Multiple disability	8. Learning difficulties 9. Outstanding capabilities and skills	10. Compensatory educational needs 11. Communitary educational needs 12. Indigenous communitary educational needs 13. Migrant educational needs
Netherlands	1. Deaf children 2. Hard of hearing 3. Language and communication disabilities 4. Visual handicap 5. Physically handicapped / motor impairment 6. Other health impairments (No long hospitalisation)	7. Learning and behaviour disabilities 13. Children in vocational training with learning difficulties	12. Children from disadvantaged backgrounds

Country	Cross-National Category A	Cross-National Category B	Cross-National Category C
Netherlands (cont.)	8. Profound mental handicap / severe learning disabilities 9. Deviant behaviour 10. Chronic conditions requiring pedagogical institutes 11. Multiply handicapped		
Poland	1. Light mental handicap 2. Multiple and severe mental handicap 3. Profound mental handicap 4. Blind 5. Partially sighted 6. Deaf 7. Partially hearing 8. Chronically sick 9. Motion handicapped 11. Autistic		10. Social disadvantages, behaviour difficulties
Spain	1. Hearing impaired 2. Motor impaired 3. Visual impaired 4. Mental handicap 5. Emotional/behavioural problems 6. Multiple impairment	7. Highly gifted 9. Programmes addressed to students in hospitals or with health problems 11. Learning difficulties	8. Students with compensatory education needs 10. Problems addressed to itinerant students
Sweden	1. Pupils with impaired hearing, vision and physical disabilities 2. Students with mental retardation 3. Students with impaired hearing and physical disabilities		4. Students receiving tuition in mother tongue (other than Swedish) and/or Swedish as a second language 5. Students in need of special support (not included in other categories)

Country	Cross-National Category A	Cross-National Category B	Cross-National Category C
Switzerland	9. Educable mental handicap – Special schools 10. Trainable mental handicap – Special schools 11. Multiply handicapped – Special schools 12. Physical disabilities – Special schools 13. Behaviour disorders – Special schools 14. Deaf or hard of hearing – Special schools 15. Language disability – Special schools 16. Visual handicap – Special schools 17. Chronic conditions/prolonged hospitalisation – Special schools 18. Multiple disabilities – Special schools	1. Learning disabilities / introductory classes – Special classes 2. Learning disabilities / special classes – Special classes 3. Learning disabilities / vocationally oriented classes – Special classes 4. Behavioural difficulties – Special classes 6. Physical disabilities – Special classes 7. Sensory & language impairments – Special classes 8. Students who are ill / hospital classes - Special classes 19. Others of the group "special curriculum" – Special classes	5. Foreign first language
Turkey	1. **Visually impaired** (includes both blind and low vision children) 2. **Hearing impaired** 3. **Orthopaedically handicapped** 4. **Educable mentally handicapped** 5. **Trainable mentally handicapped** 6. **Speech impairment** 8. **Chronically ill**	7. **Gifted and talented**	

Country	Cross-National Category A	Cross-National Category B	Cross-National Category C
United Kingdom	1. Children with statements (records) of special educational needs	2. Children with special educational needs without statements (records)	
United States	1. Mental retardation 2. Speech or language impairment 3. Visual impairments 5. Orthopaedic impairments 6. Other health impairments 8. Deaf/blindness 9. Multiple disabilities 10. Hearing impairments 11. Autism 12. Traumatic brain injury 13. Developmental delay	4. Emotional disturbance 7. Specific learning disability	14. Title 1 – Disadvantaged students

CHAPTER 4
COMPARATIVE ANALYSIS OF QUANTITATIVE DATA BASED ON CATEGORIES OF DISABILITIES, LEARNING DIFFICULTIES, AND DISADVANTAGES

Background

This chapter analyses the data provided by countries by categories of disability, learning difficulties and disadvantages based on the resources definition given in Chapter 1 that each country uses based on the returns given in Tables 2, 3 and 4 of the electronic questionnaire. Individual country data are available on the Internet, *www.oecd.org/edu/equity/senddd*. In contrast to the earlier monograph (OECD, 2000b), which only included students with disabilities or learning difficulties this revised chapter also includes students with disadvantages. The data also cover only those students who are registered by the education authorities and they suffer from the limitation of not including disabled students of the relevant age who are outside of the education system. However, earlier work (OECD, 1995a), largely confirmed by this data collection round (see Chapter 6), showed that these numbers would be either very small or non-existent since many countries have 100% of students of school age under the aegis of the education authorities.

The data are broken down by categories and presented as proportions of the total numbers of students in pre-primary, primary, lower secondary and upper secondary education. In addition, information is provided on the place or location of these students' education, *i.e.* in regular classes, special classes or special schools, expressed as proportions of the total numbers of students in that category in the particular location.

The data in this chapter have been assembled in the full knowledge of the difficulty of making international comparisons on the basis of national categories. However, it was considered useful to carry out this analysis in order to keep touch with the basic data in the form in which it was presented, using terminology that many readers would more readily follow and to provide the context for comparisons made through cross-national categories A, B and C. The method used is outlined below. Table 3.2 provides the background information revealing the inherent difficulty in making international comparisons. First, not all countries use categorical models. Second, the categories that are used are not uniform across countries. Third the definitions of the categories, when available, vary among countries. It is of course partly for these reasons that the resources model and the cross-national categorisation system have been developed.

Methodology

In order to make the comparisons across the categories provided by countries that are supplied in this chapter it is necessary to bring together the different national frameworks that exist. In order to do this, the definitions of the categories were carefully scrutinised and brought together according to the structure of the matrix given in the table in Annex 2. The data classification displayed in this matrix was used to construct the comparative charts, given in the chapter. For example, columns 1 and 2 show national categories covering students who are partially sighted or blind. The data for Belgium (Fl.) shows a "*6x*" in column 1 and a "*6x*" in column 2. The "6" refers to the national category covering students with partial sight or blindness and the "x" indicates that for instance partially sighted students are also included in the category "Blind". This means that data cannot be shown separately for these two categories. This is in contrast for instance to Canada (Alb.) in the second row where data on partially sighted students is contained in their national category 13 and for blind students in their national category 6. As the two columns reveal few countries keep data on these two groups of students separately and thus the Chart 4.1P has been constructed by bringing together the data for the two groups of students. Comparative charts are only presented if data are available for three or more countries. This means that although data are available for 22 categories only 15 of them allow for international comparisons.

Data on individual categories

Chart 4.1 (A-O) shows the percentages of students in the 15 main categories of disability, difficulties and disadvantage used by participating countries which allow for comparisons across four or more countries. Sometimes charts are presented with only three countries where a graphical presentation of the data seems particularly useful. Where possible, data on discrete categories are presented when data is available for four or more countries. The categories concerning blind and partially sighted students are presented together since the majority of countries do not keep separate data for the two individual categories. This also applies for the data on partially hearing and deaf students. Data on aboriginal and indigenous students as well as young offenders data are not analysed because only two countries provide data on each of these categories. Data on gifted and talented students are not analysed because the educational problems faced by gifted and talented children would appear to be very different from those faced by DDD students.

The percentages are calculated by dividing the number of students in each category by the total number of students in primary and lower secondary education (which are used as proxies for ISCED 1 and 2), with the exception of Belgium (Fl.) which includes upper secondary students (ISCED 3) and Poland and Turkey which only include primary education students (ISCED 1).

The figures are based on full-time study except for Finland. Data refer to the school year 1998/99, with the exception of Canada (Alb., BC, NB), Greece, Luxembourg, Japan and Mexico where data cover the period 1999/2000 and Turkey with data from 1997/98. In Germany data on students in programmes in special schools refer to year 1999/2000 and data on students in programmes in regular classes refer to year 2000/2001. The figures are based on both public and private institutions.

From the point of view of making international comparisons, Chart 4.1 reveals two major issues arising from the natural complexity of the area studied. First, comparison is hampered by the inconsistent use of categories among countries. Only seven, the blind and partially sighted (4.1A), the deaf and partially hearing (4.1B), emotional and behavioural difficulties (4.1C) physical disabilities (4.1D), speech and language difficulties (4.1E), combinatorial disabilities (4.1G), and learning disabilities (4.1L) are used by 10 or more countries. The remaining eight are used to varying degrees. All 15 categories are discussed in greater detail in the following sections. Second, close inspection of the individual categories reveals unexpectedly large differences among countries in the proportions of students identified. The information needed to understand these differences is simply not readily available.

Also note that there is some amount of double counting. This has been taken into account here and adjustments made. Nonetheless, proportions may be underestimated because of some missing data.

CHAPTER 4. COMPARATIVE ANALYSIS OF QUANTITATIVE DATA BASED ON CATEGORIES OF DDD

Chart 4.1 (A-O). Students receiving additional resources in primary and lower secondary education by disability category and by country as a percentage of all students[1]

N.B.: only includes data which can be readily placed in one of the 15 categories below.

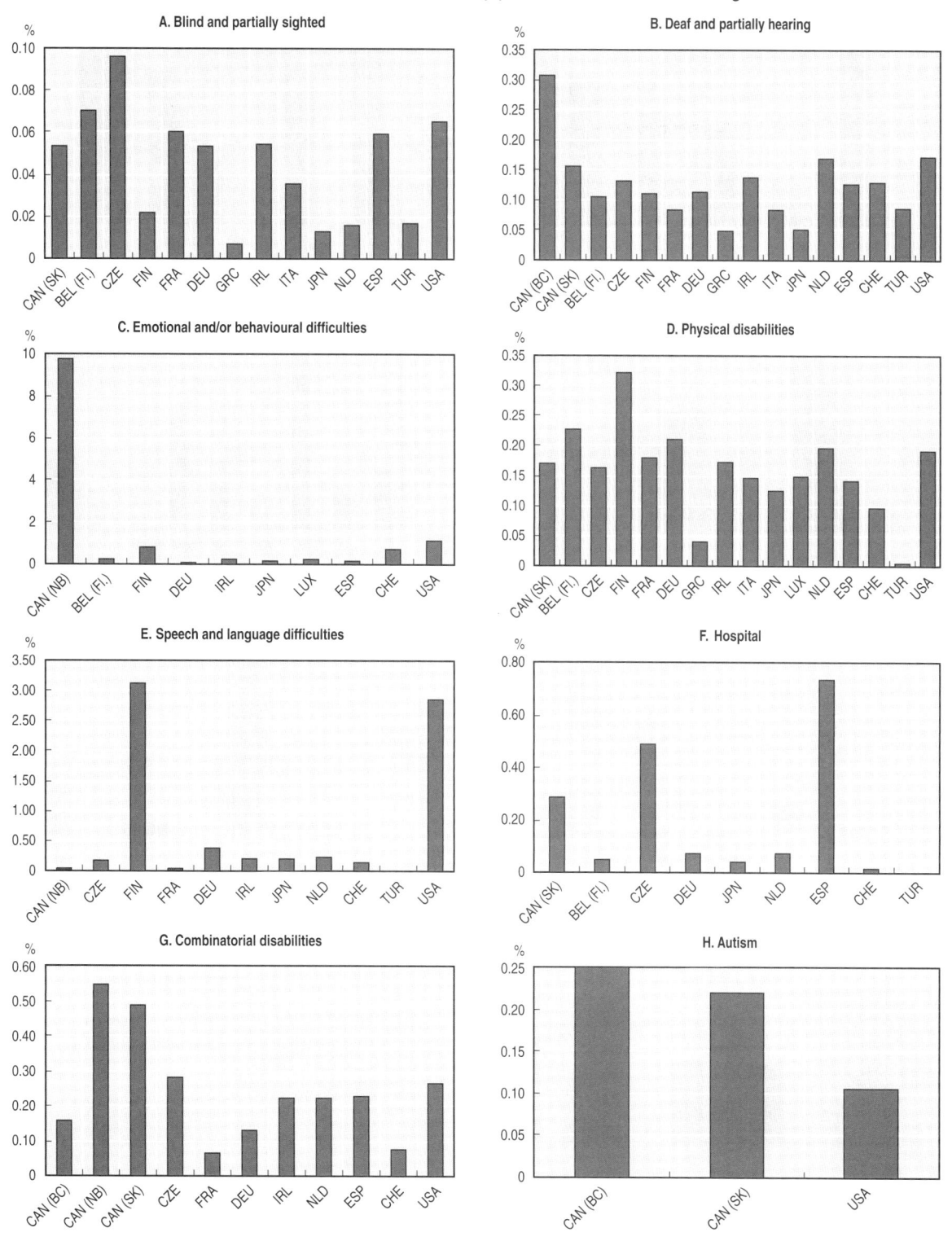

A. Blind and partially sighted

B. Deaf and partially hearing

C. Emotional and/or behavioural difficulties

D. Physical disabilities

E. Speech and language difficulties

F. Hospital

G. Combinatorial disabilities

H. Autism

1. For France, Germany, Luxembourg and Switzerland data are for the period of compulsory education.

Chart 4.1 (A-O). Students receiving additional resources in primary and lower secondary education by disability category and by country as a percentage of all students[1] *(continued)*

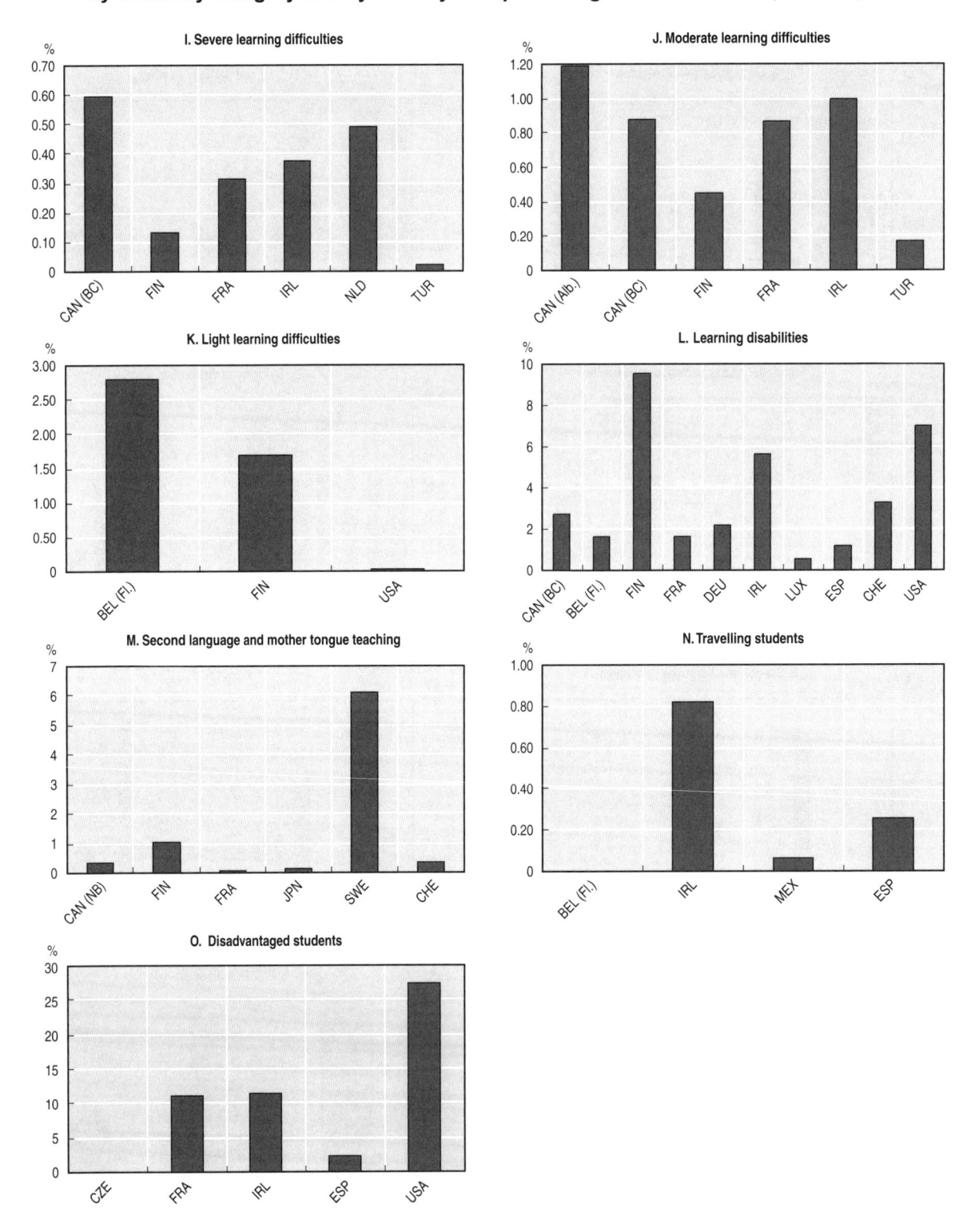

I. Severe learning difficulties

J. Moderate learning difficulties

K. Light learning difficulties

L. Learning disabilities

M. Second language and mother tongue teaching

N. Travelling students

O. Disadvantaged students

1. For France, Germany, Luxembourg and Switzerland data are for the period of compulsory education.

Description by category

Blind and partially sighted

The statistics on the categories covering blind and partially sighted students are treated separately in only a few countries (Canada [Alb.], France, Mexico and Poland) but in most are brought together as a single category which is used for reporting the data here.

As can be seen from Chart 4.1A the proportion of blind and partially sighted students receiving additional resources varies substantially from country to country, the lowest percentages being in Greece and Japan (0.01%), and the highest in the Czech Republic (0.10%). This means that some countries register in their education statistics proportionally 10 times as many as others. Even if the highest and lowest figures are ignored the differences remain substantial with the Belgium (Fl.) and the United States (0.07%) registering 3.5 times as many as Finland, Netherlands and Turkey (0.02%).

Charts 4.2 and 4.3 show where these students are being educated (regular classes, special classes or special schools). A comparison of Charts 4.1A and 4.2 suggests that the different proportions identified are independent of the nature of the placement.

Chart 4.2. **Blind and partially sighted students in primary and lower secondary education by location as a percentage of all students**[1, 2, 3, 4]

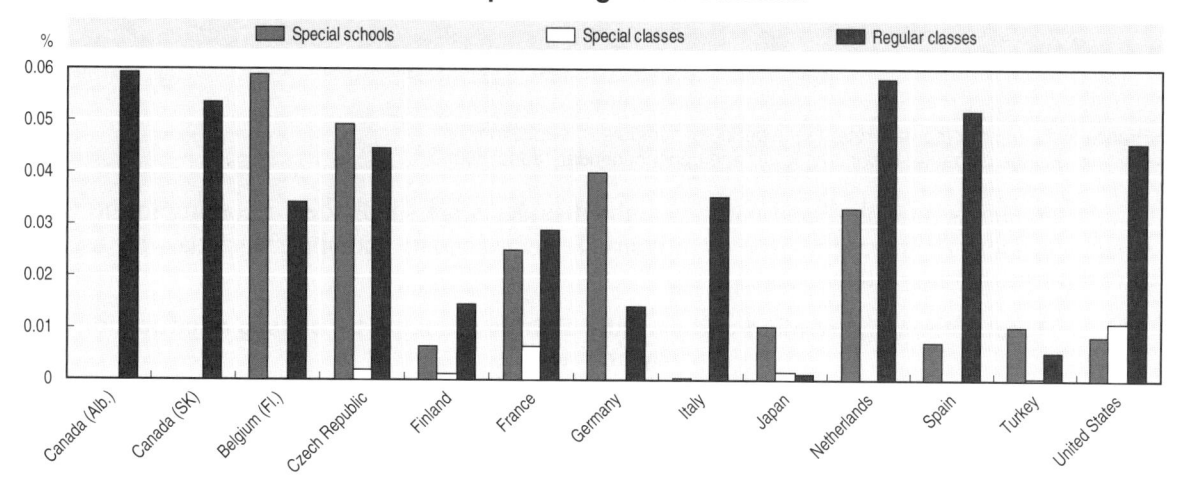

1. In France and Germany the data refer to the period of compulsory education.
2. For special schools in Canada (Alb.) data are not available; in Canada (SK) and Italy data are negligible.
3. For special classes in Belgium (Fl.), Canada (Alb.), Netherlands and Sweden data are not applicable, in Canada (SK) and Italy data are negligible; in Germany and Spain data are included in special schools.
4. In Belgium (Fl.) data refer to primary, lower secondary and upper secondary.

Chart 4.3, on the other hand, shows how variable the placement is among countries. It shows that eight countries use regular classes, special classes and special schools; the Czech Republic (46.60%, 2.18%, 51.22%), Finland (65.63%, 4.69%, 29.69%), France (47.86%, 10.77%, 41.37%), Ireland (78.47%, 0.28%, 21.25%), Italy (98.91%, 0.24%, 0.85%), Japan (9.33%, 10.75%, 79.92%), Turkey (33.18%, 3.34%, 63.48%), and the United States (70.28%, 16.91%, 12.81%).

Four countries have a binary system dividing these students between regular classes and special schools: Belgium (Fl.) (46.69%, 53.31%), Germany (26.06%, 73.94%), the Netherlands (63.76%, 36.24%), and Spain (87.92%, 12.08%). In Greece, pupils are located in special classes (27.14%) and in special schools (72.86%).

At the extremes, the location of education varies considerably. In Canada (SK) all blind and partially sighted students are educated in regular schools in contrast, for instance, to Japan and Greece where most are in special schools. In Switzerland, Sweden and Hungary the majority of students are educated in special schools but missing data prevent the calculation of the proportions in each location.

Chart 4.3. **Proportion of partially sighted and blind students in primary and lower secondary education by location and by country**[1, 2]

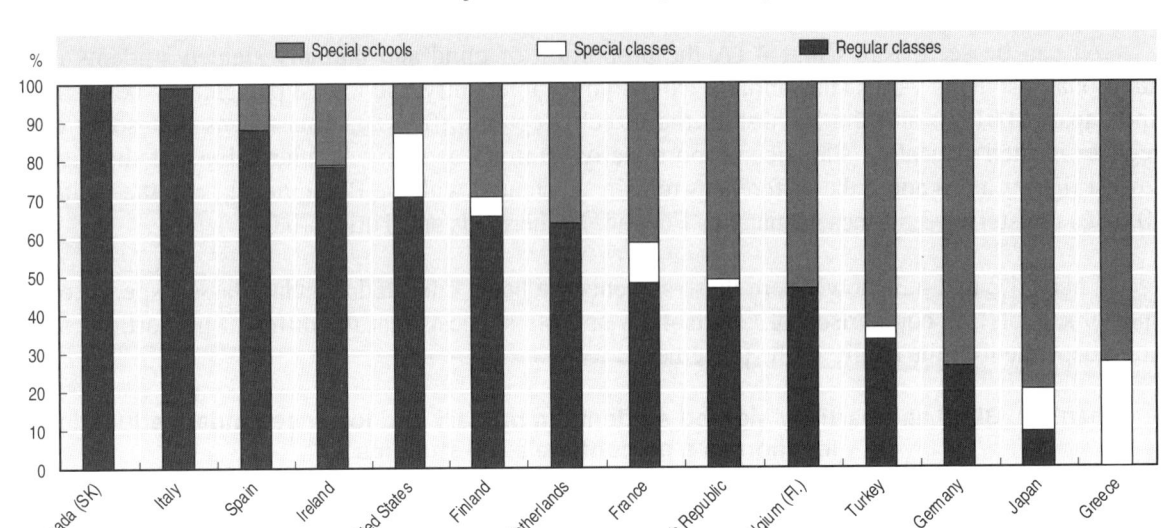

1. In France and Germany the data refer to the period of compulsory education.
2. In Belgium (Fl.) the data refer to primary, lower and upper secondary education.

Chart 4.4 shows how blind and partially sighted students are subdivided according to the various phases of education. The terms pre-primary, primary, lower secondary and upper secondary are used here as proxies for ISCED levels 0, 1, 2 and 3.

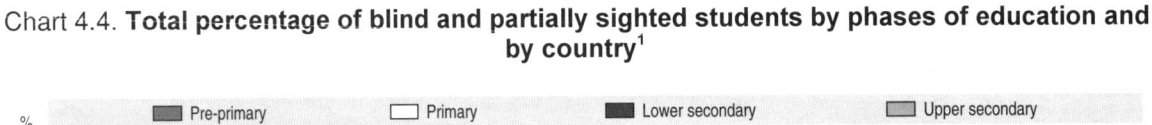

Chart 4.4. **Total percentage of blind and partially sighted students by phases of education and by country**[1]

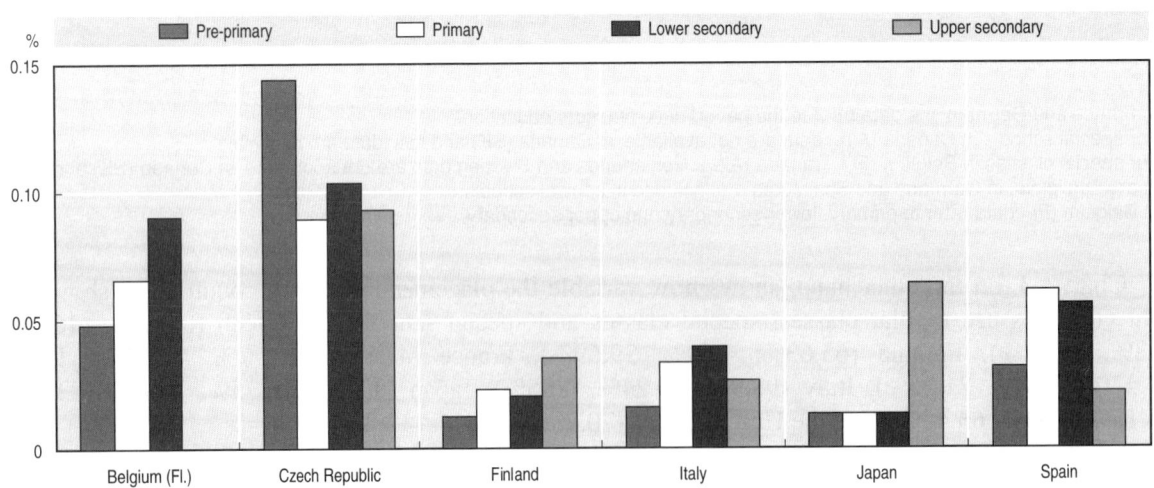

1. For Belgium (Fl.) upper secondary students are included in lower secondary.

Given the nature of the disability making up this category there appears to be little or no consistency across countries in terms of a pattern developing by age.

Deaf and partially hearing

As for blind and partially sighted students, the statistics gathered on categories covering deaf and partially hearing pupils are treated separately in only a few countries (Canada [Alb.], France, Mexico and the Netherlands). In most countries, they are treated as a single entity and this method is adopted here.

As can be seen from Chart 4.1B, the proportion of deaf and partially hearing students registered in educational statistics varies substantially from country to country, the lowest percentage being Greece and Japan (0.05%) and the highest Canada (BC) (0.31%). This means that some countries register proportionally 6.2 times as many as others. If the highest and lowest are ignored, the Netherlands and the United States (0.17%) register 2.1 times as many as Italy (0.08%).

Charts 4.5 and 4.6 show where these students are being educated (regular classes, special classes or special schools). A comparison of Charts 4.1B and 4.5 suggests that the different proportions identified are independent of the nature of the placement.

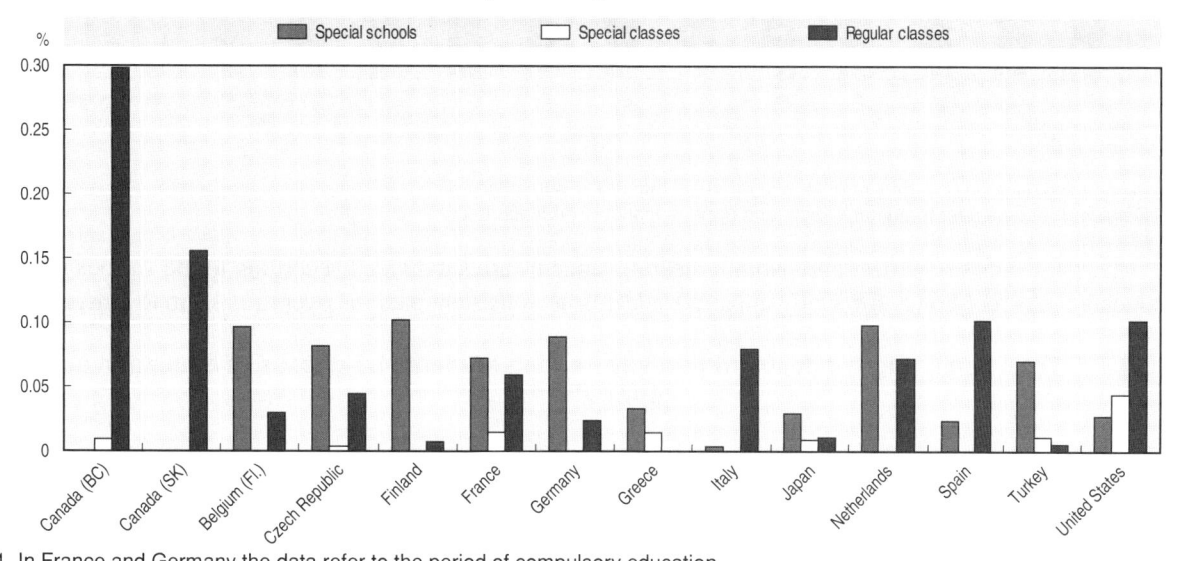

Chart 4.5. **Deaf and partially hearing students in primary and lower secondary education by location as a percentage of all students**[1, 2, 3, 4]

1. In France and Germany the data refer to the period of compulsory education.
2. For special schools in Canada (BC) data are not applicable; in Canada (SK) and Italy data are negligible.
3. For special classes in Belgium (Fl.) and the Netherlands data are not applicable; in Canada (SK) and Italy data are negligible; in Germany and Spain data are included in special schools.
4. For regular classes in Greece data are included in special classes; in Belgium (Fl.) data refer to primary, lower and upper secondary education.

Chart 4.6 on the other hand, shows how variable the placement is among countries. It reveals that seven countries divide deaf and hearing impaired pupils among regular classes, special classes and special schools: the Czech Republic (34.14%, 3.01%, 62.85%), Finland (6.56%, 0.47%, 92.97%), France (40.44%, 10.15%, 49.41%), Italy (95.16%, 0.47%, 4.36%), Japan (23.22%, 18%, 58.78%), Turkey (6.32%, 12.81%, 80.87%) and the United States (58.67%, 25.42%, 15.91%).

Five countries have a binary system. Regular classes and special schools are used in Belgium (Fl.) (33.21%, 66.79%), Germany (20.84%, 79.16%), the Netherlands (42.32%, 57.68%), and Spain (80.79%, 19.21%). In Greece, they attend either special classes (29.70%) or special schools (70.30%) because in the Greek educational system regular classes are included in special classes.

At the extremes, the location of education varies considerably with the majority being educated in regular classes in Canada (SK) in contrast to Finland, Turkey and Greece for instance where the majority are in special schools. In Switzerland and Hungary most students are educated in special schools but missing data prevent the calculation of the proportions in each location.

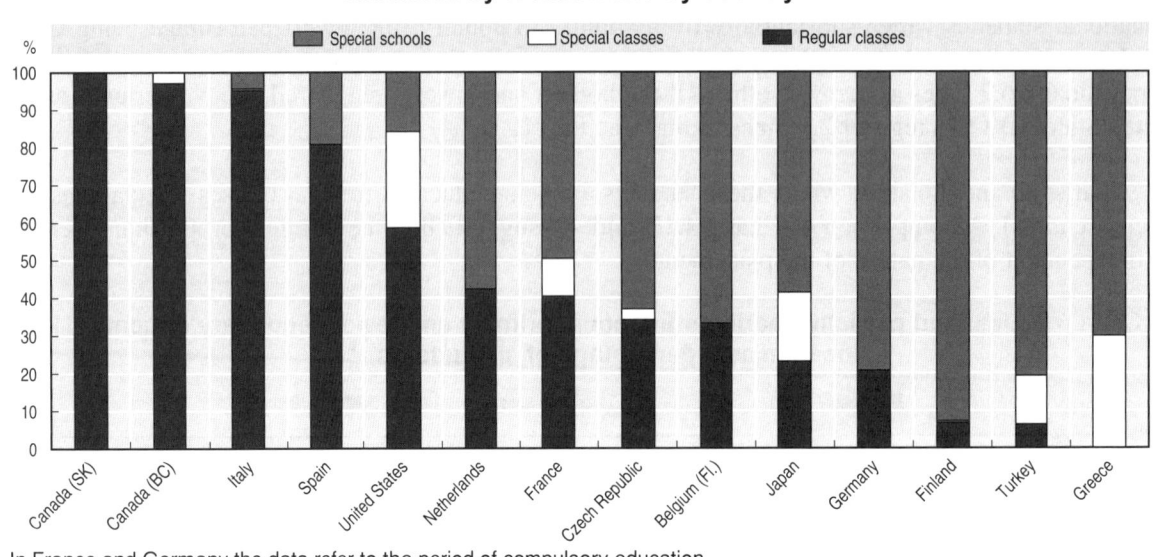

Chart 4.6. **Proportion of deaf and partially hearing students in primary and lower secondary education by location and by country** [1, 2]

1. In France and Germany the data refer to the period of compulsory education.
2. In Belgium (Fl.) data refer to primary, lower and upper secondary education.

Chart 4.7 shows how deaf and partially hearing students are subdivided according to the various phases of education. As for blind and visually impaired students no consistent patterns over time seem to emerge.

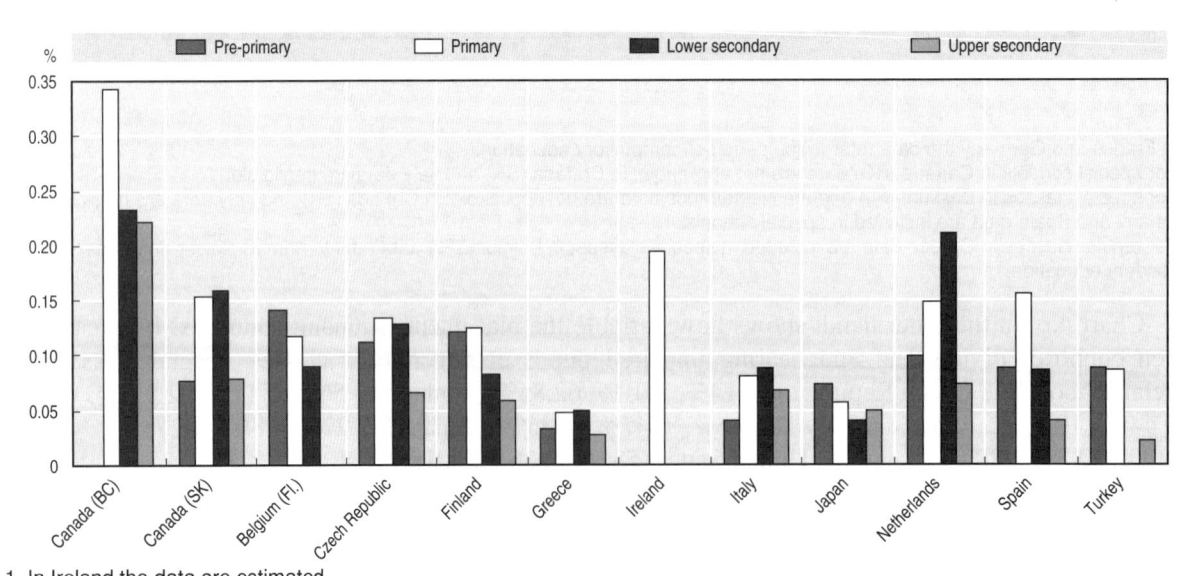

Chart 4.7. **Total percentage of deaf and partially hearing students by phases of education and by country** [1, 2, 3, 4]

1. In Ireland the data are estimated.
2. For pre-primary education in Canada (BC) data are not available; in Ireland data are not applicable.
3. For lower secondary education in Ireland data are not available; in Turkey data are not applicable.
4. For upper secondary education in Ireland data are not available; in Belgium (Fl.) data are included in lower secondary education.

Emotional and behavioural difficulties

It is of interest to note that given the apparent rise in the numbers of students described as having behaviour difficulties, not all countries use such a category. For those who do, there is evidence for a greater differentiation in terms of location than in the two preceding clusters of categories.

As can be seen from Chart 4.1C the proportion of students with emotional and behavioural difficulties varies substantially from country to country. The lowest percentage being in Germany (0.10%) and the highest in Canada (NB) (9.79%), proportionally nearly a hundred fold difference. Even if the extremes are ignored there remains substantial difference with Finland (0.78%) being 3.1 times more than Luxembourg (0.25%).

Charts 4.8 and 4.9 show where these students are being educated (regular classes, special classes or special schools). A comparison of Charts 4.1C and 4.8 suggests that the different proportions identified are independent of the nature of the placement.

Chart 4.8. **Students with emotional and/or behavioural difficulties in primary and lower secondary education by location as a percentage of all students**[1, 2, 3, 4]

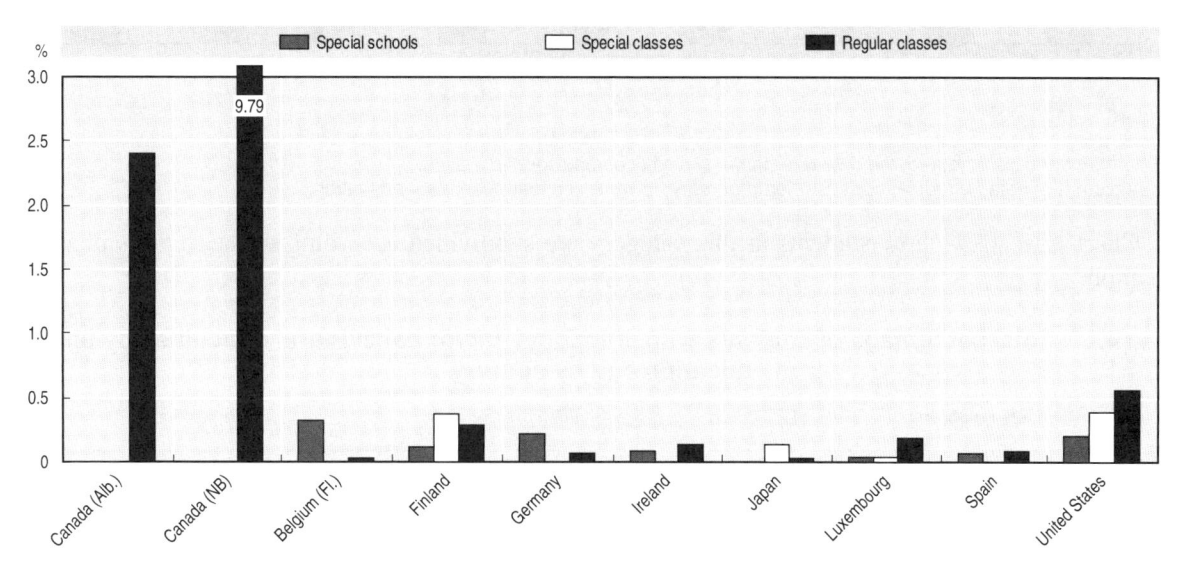

1. In Germany and Luxembourg the data refer to the period of compulsory education.
2. For special schools in Canada (Alb.) data are not available; in Canada (NB) and Japan data are not applicable.
3. For special classes in Canada (Alb.), Canada (NB) and Belgium (Fl.), data are not applicable; in Germany and Spain data are included in special schools.
4. For regular classes in Belgium (Fl.) data refer to primary, lower and upper secondary education.

Chart 4.9, on the other hand, shows how variable the placement is among countries. It shows that four countries use regular classes, special classes and special schools: Finland (36.60%, 47.05%, 16.35%), Ireland (62.73%, 2.28%, 34.99%), Luxembourg (75.52%, 10.49%, 13.99%) and the United States (48.47%, 33.87%, 17.66%).

Four countries use two locations. Regular classes and special schools are used in Belgium (Fl.) (3.34%, 96.66%), Germany (26.11%, 73.89%), and Spain (58.07%, 41.93%). Regular classes and special classes are used in Japan (13.20%, 86.80%).

At the extremes, the location of education varies considerably. In Canada (NB) all students with emotional and behavioural difficulties are educated in regular classes while in other countries the majority are in special schools or classes.

Chart 4.9. **Proportion of pupils with emotional and/or behavioural difficulties in primary and lower secondary education by location and by country**[1, 2]

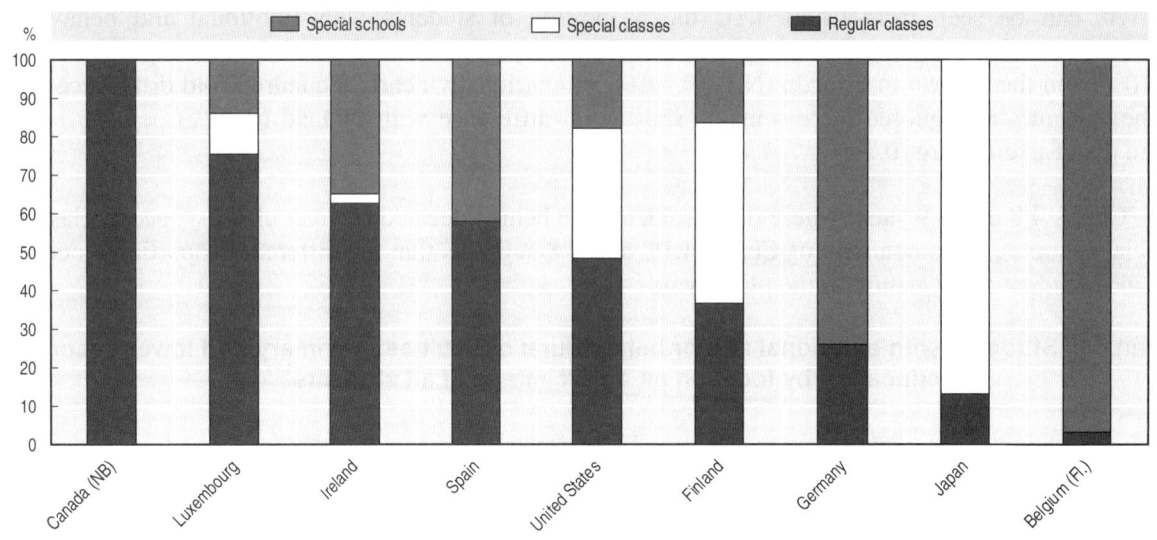

1. In Germany and Luxembourg, the data refer to the period of compulsory education.
2. In Belgium (Fl.) data for regular classes refer to primary, lower and upper secondary education.

Chart 4.10 shows how students in this category are subdivided according to the various phases of education.

Chart 4.10. **Total percentage of students with emotional and/or behavioural difficulties by phases of education and by country**[1, 2, 3]

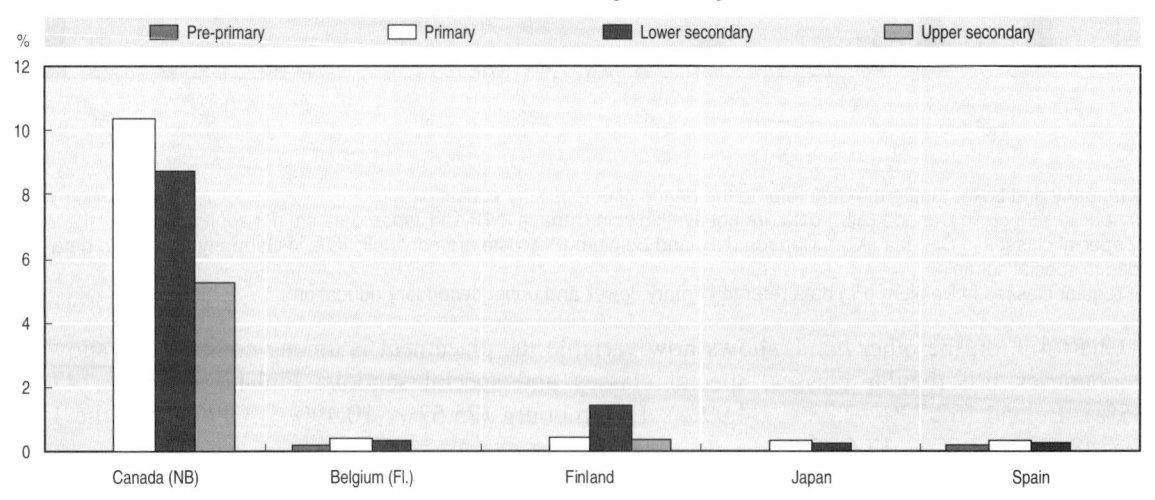

1. For upper secondary education in Belgium (Fl.) data are included in lower secondary education; in Japan data are not applicable, in Spain data are negligible.
2. For pre-primary education in Canada (NB) data are not applicable; in Finland only a negligible number; in Japan data are not applicable.
3. In Belgium (Fl.) data refer to primary, lower and upper secondary education.

No consistent patterns over time seem to emerge.

Physical disability

It is readily observable from Chart 4.1D that there is great variation in the proportion of students with physical disabilities in all countries. Finland (0.32%) has the highest percentages, while the lowest is in Greece (0.04%) which means that proportionally Finland registers in educational statistics 8 times as many students as Greece. Even if the most extreme countries are not considered, Germany (0.21%) registers 2.1 times more than Switzerland (0.10%).

Charts 4.11 and 4.12 show where these students are being educated (regular classes, special classes or special schools). A comparison of Charts 4.1D and 4.11 suggests that the different proportions identified are independent of the nature of the placement.

Chart 4.11. **Students with physical disabilities in primary and lower secondary education by location as a percentage of all students**[1, 2, 3, 4]

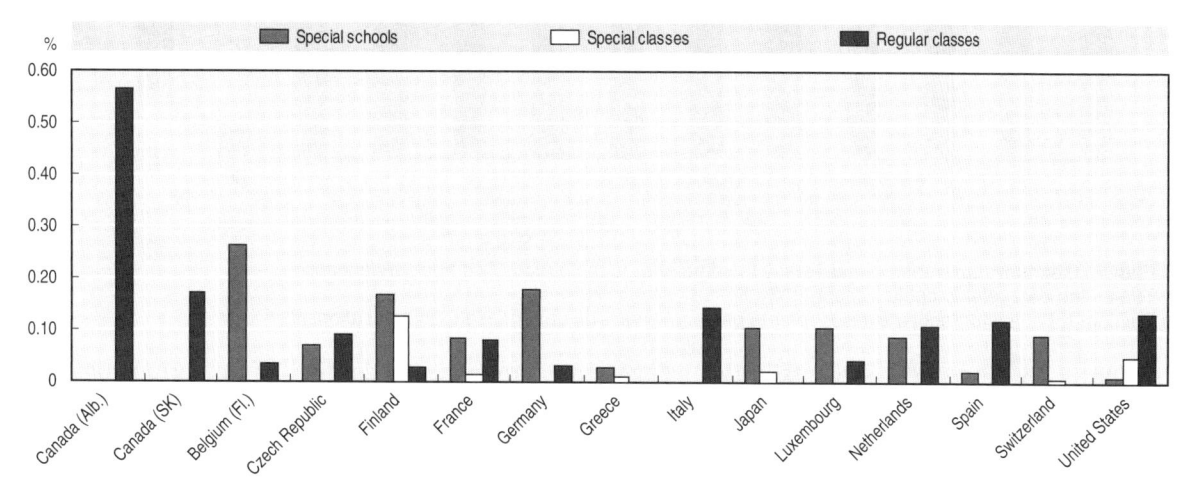

1. In France, Germany, Luxembourg and Switzerland the data refer to the period of compulsory education.
2. For special schools in Canada (Alb.) data are not available; in Canada (SK) and Italy data are negligible.
3. For special classes in Canada (SK), Czech Republic and Italy data are negligible; in Canada (Alb.), Belgium (Fl.) and the Netherlands data are not applicable; in Germany and Spain data are included in special schools.
4. For regular classes in Greece data are included in special classes; in Japan data are negligible; in Switzerland data are not available; in Belgium (Fl.) data refer to primary, lower and upper secondary education.

Chart 4.12 on the other hand, shows how variable the placement is among countries.

As shown in Chart 4.12, six countries use all three locations, regular classes, special classes and special schools; the Czech Republic (55.78%, 0.41%, 43.81%), Finland (9.17%, 38.88%, 51.95%), France (45.03%, 7.11%, 47.86%), Italy (99.30 %, 0.30%, 0.40%), Japan (0.05%, 15.48%, 84.48%) and the United States (69.20%, 25.28%, 5.52%).

Six countries have systems which distribute these students between regular classes and special schools: Belgium (Fl.) (16.35%, 83.65%), Germany (15.35%, 84.65%), Luxembourg (27.71%, 72.29%), the Netherlands (55.03%, 44.97%), Spain (85.34%, 14.66%), and Turkey (50.38%, 49.62%). One country uses special classes and special schools and special classes are equals to regular classes in their educational system: Greece (27.16 %, 72.84%).

At the extremes the location of education varies considerably. In Canada (SK) and Italy the majority of students are educated in regular schools in contrast to Belgium (Fl.) and Germany where the majority are in special schools. In Switzerland and Hungary where the majority of students remain in special schools but missing data prevent the calculation of the proportions in each location.

Chart 4.12. **Proportion of students with physical disabilities in primary and lower secondary education by location and by country**[1, 2, 3]

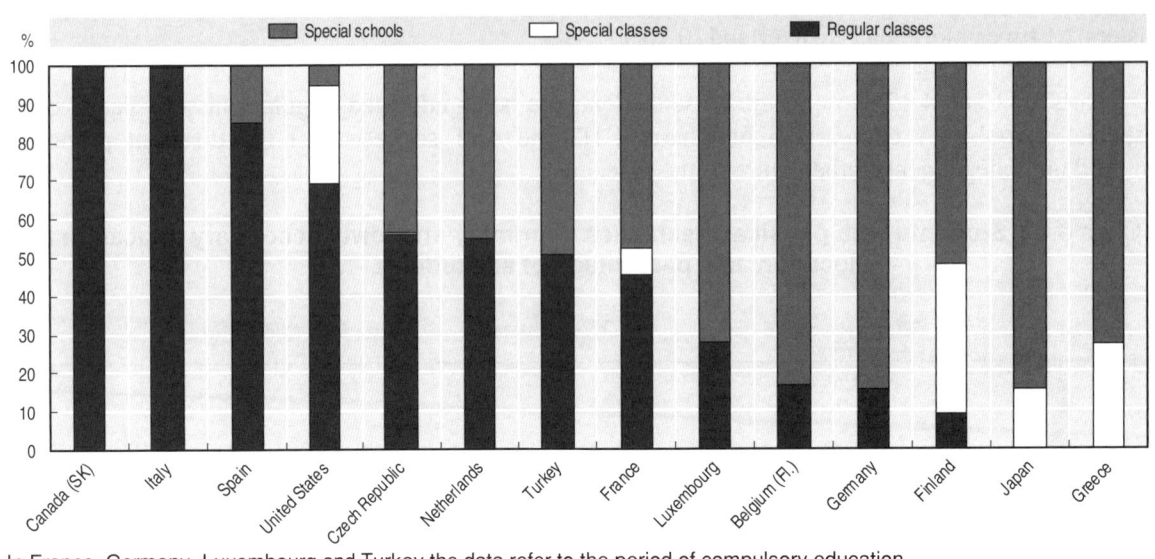

1. In France, Germany, Luxembourg and Turkey the data refer to the period of compulsory education.
2. In Turkey the data refer to public schools only.
3. In Belgium (Fl.) data for regular classes refer to primary, lower and upper secondary education.

Chart 4.13 shows how students in this category are subdivided according to the various phases of education. Again no consistent pattern emerges although in some countries more students with physical disabilities receive additional resources in the primary period.

Chart 4.13. **Total percentage of students with physical disabilities by phases of education and by country**[1]

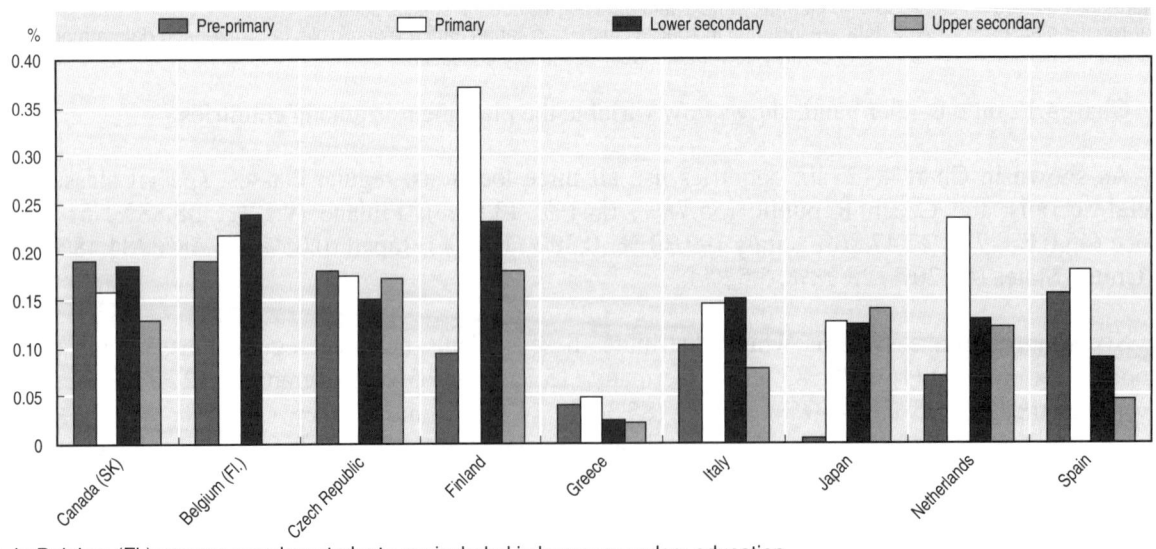

1. In Belgium (Fl.) upper secondary students are included in lower secondary education.

Speech and language difficulties

As can be seen from Chart 4.1E the percentages of students registered with speech and language difficulties also vary substantially from country to country, the lowest percentage being in Turkey (0.01%) and the highest in Finland (3.12%). This means that some countries register proportionally 312 times as many as others. If the extremes are ignored, the variation is reduced with Germany (0.37%) registering 18.5 times more than France (0.02%). Nonetheless, the differences remain substantial.

Charts 4.14 and 4.15 show where these students are being educated (regular classes, special classes or special schools). A comparison of Charts 4.1E and 4.14 suggests that the different proportions identified are independent of the nature of the placement.

Chart 4.14. **Students with speech and language difficulties in primary and lower secondary education by location as a percentage of all students**[1, 2, 3, 4]

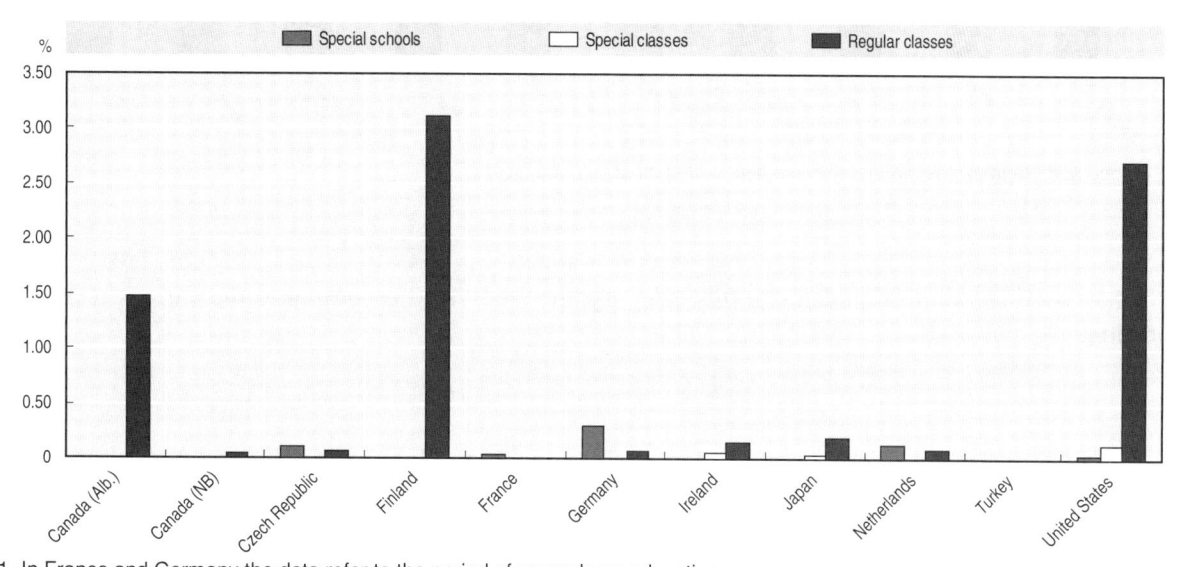

1. In France and Germany the data refer to the period of compulsory education.
2. For special schools in Canada (Alb.) data not available; in Canada (NB), Finland, Ireland, Japan and Turkey data not applicable.
3. For special classes in Canada (Alb.), Canada (NB), Finland, France, the Netherlands and Turkey data not applicable; in the Czech Republic data are negligible; in Germany data are included in special schools.
4. For regular classes in France data are negligible.

Chart 4.15 on the other hand, shows how variable the placement is among countries showing that that two countries use regular classes, special classes and special schools: the Czech Republic (39.61%, 2.31%, 58.07%), and the United States (95.17%, 4.39%, 0.44%).

Five countries use only two locations. Regular classes and special schools are used in France (13.08%, 86.92%), Germany (19.08%, 80.92%), and Netherlands (39.56%, 60.44%). Regular classes and special classes are used by Japan (94.42%, 5.58%) and Ireland (76.55%, 23.45%).

In Canada (NB), Finland and Turkey all students in this category are in regular classes while in Germany and France they are nearly all in special schools.

Chart 4.15. **Proportion of students with speech and language difficulties in primary and lower secondary education by location and by country[1]**

1. In France and Germany the data refer to the period of compulsory education.

Chart 4.16 shows how students in this category are subdivided according to the various phases of education.

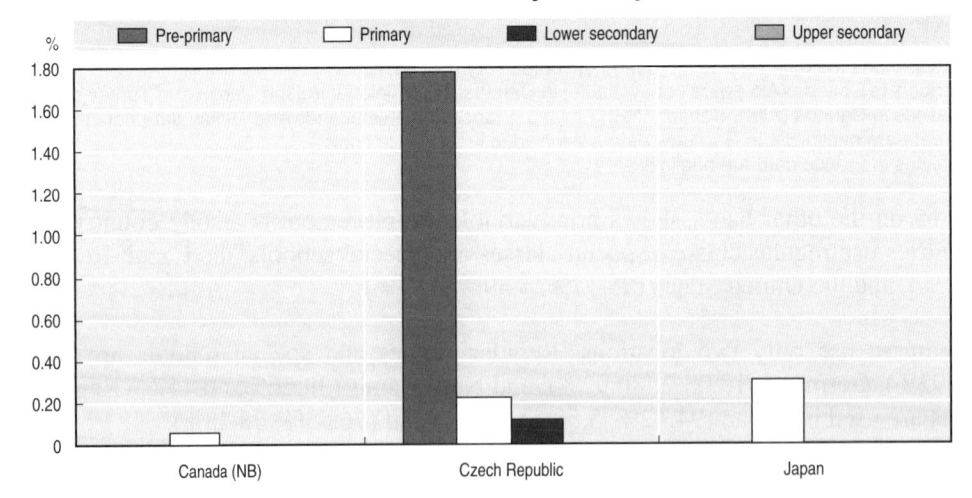

Chart 4.16. **Total percentage of students with speech and language difficulties by phases of education and by country**

Only three countries provided data allowing for a breakdown by ISCED levels. As with most of the other categories these data show no consistent pattern between proportions of students identified and ISCED level.

Hospital

As can be seen from Chart 4.1F, the percentage of students registered as receiving education while hospitalised varies substantially from country to country, the lowest percentage being in Switzerland (0.01%) and the highest in Spain (0.73%). This means that some countries register proportionally 73 times as many as others. However if the extremes are ignored the differences are considerably reduced, with the Czech Republic hospitalising 12.25 times more than Japan.

Charts 4.17 and 4.18 show where these students are being educated (regular classes, special classes or special schools). A comparison of Charts 4.1F and 4.17 suggests that the different proportions identified are independent of the nature of the placement.

Chart 4.17. **Students in hospitals in primary and lower secondary education by location as a percentage of all students**[1, 2, 3, 4, 5]

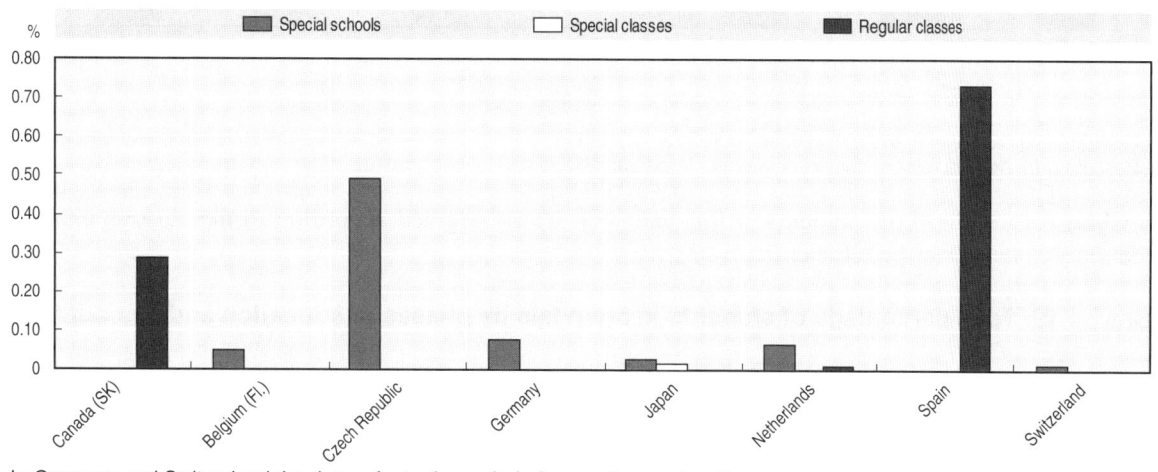

1. In Germany and Switzerland the data refer to the period of compulsory education.
2. For special schools in Canada (SK) data are negligible; in Spain data are not applicable; in Belgium (Fl.) data refer to primary, lower and upper secondary education.
3. For special classes in Belgium (Fl.), the Netherlands and Spain data are not applicable; in the Czech Republic data are nil; in Canada (SK) data are negligible; in Germany data are included in special schools.
4. For regular classes in Belgium (Fl.) data are not applicable; in the Czech Republic and Germany data are nil; in Switzerland data are not available.
5. In Spain data refer to the total number of students regardless of the period of time they spend in hospital.

Chart 4.18 on the other hand, shows how variable the placement is among countries. Note that this divergence could be due to different criteria in data gathering. The chart shows that with the exception of the Netherlands which places these students in regular classes (12.93%) and special schools (87.07%), and Japan which uses special schools (62.94%) and special classes (37.06%), all other countries use one location only, either special schools or regular schools. In Spain, those students identified who are located in regular classes are those who need only periodic hospitalisation. The data thus confirm the wide variety of provision which is utilised for these students. In Belgium (Fl.) students are in the so-called "hospital schools" for a limited period of time; in the meantime they remain also registered in their usual special or regular school.

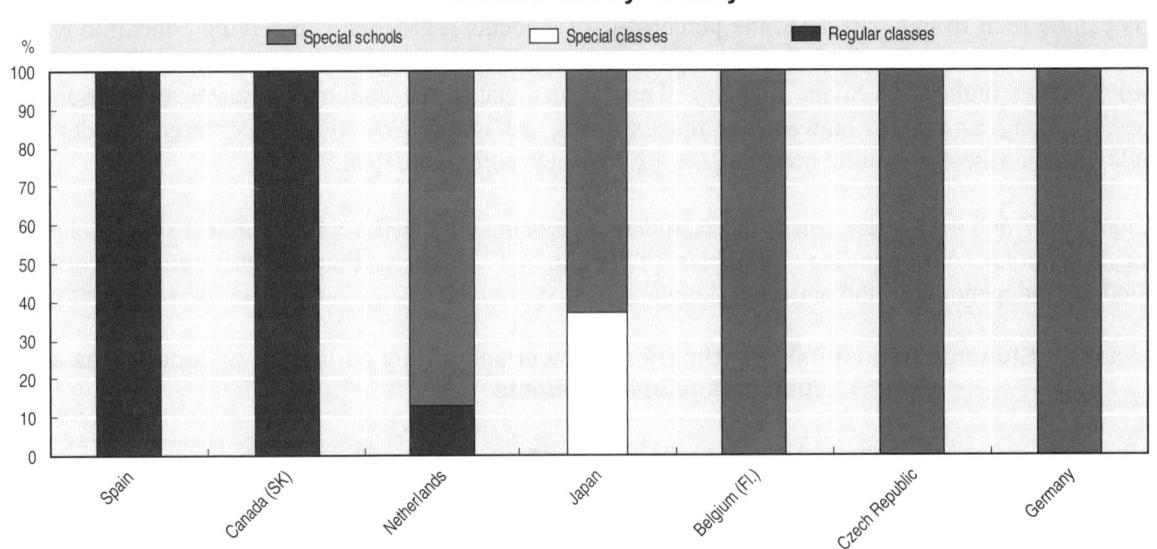

Chart 4.18. **Proportion of students in hospitals in primary and lower secondary education by location and by country**[1, 2]

1. In Germany the data refer to the period of compulsory education.
2. In Belgium (Fl.) the data refer to primary, lower and upper secondary education.

Chart 4.19 shows how students in this category are subdivided according to the various phases of education. No particular patterns emerge.

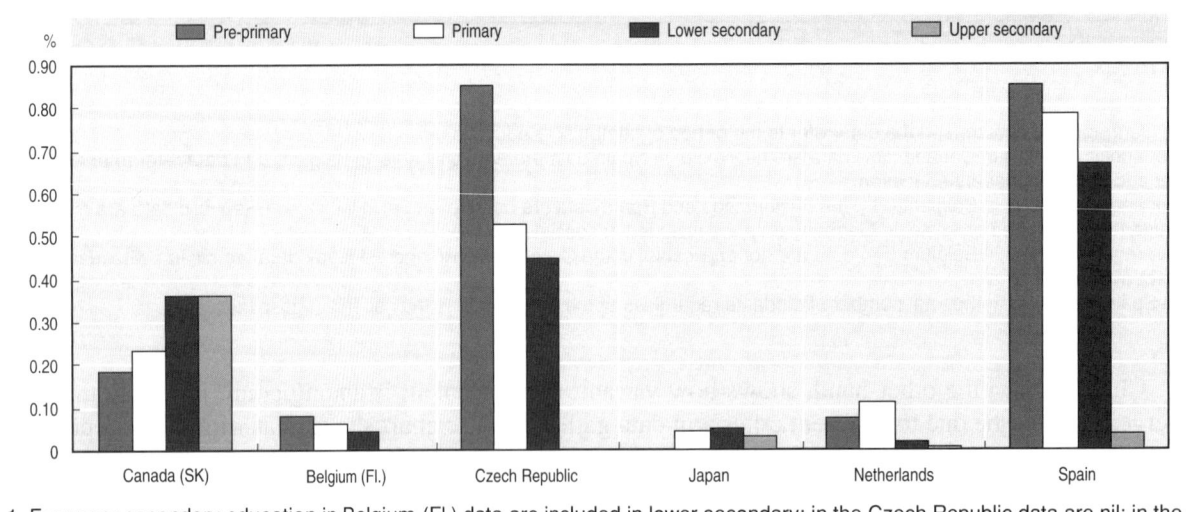

Chart 4.19. **Total percentage of students in hospitals by phases of education and by country**[1]

1. For upper secondary education in Belgium (Fl.) data are included in lower secondary; in the Czech Republic data are nil; in the Netherlands data are negligible.

Combinatorial disabilities

Combinatorial disabilities is a new term that has been coined by the Secretariat to avoid the confusion in the 2000 monograph over the use of "multiple disability" which in the United States is a legally defined category but which is too precisely defined to cover the range of students included in the "combinatorial" category used here.

Chart 4.1G shows that again the proportions of students in this category vary substantially from country to country. The lowest percentage is found in France (0.06%) and the highest in the Canada (NB) (0.54%). This means that some countries register in educational statistics proportionally 9 times as many as others do. If the extremes are ignored, the differences are substantially reduced, with Canada (SK) (0.49%) registering 1.88 times more than the Unites States (0.26%).

Charts 4.20 and 4.21 show where these students are being educated (regular classes, special classes or special schools). A comparison of Charts 4.1G and 4.20 suggests that the different proportions identified are independent of the nature of the placement.

Chart 4.20. **Students with combinatorial disabilities in primary and lower secondary education by location as a percentage of all students**[1, 2, 3, 4]

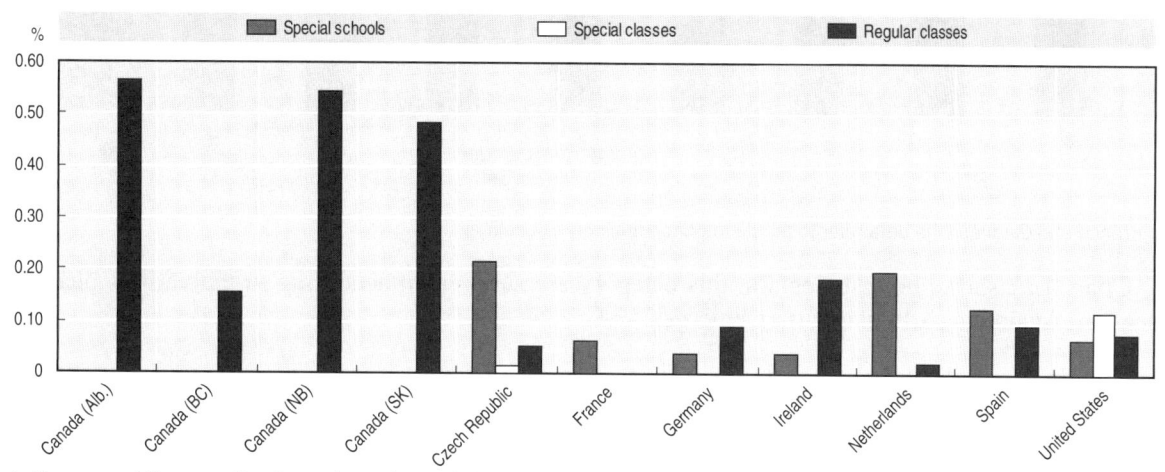

1. In France and Germany the data refer to the period of compulsory education.
2. For special schools in Canada (Alb.) data are not available; in Canada (BC) and Canada (NB) data are not applicable; in Canada (SK) data are negligible.
3. For special classes in Canada (Alb.) and Canada (NB) data are not applicable; in Canada (BC) data are not available; in Canada (SK) data are negligible; in France, Ireland and the Netherlands data are not applicable; in Germany and Spain data are included in special schools.
4. For regular classes in France data are not applicable.

Chart 4.21, on the other hand, shows how variable the placement is among countries and shows that two countries have systems which use regular classes, special classes and special schools: the Czech Republic (19.10%, 3.69%, 77.21%), and the United States (29.10%, 45.48%, 25.42%).

Four countries use only two locations, regular classes and special schools: Ireland (82.19%, 17.81%), Germany (70.19%, 29.81%), the Netherlands (10.12%, 89.88%) and Spain (43.03%, 56.97%). France places all of these students into special schools. In Switzerland the majority of these students are educated in special schools but missing data prevent the calculation of the proportions in each location.

It is noticeable that in Canada (NB, SK) regular classes are used to educate the majority of these very impaired students.

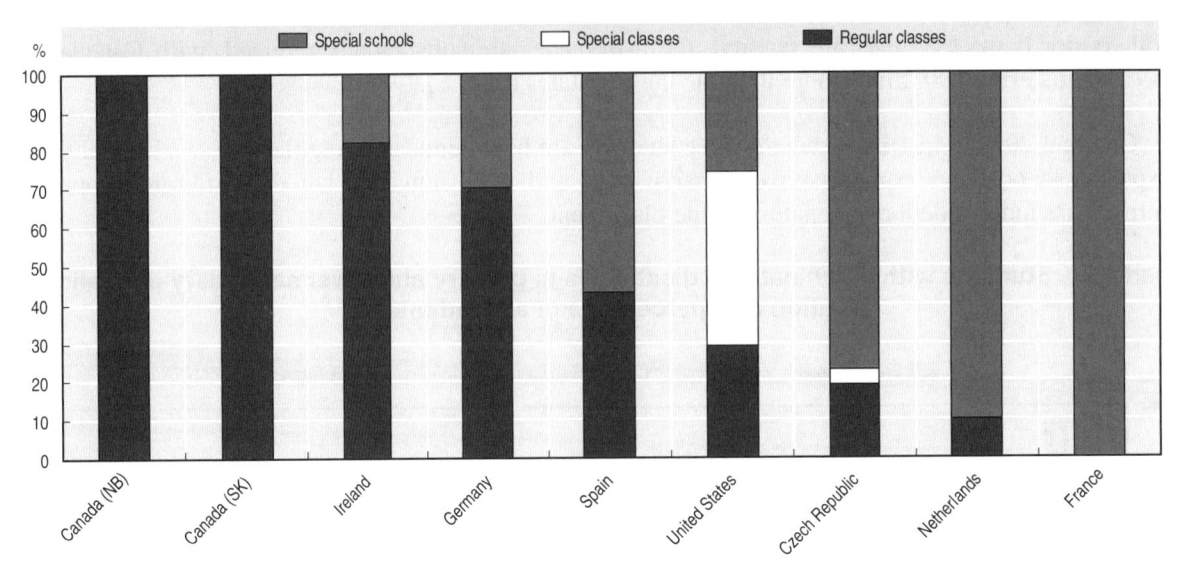

Chart 4.21. **Proportion of students with combinatorial disabilities in primary and lower secondary education by location and by country**[1]

1. In France and Germany the data refer to the period of compulsory education.

Chart 4.22 shows how students in this category are subdivided according to the various phases of education. Again, no particular pattern emerges.

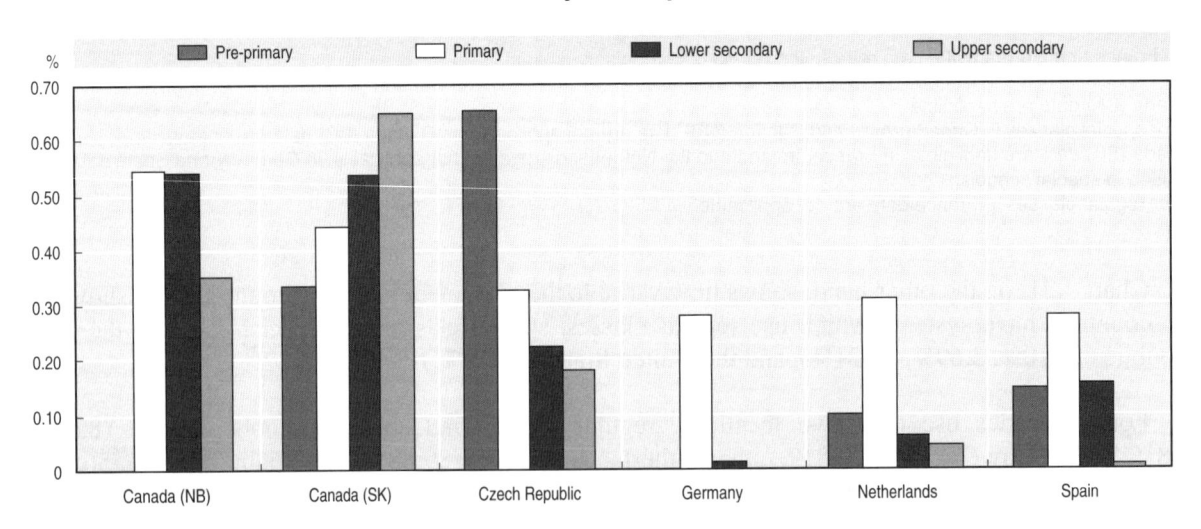

Chart 4.22. **Total percentage of students with combinatorial disabilities by phases of education and by country**[1, 2]

1. In Germany the data refer to the period of compulsory education. The breakdown is for regular classes only. For upper secondary data are negligible.
2. For pre-primary in Canada (NB) data are not applicable.

Autism

Although there is great interest world wide in the topic of autism only two countries, Canada (BC, SK), and the United States, use this as a clear category to gather statistics and Chart 4.1H shows the variation between them. Canada (BC) (0.25%) registers proportionally 2.3 times as many as the United States (0.11%).

As with other categories the different proportions identified appear independent of the nature of the placement.

The data show that in Canada (BC, SK) the majority of students are educated in regular classes in contrast to the United States where special classes are the preferred provision.

Chart 4.23 shows how students in this category are subdivided according to the various phases of education. Here a consistent pattern emerges with fewer students identified in the older age groups. This is especially true in Canada (BC) but more information is needed to interpret this difference.

Chart 4.23. **Total percentage of students with autism by phases of education and by country**[1, 2]

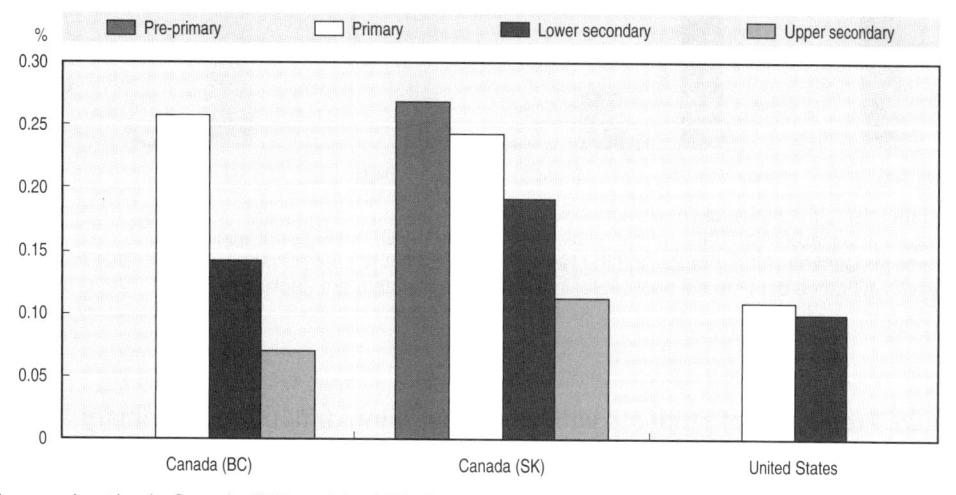

1. For pre-primary education in Canada (BC) and the USA data are not available.
2. For upper secondary education in the USA data are included in lower secondary.

Severe learning difficulties

Five countries keep statistics for students with severe learning difficulties as Chart 4.1I shows.

As can be seen from Chart 4.1I the proportion of students registered with severe learning difficulties varies substantially from country to country, the lowest percentage being in Turkey (0.02%) and the highest in Canada (BC) (0.59%). This means that Canada (BC) registers proportionally 29.5 times as many as Turkey. However, if the extremes are ignored, the differences are substantially reduced with the Netherlands (0.49%) registering 1.32 times more than Ireland (0.37%).

Charts 4.24 and 4.25 show where these students are being educated – regular classes, special classes or special schools. A comparison of Charts 4.1I and 4.24 suggests that the different proportions identified are independent of the nature of the placement.

Chart 4.25 shows the three countries that provided data allowing for partitioning students with severe learning difficulties in primary and lower secondary education between regular classes, special classes and special schools. The data show that 2 countries use regular classes, special classes and special schools; Finland (4.22%, 30.43%, 65.30%), Ireland (3.88%, 4.30%, 91.82%). The Netherlands uses regular classes (0.42%) and special schools (99.58%). Thus in these countries the majority of students with severe learning difficulties in primary and lower secondary education are educated in special schools.

Chart 4.24. **Students with severe learning difficulties in primary and lower secondary education by location as a percentage of all students**[1, 2, 3, 4]

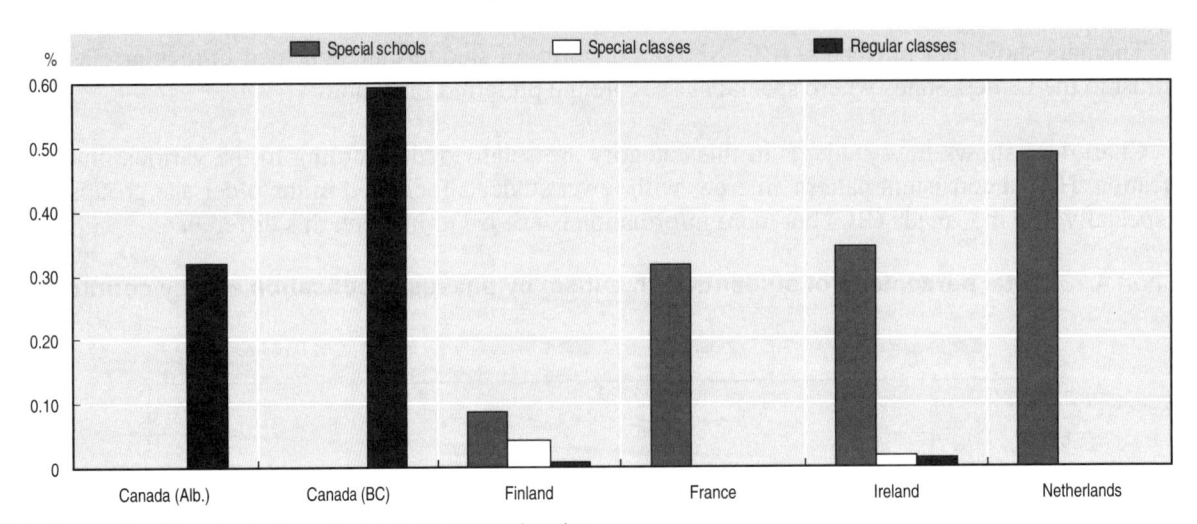

1. In France the data refer to the period of compulsory education.
2. For special schools in Canada (Alb.) data are not available; in Canada (BC) data are not applicable.
3. For special classes in Canada (Alb.), France and the Netherlands data are not applicable; in Canada (BC) data are not available.
4. For regular classes in France data are not applicable; in the Netherlands data are negligible.

Chart 4.25. **Proportion of students with severe learning difficulties in primary and lower secondary education by location and by country**

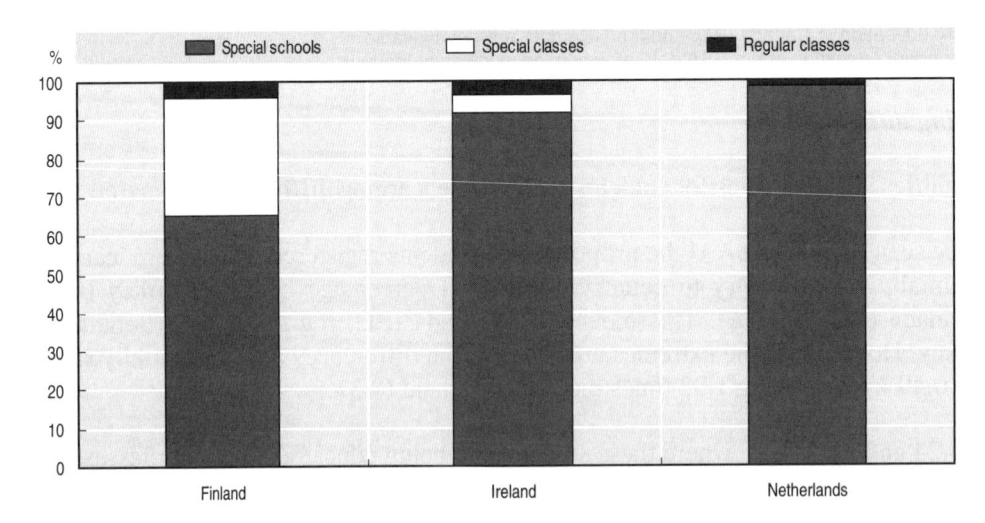

Chart 4.26 shows how students in this category are subdivided according to the various phases of education. Again, no particular pattern emerges.

Chart 4.26. **Total percentage of students with severe learning difficulties by phases of education and by country**[1, 2, 3]

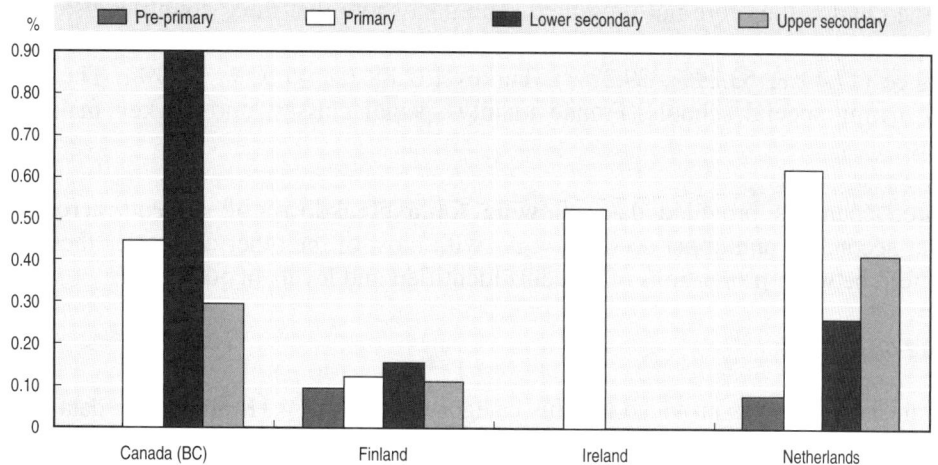

1. For pre-primary in Canada (BC) data are not available; in Ireland data are not applicable.
2. For lower secondary in Ireland data are not available.
3. For upper secondary in Ireland data are not available.

Moderate learning difficulties

As can be seen from Chart 4.1J the proportions of students experiencing moderate learning difficulties vary substantially from country to country, the lowest percentage being in Turkey (0.17%) and the highest in Canada (Alb.) (1.19%). This means that Canada (Alb.) registers proportionally 7 times as many as Turkey. If the extremes are removed the variation between countries still remains with Ireland (0.99%) registering 2.2 times as many as Finland (0.45%).

Chart 4.27 shows where these students are being educated (regular classes, special classes or special schools). A comparison of Charts 4.1J and 4.27 suggests that the different proportions identified are independent of the nature of the placement.

Chart 4.27. **Students with moderate learning difficulties in primary and lower secondary education by location as a percentage of all students**[1, 2, 3]

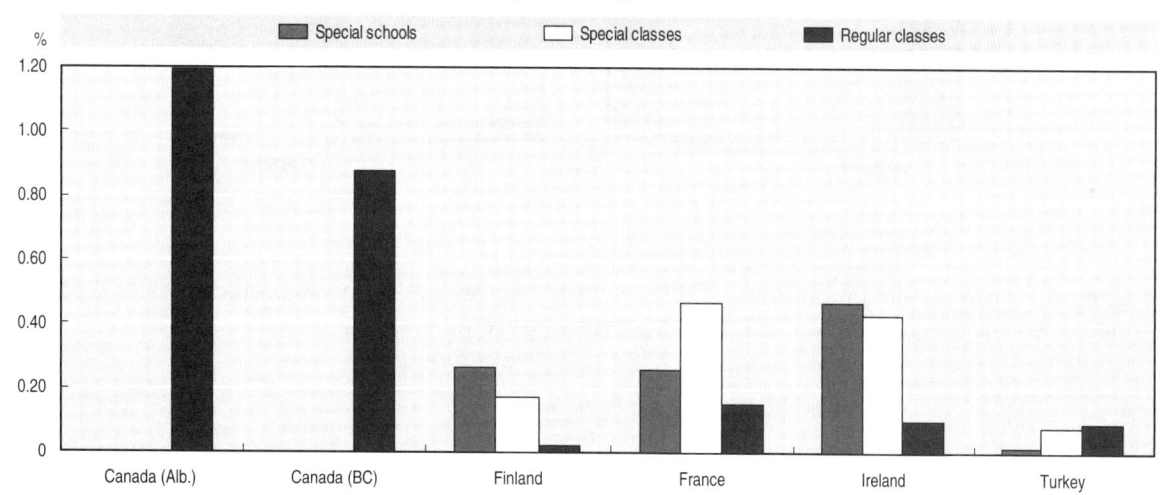

1. In France the data refer to the period of compulsory education.
2. For special schools in Canada (Alb.) data are not available; in Canada (BC) data are not applicable; in Turkey data are negligible.
3. For special classes in Canada (Alb.) data are not applicable; in Canada (BC) data are not available.

Only three countries provided data allowing for partitioning students with moderate learning difficulties in primary and lower secondary education between regular classes, special classes and special schools and the chart is therefore not presented. The data show that three countries use regular classes, special classes and special schools for educating students in this category: Finland (2.45%, 38.62%, 58.93%), France (17.49%, 53.29%, 29.22%), Turkey (52.88 %, 45.02%, 2.10%). The data show that Finland uses mainly special schools, France mainly special classes, and Turkey mainly regular and special classes.

Only three countries provided data allowing for a breakdown of students across pre-primary, primary, lower secondary and upper secondary. As with most of the other categories these data show no consistent pattern between proportions of students identified and levels of education.

Light learning difficulties

In general, little data was provided for this category and Chart 4.1K shows the data from those that could. They indicate large variations in the proportions of students resourced. Proportionally, as per Chart 4.28, Belgium (Fl.) resources 141 times more students with light learning difficulties than Finland or the United States. In addition, the location of education varies considerably among the countries providing data, Chart 4.29 reveals.

Chart 4.28. **Students with light learning difficulties in primary and lower secondary education by location as a percentage of all students**

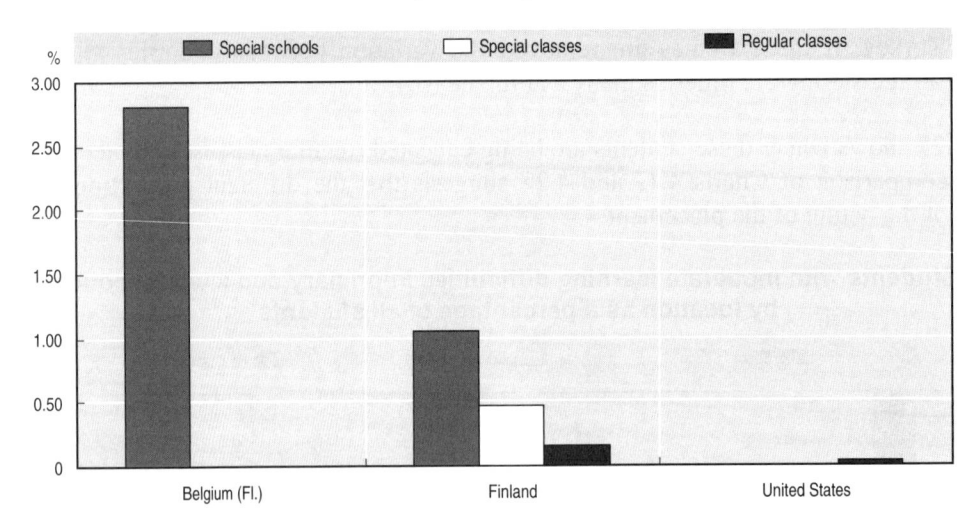

Chart 4.30 reveals the proportions of these students across pre-primary, primary, lower secondary and upper secondary. Again there seems to be no evident pattern.

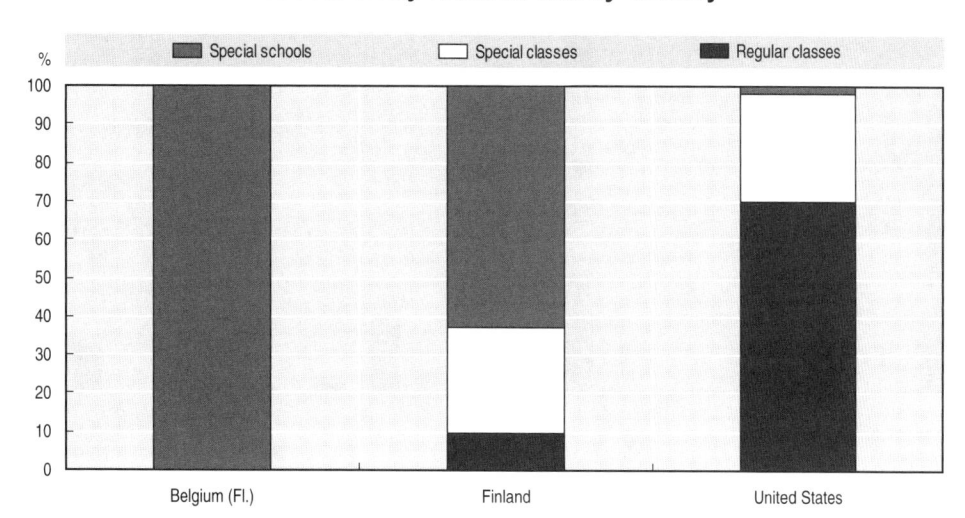

Chart 4.29. **Proportion of pupils with light learning difficulties in primary and lower secondary education by location and by country**

Chart 4.30. **Total percentage of students with light learning difficulties by phases of education and by country[1, 2]**

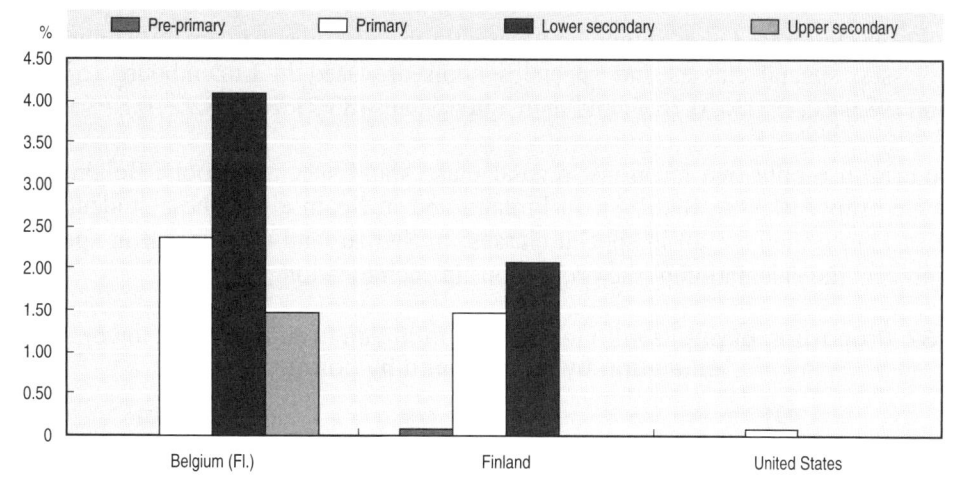

1. In Belgium pre-primary data are not applicable.
2. For the USA pre-primary data are not available; upper secondary data are included in lower secondary.

Learning disabilities

Chart 4.1L shows that, as for many of the other categories, there is substantial variation among countries of proportions of students categorised with learning disabilities. The highest proportion is in Finland (9.56%) who registers proportionally 18 times as many as in Luxembourg (0.53%). Even if the extremes are removed the United States (7.01%) still identifies 5.7 times the students in Spain (1.23%).

Charts 4.31 and 4.32 show where these students are being educated (regular classes, special classes or special schools). A comparison of Charts 4.1K and 4.31 suggests that the different proportions identified are independent of the nature of the placement.

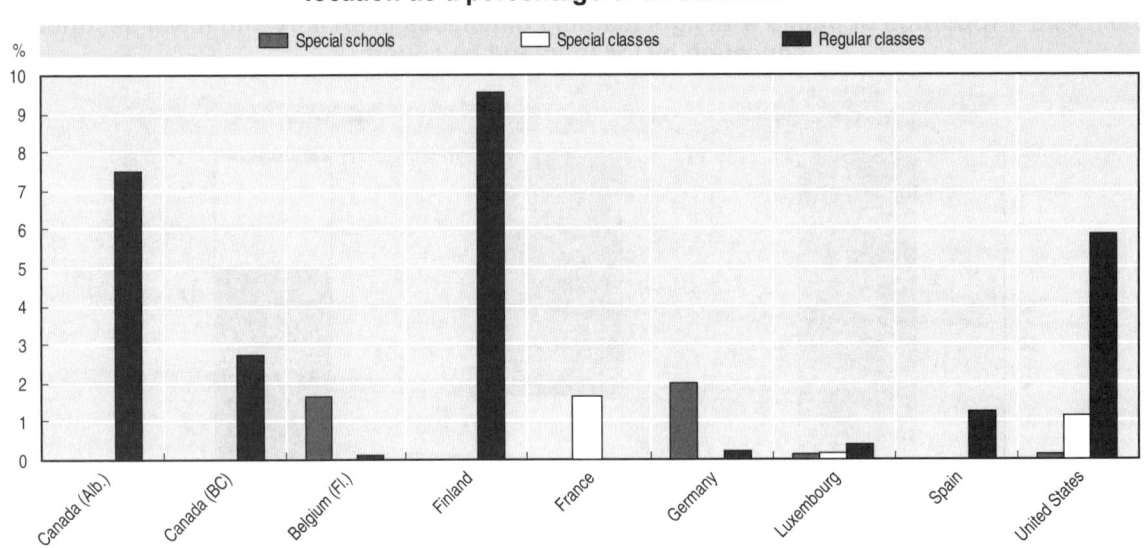

Chart 4.31. **Students with learning disabilities in primary and lower secondary education by location as a percentage of all students**[1, 2, 3, 4]

1. In France, Germany and Luxembourg the data refer to the period of compulsory education.
2. For special schools in Canada (Alb.) data are not available; in Canada (BC), Finland, France and Spain data are not applicable.
3. For special classes in Canada (Alb.), Canada (NB), Belgium (Fl.) and Finland data are not applicable; in Canada (BC) data are not available; in Germany data are included in special schools.
4. For regular classes in France data are not applicable.

Chart 4.32, on the other hand, shows how variable the placement is among countries and reveals that regular classes, special classes and special schools are used in Luxembourg (68.23%, 22.07%, 9.70%), Ireland (98.94%, 0.31%, 0.76%) and the United States (83.31%, 15.82%, 0.87%).

Two countries use only two locations, regular classes and special schools, Belgium (Fl.) (1.95%, 98.05%) and Germany (10.39%, 89.61%). In Finland and in Spain all of these students are in regular classes while in France they are all in special classes. In Switzerland they are all in special classes but missing data prevent the calculation of the proportions in each location.

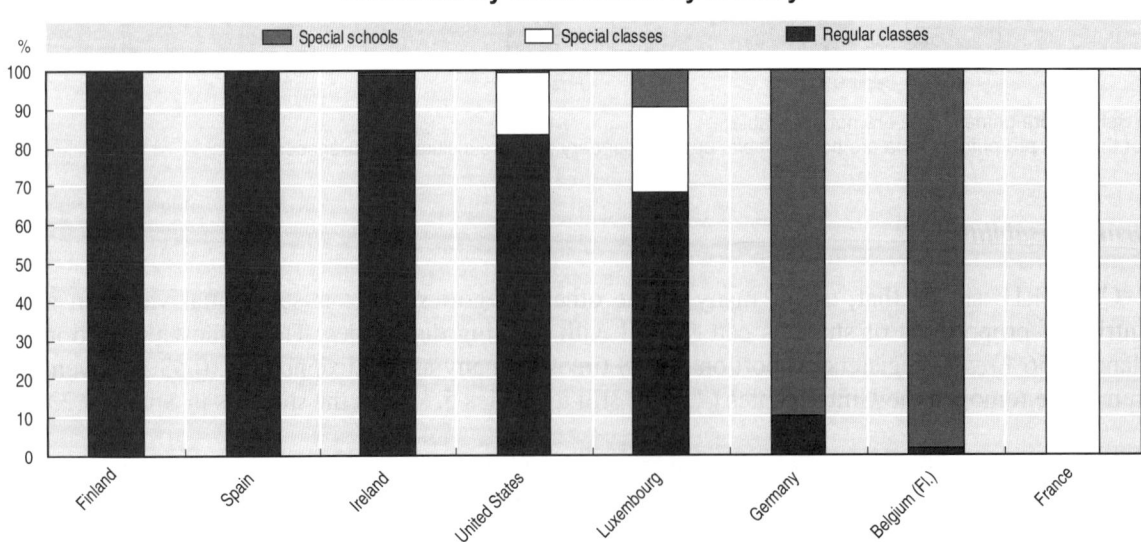

Chart 4.32. **Proportion of pupils with learning disabilities in primary and lower secondary education by location and by country**[1]

1. In France, Germany and Luxembourg the data refer to the period of compulsory education.

Only three countries provided data allowing for a breakdown of students across pre-primary, primary, lower secondary and upper secondary. As with most of the other categories these data show no consistent pattern between proportions of students identified and ISCED level.

Additional categories related to disadvantage

The analysis presented in the following section is based on data on national categories related to disadvantage where common categories could be provided for making international comparisons. Three of these emerged covering: second language and mother tongue students; travelling students; and disadvantaged students.

Second language and mother tongue teaching

This category brings together data on students who do not speak the national language of instruction (second language) with mother tongue teaching comprising courses which allow foreign students to maintain their mother tongue since some countries do not separate out these two types of provision in their statistical return.

Chart 4.1M shows the countries providing data for this category. They indicate large variations in the proportions of students resourced, Sweden (6.13%) resources being proportionally 102 times more than in France (0.06%). If the extremes are removed the difference still remains large with Finland (1.04%) resourcing 6.5 times that of Japan (0.16%).

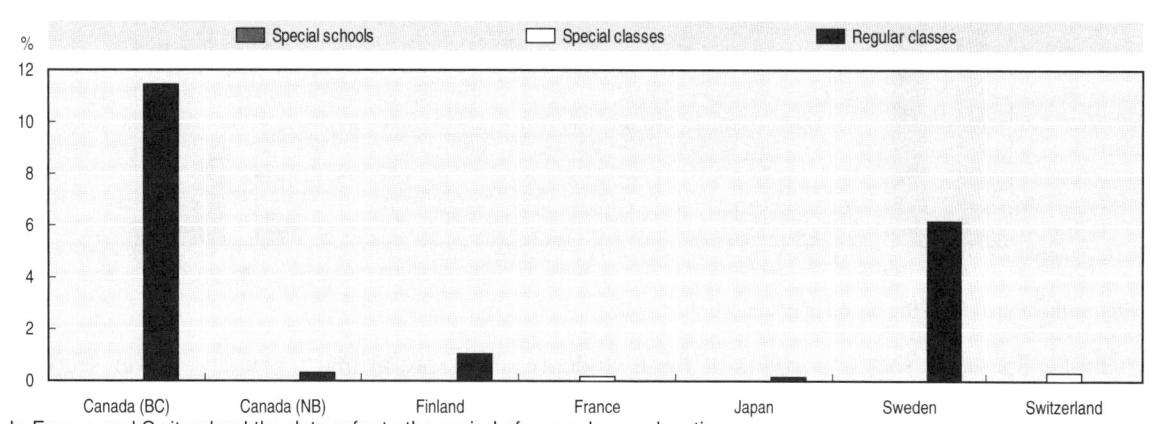

Chart 4.33. **Second language and mother tongue teaching students in primary and lower secondary education by location as a percentage of all students**[1, 2]

1. In France and Switzerland the data refer to the period of compulsory education.
2. In Japan, special classes data are included in data for regular classes.

Charts 4.33 and 4.34 show that the location of education only varies between regular classes and special classes. Canada (BC, NB), Finland, Japan and Sweden use only regular classes while France and Switzerland use exclusively special classes.

Chart 4.34. **Proportion of second language and mother tongue teaching students in primary and lower secondary education by location and by country**[1]

1. In France and Switzerland the data refer to the period of compulsory education.

Chart 4.35. **Total percentage of second language and mother tongue teaching students by phases of education and by country**[1]

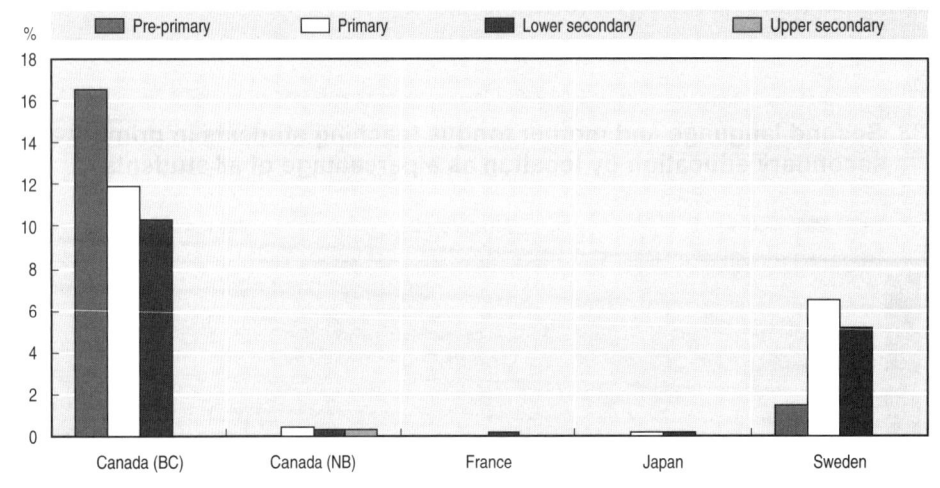

1. In France the data refer to the period of compulsory education.

Chart 4.35 shows the proportions of these students across pre-primary, primary, lower secondary and upper secondary. Again there seems to be no evident pattern.

Travelling children

Chart 4.1N shows the countries providing data for this category with Ireland (0.81%) resourcing proportionally 162 times as many students as Belgium (Fl.) (0.005%). The traveller community is Ireland's only nomadic community and is widely acknowledged as one of the most marginalised groups in Irish society, thus accounting for the relatively large proportions of students resourced in this category.

Chart 4.36. **Travelling students in primary and lower secondary education by location as a percentage of all students**[1]

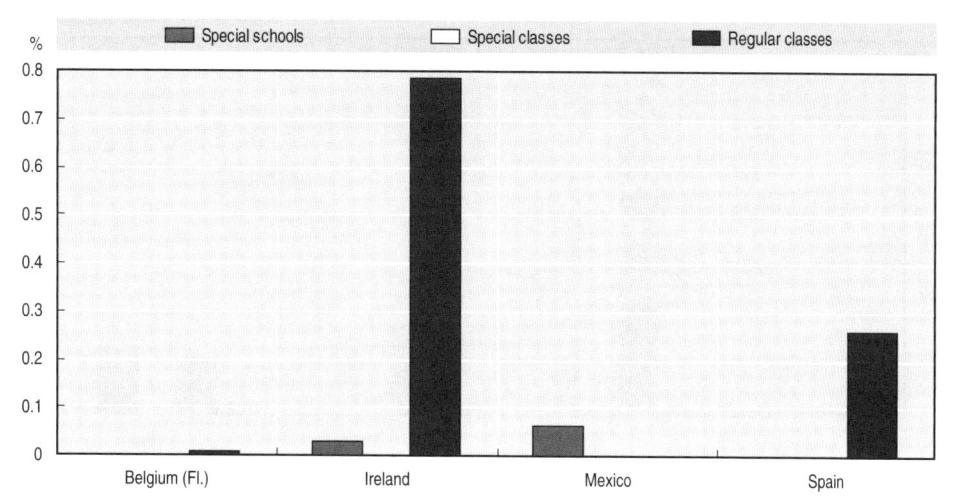

1. In Belgium (Fl.) data for special schools and special classes are not applicable. Education for travelling students is only organised in regular classes at pre-primary and primary levels.

Chart 4.37. **Proportion of travelling students in primary and lower secondary education by location and by country**[1]

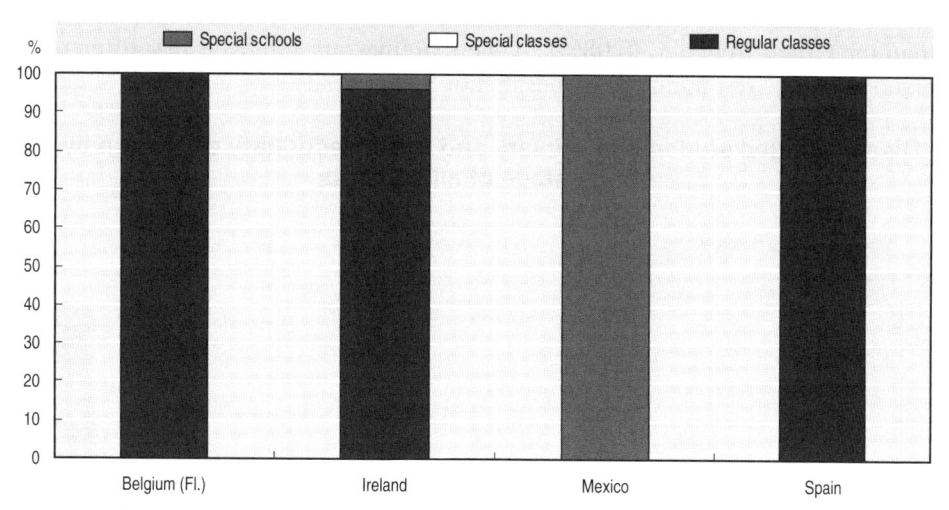

1. In Belgium data for special schools and special classes are not applicable. Education for travelling students is only organised in regular classes at pre-primary and primary levels.

Charts 4.36 and 4.37 show that the location of education varies between regular classes and special schools. Belgium (Fl.) and Spain use only regular classes while Mexico uses only special schools. Ireland uses mainly regular classes (96.30%) with some special school provision (3.70%).

Chart 4.38 shows the proportions of these students across pre-primary, primary, lower secondary and upper secondary. As with most of the other categories these data show no consistent pattern between proportions of students identified and ISCED level.

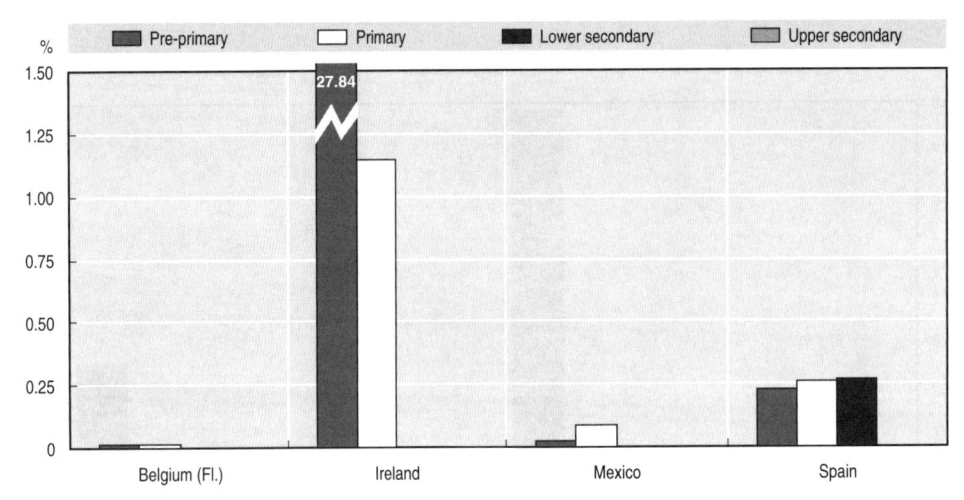

Chart 4.38. **Total percentage of travelling students by phases of education and by country**[1]

1. In Belgium (Fl.) data for special schools and special classes are not applicable. Education for travelling students is only organised in regular classes at pre-primary and primary levels.

Disadvantaged students

Chart 4.10 shows the countries providing data for this category. They indicate large variations in the proportions of students resourced. The United States (27.46%) resource proportionally about 350 times more than the Czech Republic (0.08%). If the extremes are removed the difference still remains large with Ireland (11.34%) resourcing 4.9 times that of Spain (2.33%).

Chart 4.39. **Disadvantaged students in primary and lower secondary education by location as a percentage of all students**

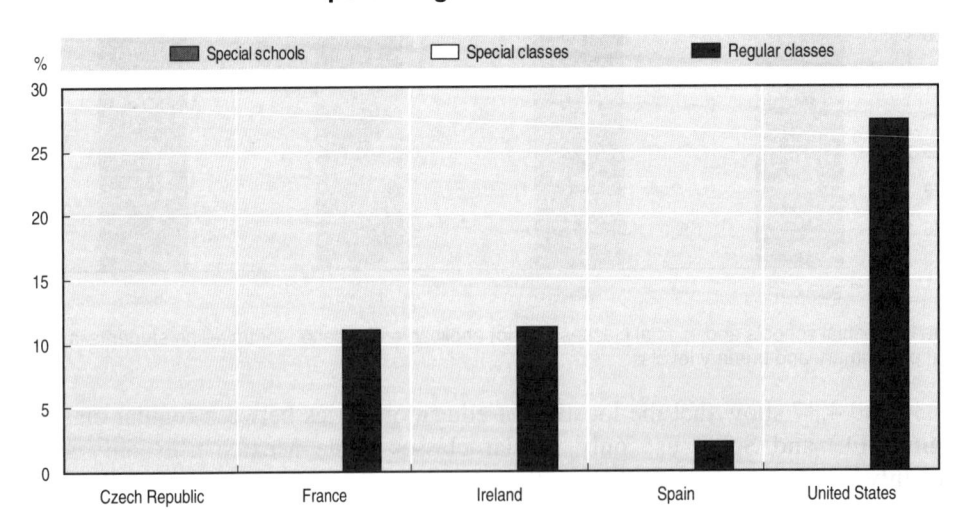

Chart 4.40. **Proportion of disadvantaged students in primary and lower secondary education by location and by country**[1]

1. In France the data refer to the period of compulsory education.

Charts 4.39 and 4.40 show that France, Ireland, Spain and the United States only use regular classes. In the Czech Republic all of these students are in special schools.[1]

Chart 4.41. **Total percentage of disadvantaged students by phases of education and by country**[1]

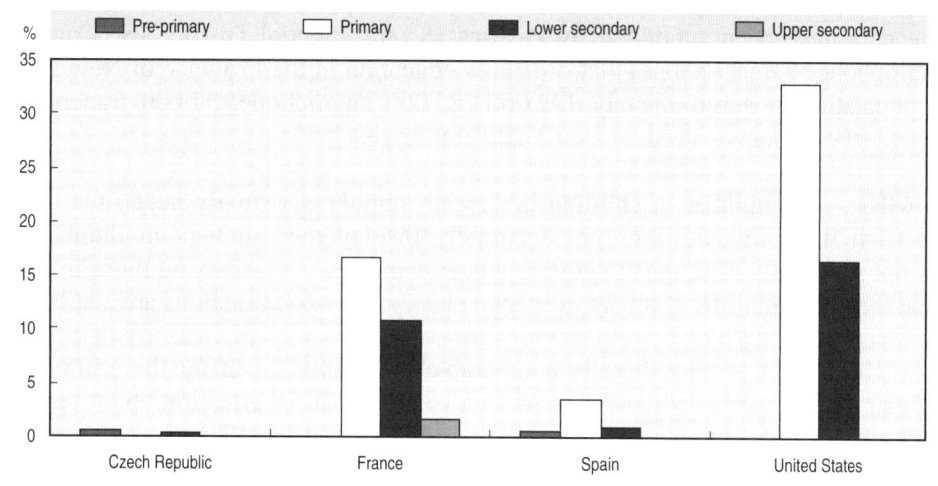

1. In France the data refer to the period of compulsory education.

Chart 4.41 shows the proportions of these students across pre-primary, primary, lower secondary and upper secondary. Again there seems to be no evident pattern.

---

1. The data from the Czech Republic include "socially disadvantaged children in preparatory classes and regular schools". These category 11 students are educated in special schools.

Conclusions

This chapter has considered the data based on the national categories of disabilities, difficulties and disadvantages as supplied by participating countries. It has looked at the proportions registered in educational statistics by category and by location of education. The data show substantial variation in categories used by countries and in the country prevalence rates for the school years covering pre-primary, primary, lower secondary and upper secondary education. Furthermore, the location of education, regular schools, special classes, or special schools varies greatly from country to country. For almost all categories at the extremes the education experiences of similar students would be vastly different in different countries. For instance, in one they might be educated in regular classes while in another they may be fully segregated from mainstream education.

Because of the different definitions in use of national categories for students with disabilities, difficulties and disadvantages the present study has adopted a simplified tri-partite cross-national categorisation, referred to as A, B and C within the context of a resources model which has been outlined in previous chapters. The following chapters use this framework to describe the remainder of the data gathered by the quantitative part of the instrument.

General notes

Canada (BC) – The province has no special schools. Provincial Resource Programs which are directly funded by the Ministry and operated by individual districts are considered to be "special classes".

Canada (NB) – Pre-primary students are not part of the public school system. Note that for New Brunswick the data have been submitted by District 18 only. School District 18 is one of 13 school districts (9 anglophone, 4 francophone) that organises education in the Province of New Brunswick. The total student population is approximately 122 000 (85 000 anglophone, 37 000 francophone). School District 18 has 12 919 students served by over 1 200 employees.

Canada (SK) – The number of children in special schools is virtually negligible in the province. The database from this province does not accurately display the numbers in these situations. The database does not accurately distinguish between students in special classes and those in regular classes. It is known that there are minimal numbers in special classes; but no estimations are available.

Finland – The figures are not directly comparable with those given for the school year 1994/95. Information about students is based on different data sources than information about teachers and they are not directly comparable. In regular classes, figures in categories 17 and 18 may to some extent overlap with figures in categories 1-16.

Germany – Data on students in special classes are included in special schools (for all categories). The distribution of pre-primary to public and private institutions is estimated for all categories.

Greece – Special schools: the available data for lower and upper secondary education are combined. Regular classes: in the Greek educational system these are under special classes.

Ireland – All ages special schools (4-18 yrs). Data gathered in Ireland (Department of Education 1997, 1999) indicate that between the school years 1994-1995 and 1998-1999 the number of pupils with special needs in mainstream primary schools increased by approximately 40%. The experience of those closely involved with these developments clearly indicates that these increases were associated with an identifiable range of categories and, on the other hand, that a small number of categories were not influenced by this overall increase. The figures provided here are designed to take these factors into account.

Italy – Pre-primary schools dependent on municipalities are not included in the data on regular classes: there are about 1 700 (estimated) children with disabilities of pre-primary age. Figures are estimated for the total number of students in the different phases of education.

Mexico – Upper secondary education does not apply. Special classes: Totals only are available, there is no individual breakdown of category.

Poland – Data are available for special schools only.

Spain – The numbers of students in special classes are included in special schools. There are a small number of students in special classes, but for the Spanish educational system these classes are considered to be special schools.

Switzerland – Data regarding students in regular classes are missing. Data relating to the Swiss education statistics has been compiled according to classes. Therefore there are no statistical data on aspects of integrated education. Data on students, teachers and financial resources are not derived from a single source. As a consequence it is not possible to combine the various information in a regular manner. Besides, information on financial resources is difficult to obtain on a reliable basis and therefore not provided. Teachers are the only category on which statistical data on staff exist. Nevertheless even such information is limited and not as detailed as the categories of disabilities in students. The entire data on special education is limited to a single description of "compulsory schooling". The different ISCED levels cannot be separated out.

United Kingdom – Special classes are included in regular classes.

CHAPTER 5
ANALYSIS OF THE QUANTITATIVE DATA FOR CROSS-NATIONAL CATEGORIES A, B AND C

Background

In addition to the data on national categories discussed in Chapter 4, information about the quantitative aspects of provision for students receiving additional resources for disabilities, difficulties, or disadvantages was obtained by further analysis of the data collection tables. As in the earlier data collection described in the previous monograph (OECD, 2000b), the amount of information which countries were able to provide varied widely from country to country. There was still an overall trend for the most detailed information to be available about provision in special schools, for substantially less information about special classes in regular or mainstream schools, and for there to be very patchy data on students fully integrated in regular classes in regular schools.

As discussed earlier (see Chapter 1) the three cross-national categories correspond broadly to students with ***disabilities*** (A); students with ***difficulties*** (B); and those with ***disadvantages*** (C). To avoid extensive repetition of the clumsy "students within cross-national category", the terms disabilities, difficulties and disadvantages are frequently used in this chapter as synonyms for the three cross-national categories. There are more extensive and reliable data for students with disabilities (relating broadly to what might be called organic defects relating to sensory, motor, or neurological systems) than for those with difficulties or disadvantages.

The chapter is divided into sections covering each of the cross-national categories in turn. Within each section there is an initial discussion of data on students receiving additional resources over the period of compulsory education. This is followed by discussion of data on the various phases of education in turn (*i.e.* pre-primary, primary or basic school education, lower secondary education and upper secondary education).

The earlier monograph (OECD, 2000b) attempted an analysis of data covering all students receiving additional resources, effectively by adding totals for the three cross-national categories. Following discussions with national representatives, and on further consideration, this has not been attempted in the present monograph. It is felt that such summations can be misleading as they are in danger of putting together non-comparable data. The basis for determining the number of students receiving additional resources because of disabilities or difficulties (cross-national categories A and B respectively) is typically relatively straightforward and non-controversial. However, when countries provide additional resources for students with disadvantages (cross-national category C), not only are the data often not available at national level, but also there are typically complexities in arriving at a reliable figure for the actual number of students receiving additional resources.

For example, numbers of students receiving additional resources for disabilities (and also for difficulties) are typically based on head-counts. All such students need these resources to access the regular curriculum. Numbers of students with social and other disadvantages may be computed on a group or class basis where the resources are provided for all falling within that classification irrespective of the needs of specific individuals. In these circumstances an inflated figure (compared with that for disabilities or disadvantages) may be produced.

Availability of data

The table in Annex 3 illustrates the availability of data for the cross-national categories for different countries, split according to the location of education (special schools, special classes and regular classes), and its level or phase (compulsory education, pre-primary, primary, lower secondary and upper secondary). It is clear that, as discussed above, there are considerable gaps in data availability, particularly for categories B and C.

The table in Annex 3 and the charts presented below, and in the following chapter, generally exclude countries where data are wholly, or partially, not available (coded as "m" or "m:" respectively) for the aspect covered in the table or chart. Use of this coding implies that while it is known that there are such students within the national system, the actual numbers of students are not known. Hence it is not possible to make meaningful comparisons. The "m:" coding is typically used when data are available for some national categories falling within the cross-national category under consideration, but not for others. With such partial information it is possible to say that the number of students given in the category is at least equal to that provided in the data collection, which can be of value (particularly when the number of students in the national category or categories for which data are not available can be reasonably inferred as being likely to be small – although the coding of "n" should have been used if the number was considered to be negligible). These analyses have not been attempted.

Codings of "a" and "n" (indicating that the category is "not applicable" or known to be "nil" respectively) are effectively interchangeable for most analysis purposes as they indicate that there are no students falling within the category under consideration. This is helpful as inspection of the data returns indicates some uncertainty about their relative use ("n" implying that while the figure is actually zero, it would be possible within the national system to take on a non-zero value; "a" implying that the national system is such, that it is not possible for the category to take on a non-zero value).

Use of "x", indicating that the relevant data have been included in another cell of the data return (*e.g.* where data for special classes are included in returns for special schools) is typically covered in charts or tables by an appropriate annotation.

Quantitative data on cross-national category A (students receiving additional resources for disabilities)

Cross-national category A, as discussed and defined in Chapter 1, roughly corresponds to needs arising from impairing conditions. All countries using categorical systems for special educational needs have national categories which they consider to fall within cross-national category A, although the number of such categories varies widely from country to country (see Table 3.2 in Chapter 3 and Annex 1 for details).

The period of compulsory education

Chart 5.1 shows the number of students receiving additional resources within the period of compulsory education who are considered to fall within cross-national category A for different countries, as a percentage of all students in compulsory education (the period of compulsory education differs from country to country – see Annex 4. Values range from 0.64% (Mexico) to 4.55% (the United States). The median number of students receiving additional resources for disabilities, for the 16 countries reporting data, as a percentage of all students in compulsory education is 2.12%, with an inter-quartile range[1] of 1.61% to 3.07%.

Chart 5.1. **Number of students receiving additional resources over the period of compulsory education in cross-national category A as a percentage of all students in compulsory education**[1]

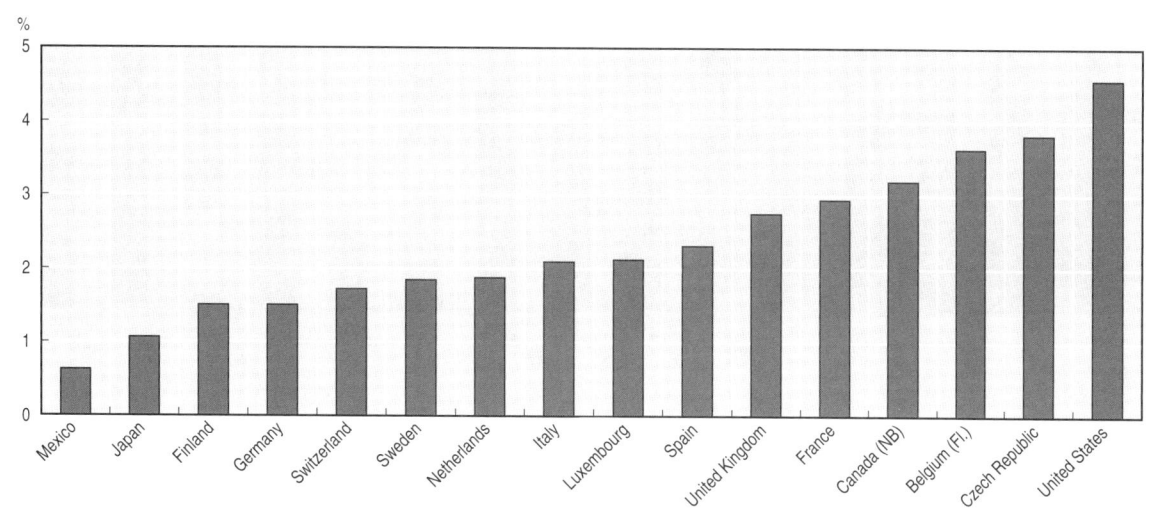

1. France: For the sake of international comparability French students administered by the Ministry of Health have been added to these data provided by the Ministry of Education. This probably has the effect of slightly inflating the percentage for France in contrast to other countries that have an unknown number of students outside the education system.

Although wide variation continues to exist between countries in terms of students receiving additional resources for disabilities, the differences are substantially less than the differences between countries for some individual categories discussed in the previous chapter. This confirms the use of an overall disability category as part of the tri-partite approach and increases confidence that like is being compared with like. However, the remaining differences still require explanation. The gross differences between countries may well reflect levels of national wealth although correlation between these data and GDP per capita are not statistically significant.

The extent to which students receiving additional resources for disabilities are educated within segregated settings also varies widely between countries as shown in Chart 5.2. All students with disabilities are educated in regular mainstream classes in Canada (NB) and over 98% of them in Italy. Over 80% of such students are in special schools in Belgium (Fl.), the Czech Republic, Germany and the Netherlands.

---

1. The statistics reported here (and for other phases of education) are a simplified version of quartiles. The median (Mdn) (or second quartile) is the central data point in an ordered set of data points. The first quartile (Q_1) is taken as the central data point of those points below the median. The third quartile (Q_3) is taken as the central data point of those points above the median. The inter-quartile range is ($Q_3 - Q_1$). For an even number of data points a quartile is taken as the average of the two central points. It is only reported when data are available from at least nine countries.
Examples:
15 data points – Q_1= 4th, Mdn = 8th, Q_3 = 12th point;
10 data points – Q_1= 3rd, Mdn = ave of 5th & 6th, Q_3 = 8th point);
12 data points – Q_1= ave of 3rd & 4th, Mdn = ave of 6th & 7th, Q_3 = ave of 9th & 10th point.

Chart 5.2. **Percentages of students receiving additional resources over the period of compulsory education in cross-national category A by location**[1, 2, 3, 4]

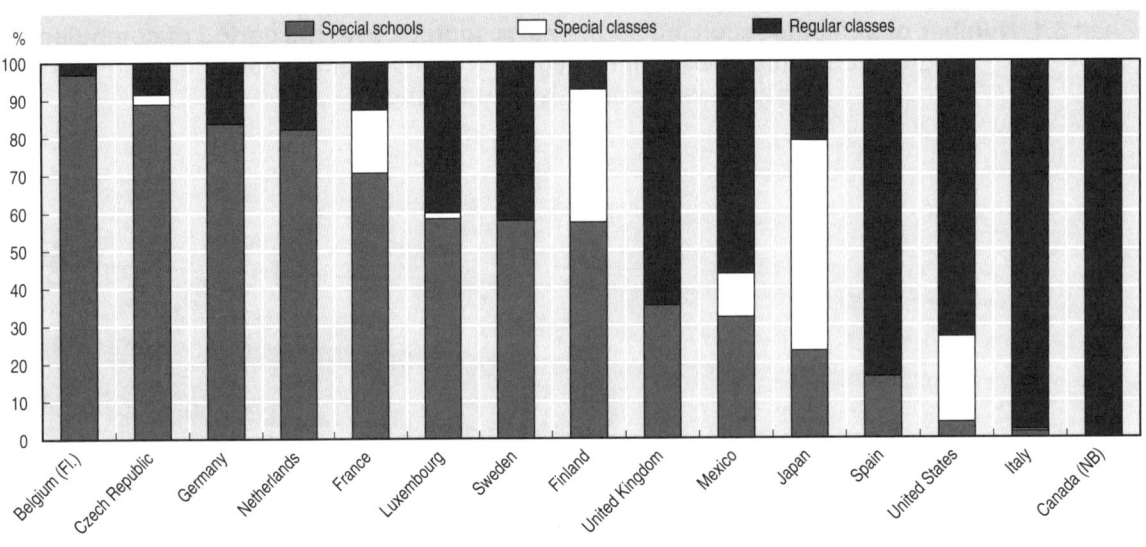

1. In Germany and Spain students in special classes are included in special schools.
2. In the United Kingdom students in special classes are included in regular classes.
3. In Sweden special schools are located in regular schools as a first step towards inclusion.
4. France – For the sake of international comparability French students administered by the Ministry of Health have been added to these data provided by the Ministry of Education. This probably has the effect of slightly inflating the percentage in special schools for France in contrast to other countries that have an unknown number of students outside the education system.

Pre-primary education

Pre-primary education (*i.e.* that which is provided before the normal age at which children are required to attend school) is regarded by many as an important service for students with disabilities, difficulties, and disadvantages. By providing early intervention for those who are likely to have difficulties in accessing the school curriculum, it may well be that such later problems are reduced.

Chart 5.3. **Number of children receiving additional resources in pre-primary education in cross-national category A as a percentage of all children in pre-primary education**[1]

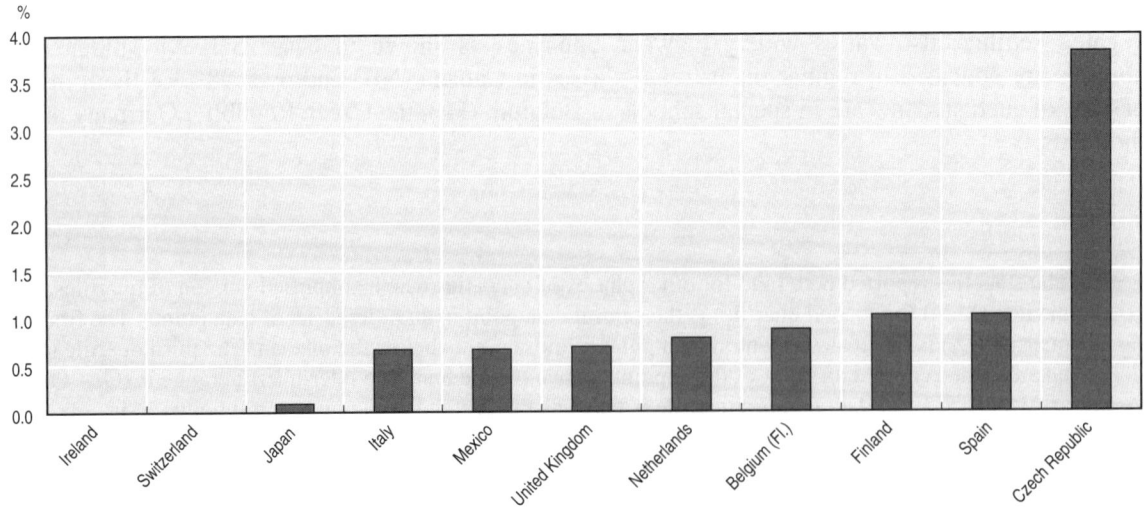

1. Although there are national categories falling within cross-national category A in Ireland and Switzerland no children are in this category in pre-primary education.

Eleven countries were able to provide data on this phase of education (for Ireland and Switzerland the data were that this category was not applicable within their system; *i.e.* that there is no pre-school provision for children with disabilities). Chart 5.3 indicates the number of children receiving additional resources in pre-primary education who are considered to fall within cross-national category A for different countries, as a percentage of all children in pre-school education.

The median number of students receiving additional resources for disabilities, for the eleven countries reporting data, as a percentage of all children in pre-primary education is 0.70%, with an inter-quartile range of 0.09% to 1.03%.

It is noteworthy that, as shown in Table 5.1, for all of the ten countries for which comparisons can be made, these percentages are smaller than the corresponding percentages at primary level (see also Chart 5.5). Median values are 0.77% at pre-primary and 2.49% at primary level. The Wilcoxon test (n=10, T=0, p<0.5) indicates that there are significantly more students with disabilities being educated in primary schools than in pre-primary.

Table 5.1. **Comparison of numbers of children with disabilities receiving additional resources in pre-primary and primary education as a percentage of all children in that phase of education**

	IRE	JPN	ITA	MEX	NDL	BEL(Fl.)	FIN	ESP	CZE	GBR
Pre-primary	0	0.09	0.65	0.66	0.77	0.88	1.03	1.03	3.83	0.70
Primary	3.21	1.35	1.89	0.86	2.40	3.50	1.36	3.01	3.90	2.57

Chart 5.4 shows that, in six of the nine countries for which data are available, most pre-primary children with disabilities attend segregated special centres. In Japan and the Netherlands all of the provision for such children is of this type. In Spain and Italy, however, nearly all such children are integrated into regular provision (80% and over 98% respectively).

Chart 5.4. **Percentages of children receiving additional resources in pre-primary education in cross-national category A by location**[1, 2]

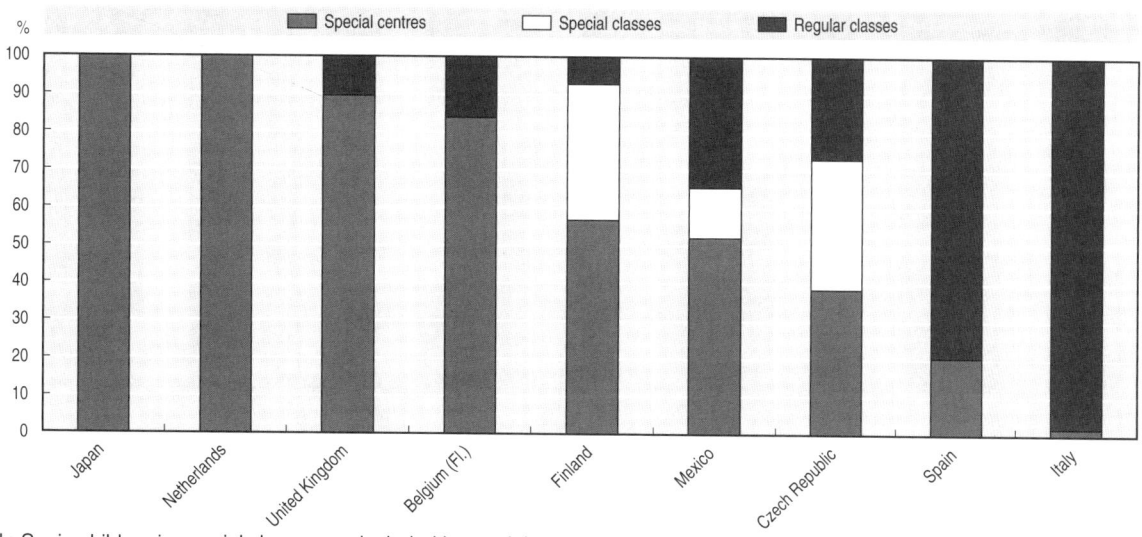

1. In Spain children in special classes are included in special centres.
2. In the United Kingdom children in special classes are included in regular classes.

Primary education

As indicated above there are typically higher percentages of students with disabilities receiving additional resources at primary level than at pre-primary. Chart 5.5 provides details. The overall median value for the fourteen countries providing data is 2.26%, with an inter-quartile range of 1.68% to 3.21%. The two countries providing outliers are again Mexico at 0.86% at the low end of the distribution, and the United States at 5.81% at the high end.

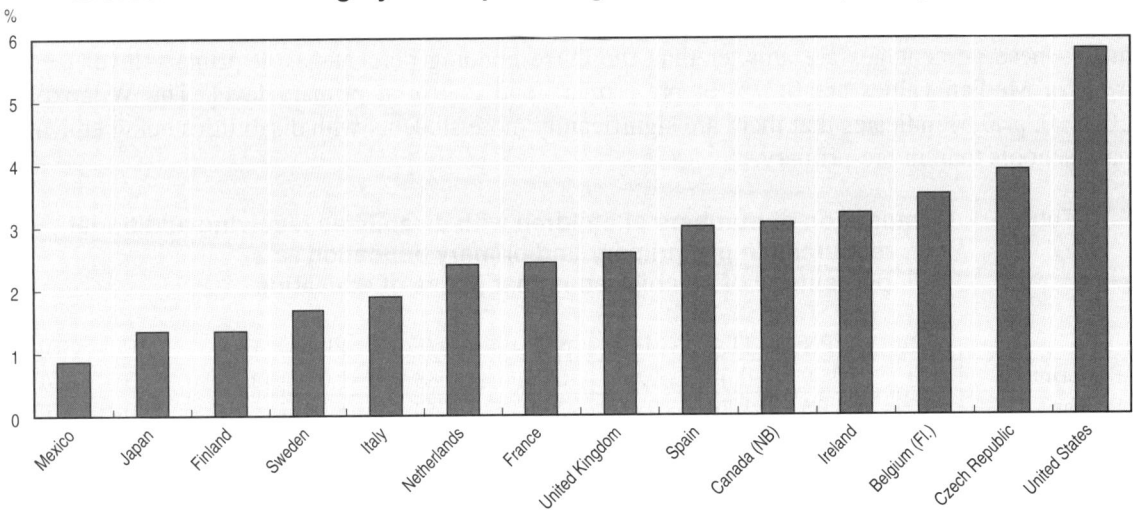

Chart 5.5. **Number of students receiving additional resources in primary education in cross-national category A as a percentage of all students in primary education**[1]

1. France: For the sake of international comparability French students administered by the Ministry of Health have been added to these data provided by the Ministry of Education. This probably has the effect of slightly inflating the percentage for France in contrast to other countries that have an unknown number of students outside the education system.

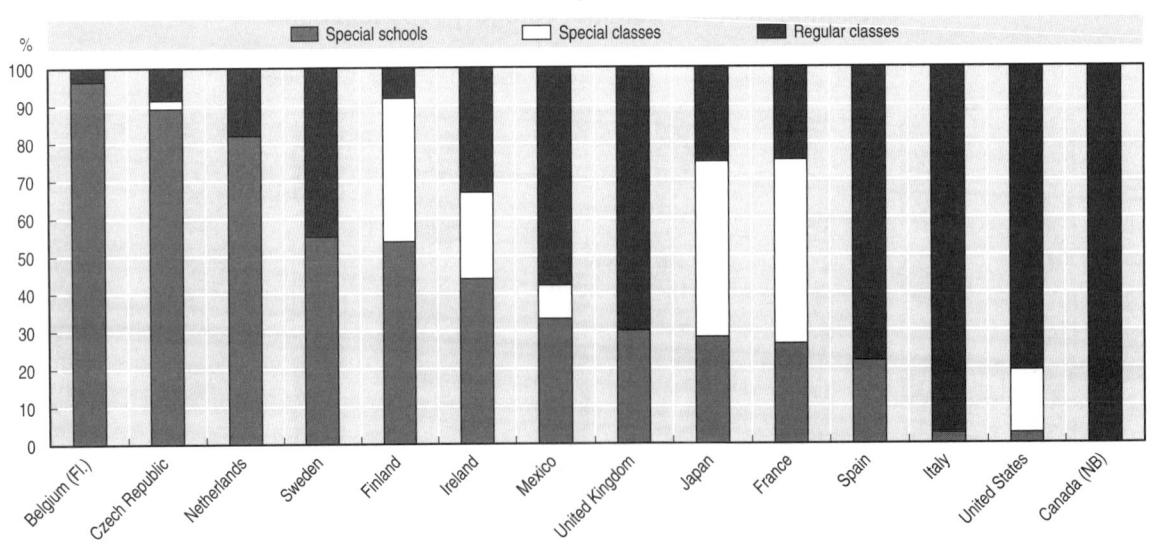

Chart 5.6. **Percentages of students receiving additional resources in primary education in cross-national category A by location**[1, 2, 3]

1. In Spain students in special classes are included in special schools.
2. In the United Kingdom students in special classes are included in regular classes.
3. France: For the sake of international comparability French students administered by the Ministry of Health have been added to these data provided by the Ministry of Education. This probably has the effect of slightly inflating the percentage in special schools for France in contrast to other countries that have an unknown number of students outside the education system.

Fourteen countries provided usable data on the location of the education of cross-national category A students at primary level, as shown in Chart 5.6. The picture is again of the full range between large-scale integration in the regular classes of mainstream schools (Canada [NB], 100%, Italy, 96.98%) and virtually total (96.24%) segregation in special schools in Belgium (Fl.). This divergence is further illustrated by the fact that five of the fourteen countries have a majority of these students receiving additional resources for disabilities in segregated special schools, while five of the fourteen have a majority of these students in fully integrated regular classes (the United Kingdom presents aggregate figures where students in special classes are included in regular classes, hence the percentage in regular classes can not be determined). France (48.87%), Finland (38.27%), Ireland (22.65%), Japan (46.82%), Mexico (9.28%) and the United States (16.88%) make more substantial use of special classes.

Lower secondary education

Chart 5.7 shows the number of students with disabilities receiving additional resources in lower secondary education (again as a percentage of all students at that level). The overall median value for the twelve countries providing data is 2.32% with an inter-quartile range of 1.23% to 4.07%. This shows somewhat greater variability than was found at primary level, also with more extreme outliers (0.23% in Mexico to 5.23% in the USA). However there is no consistent pattern for the relative size of percentages in the two phases of education. The median value at primary level for the 12 countries for which there are data at lower secondary is slightly lower (2.02% as against 2.32%), but 7 countries show a decreased percentage at lower secondary compared with primary while 4 countries show an increased percentage.

Chart 5.7. **Number of students receiving additional resources in lower secondary education in cross-national category A as a percentage of all students in lower secondary education**[1, 2]

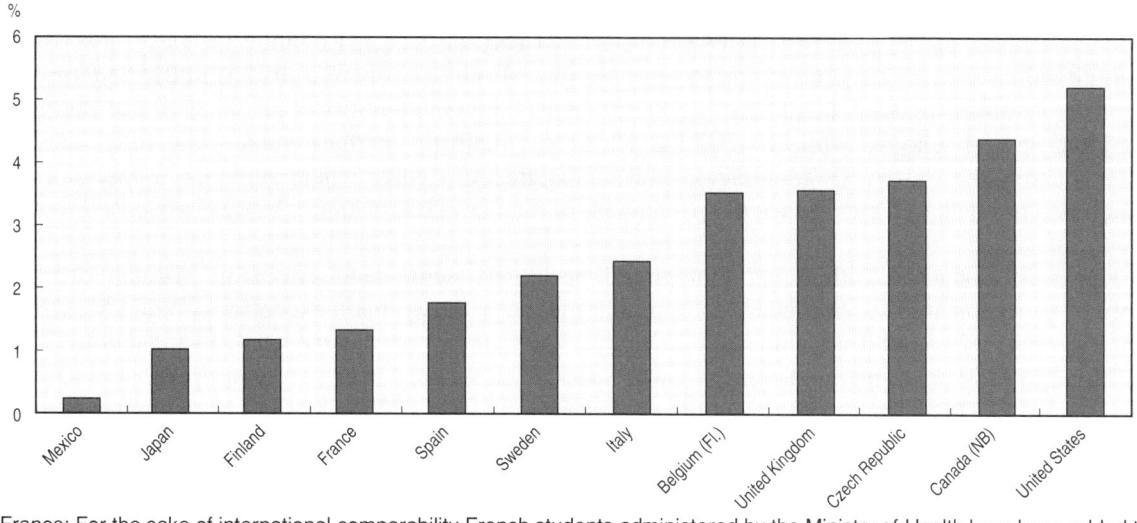

1. France: For the sake of international comparability French students administered by the Ministry of Health have been added to these data provided by the Ministry of Education. This probably has the effect of slightly inflating the percentage for France in contrast to other countries that have an unknown number of students outside the education system.
2. In Belgium (Fl.) upper secondary data are included.

Data on the location of the education of students with disabilities receiving additional resources shows a very similar pattern at lower secondary to that at primary level and is displayed in Chart 5.8.

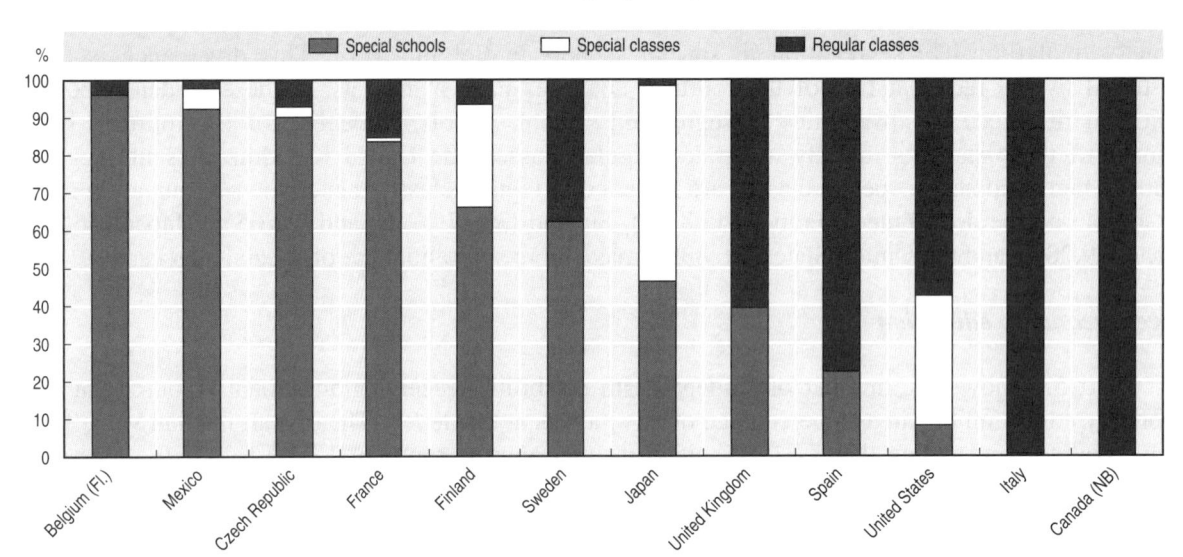

Chart 5.8. **Percentages of students receiving additional resources in lower secondary education in cross-national category A by location**[1, 2, 3, 4]

1. In Spain students in special classes are included in special schools.
2. In the United Kingdom students in special classes are included in regular classes.
3. France: For the sake of international comparability French students administered by the Ministry of Health have been added to these data provided by the Ministry of Education. This probably has the effect of slightly inflating the percentage in special schools for France in contrast to other countries that have an unknown number of students outside the education system.
4. In Belgium (Fl.) the very small percentage in regular classes is an overestimate because it includes students in upper as well as in lower secondary education.

The picture is once more of the full range between large-scale integration in the regular classes of mainstream schools (again Canada [NB], 100%; Italy, 99.49%) and virtually total (96.18%) segregation in special schools in Belgium (Fl.). Mexico (92.21 %) and the Czech Republic (90.03%) also display very high values of segregated provision in separate special schools. There is also a similar pattern in that five of the 12 countries have a majority of these students receiving additional resources for disabilities in segregated special schools, while five of the 12 have a majority of these students in fully integrated regular classes (the United Kingdom again presents aggregate figures where students in special classes are included in regular classes, hence the percentage in regular classes can not be determined).

Generally countries with largely integrated or largely segregated provision maintain the same pattern of provision at lower secondary as at primary level, with two main exceptions. While Mexico had a majority (57.75%) of students with disabilities in regular classes at primary level, as noted above this is very largely (92.21%) transferred to segregated special schools at lower secondary level. France made use of special classes in mainstream schools at primary level (48.87%), while almost a quarter (24.69%) were fully integrated in regular classes, and in special schools (26.44%) including children outside the Ministry of Education. At lower secondary level the picture changes dramatically with little use of special classes (6.07%), 15.26% integrated into regular classes and a substantially increased use of special schools (83.66%).

Upper secondary education

Chart 5.9 shows the number of students with disabilities receiving additional resources in upper secondary education (again as a percentage of all students at that level). The overall median value for the nine countries providing data is 2.15% with an inter-quartile range of 0.76% to 2.61%. Three of the nine show values less than 1% (Spain 0.28%, Italy 0.61% and Japan 0.91%). The United Kingdom provides an upper value outlier at 4.04% which suggests a concern for extending the age range of educational provision where additional resources are provided for students with disabilities. There is a slight tendency for the relative size of percentages in upper secondary to be smaller than those at lower secondary. The median value at upper secondary level for the nine countries for which there are data at lower secondary is lower (2.15% as against 2.32%), and six countries show a decreased percentage at upper secondary compared with lower, while three countries show an increased percentage.

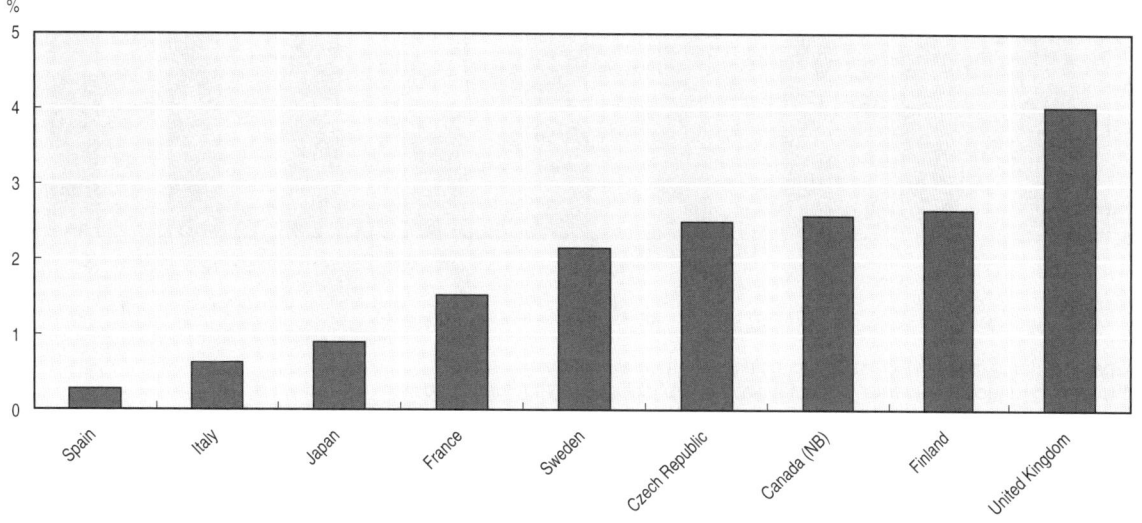

Chart 5.9. **Number of students receiving additional resources in upper secondary education in cross-national category A as a percentage of all students in upper secondary education**[1]

1. France: For the sake of international comparability French students administered by the Ministry of Health have been added to these data provided by the Ministry of Education. This probably has the effect of slightly inflating the percentage for France in contrast to other countries that have an unknown number of students outside the education system.

Data on the location of the education of students with disabilities receiving additional resources shows a very similar pattern at upper secondary to that at primary and lower secondary level and is displayed in Chart 5.10. The picture is again of the full range between large-scale integration in the regular classes of mainstream schools (again Canada [NB], 100%; Italy, 97.89%) and total or virtually total segregation in special schools in Japan (100%) and the Czech Republic (96.13%). There is again a similarly contrasting pattern in that four of the ten countries have a majority of these students receiving additional resources for disabilities in segregated special schools, while three of the ten have a majority of these students in fully integrated regular classes, and a fourth country (Finland) has a greater proportion of students in regular classes than the other two locations (the United Kingdom again presents aggregate figures where students in special classes are included in regular classes, hence the percentage in regular classes can not be determined).

In most cases countries with largely integrated or largely segregated provision at lower secondary level maintain the same pattern of provision at upper secondary, although there are dramatic exceptions. In Japan, while over half of the students with disabilities (51.80%) are in special classes and just fewer than half (46.59%) in special schools at lower secondary level, upper secondary education for these students is exclusively (100%) in special schools. In Finland, two thirds (66.27%) of lower secondary students with disabilities are in special schools, with nearly all the rest (27.08%) educated in special classes. At upper secondary level, the percentage in segregated special schools halves to 34.24%, those in special classes remain essentially the same percentage (23.51%), but the percentage in fully integrated settings increases six-fold to 42.26%.

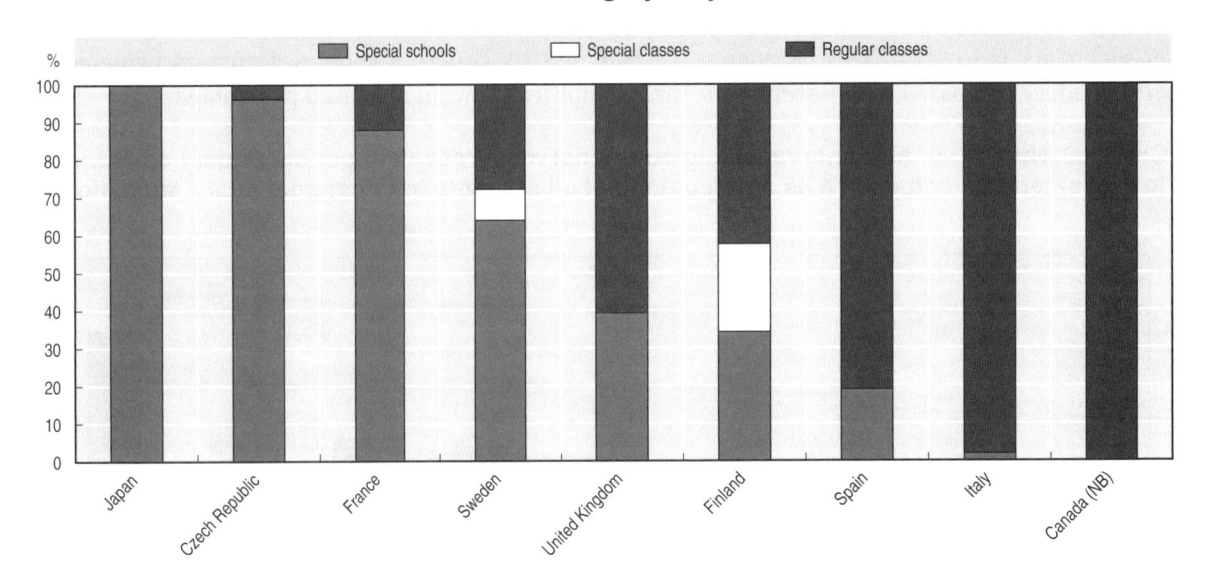

Chart 5.10. **Percentages of students receiving additional resources in upper secondary education in cross-national category A by location**[1, 2, 3]

1. In Spain students in special classes are included in special schools.
2. In the United Kingdom students in special classes are included in regular classes.
3. France: For the sake of international comparability French students administered by the Ministry of Health have been added to these data provided by the Ministry of Education. This probably has the effect of slightly inflating the percentage in special schools for France in contrast to other countries that have an unknown number of students outside the education system.

Quantitative data on cross-national category B (students receiving additional resources for difficulties)

As previously discussed the quantity and quality of data relating to cross-national categories B and C are inferior to that for cross-national category A, although differences do not appear to be as marked as in the previous data collection discussed in the earlier monograph (OECD, 2000b). Cross-national category B, as discussed and defined in Chapter 1, is formally a residual category covering those national categories referring to students whose special needs are not clearly ascribed to either organic defects or to disadvantages in their socio-economic background – in other words students who appear to have difficulties in accessing the curriculum for other reasons.

While all countries using categorical systems for students with disabilities, difficulties, and disadvantages have national categories which they consider to fall within cross-national category A, in 1999 four countries (Italy, Japan, Poland and Sweden) placed no categories in cross-national category B.

The period of compulsory education

Chart 5.11 shows the number of students receiving additional resources within the period of compulsory education who are considered to fall within cross-national category B for different countries, as a percentage of all students in compulsory education. Those countries that have no national categories falling within cross-national category B (*i.e.* for whom a zero is entered because the category is not applicable) are included in the chart as this implies that there are no cross-national category B students receiving additional resources. Including these, 17 countries provide data, the median number of category B students as a percentage of all students in compulsory education being 1.96%. The inter-quartile range from 0% to 7.45% indicates an amount of variability far in excess of that found in the corresponding data for students with disabilities.

CHAPTER 5. ANALYSIS OF THE QUANTITATIVE DATA FOR CROSS-NATIONAL CATEGORIES A, B AND C – **89**

Chart 5.11. **Number of students receiving additional resources over the period of compulsory education in cross-national category B as a percentage of all students in compulsory education**[1, 2, 3]

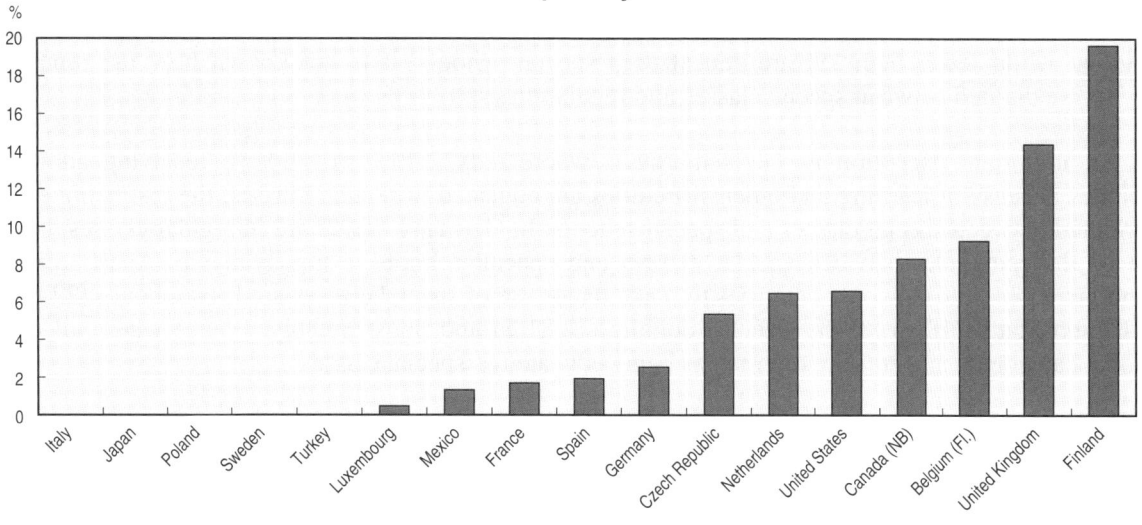

1. In Italy, Japan, Poland and Sweden there are no national categories falling within cross-national category B.
2. In Turkey the only national category falling within cross-national category B is "Gifted & talented" which has been excluded from the analysis.
3. In Finland the vast majority of pupils recognised as having special educational needs in category B receive part-time special education, in which they are given special support, for their minor learning or adjustment problems.

Limiting the analysis to those countries with national categories falling within cross-national category B, data are available from 12 countries (median percentage 5.91%; with an inter-quartile range of 1.81% to 8.79%). Taking these figures together with the high values of 8.29% (Canada [NB]), 9.29% Belgium (Fl.), 14.41% (United Kingdom) and 19.65% (Finland) which greatly exceed corresponding percentages for students with disabilities, it appears that when such categories are recognised in national systems the numbers of students receiving additional resources are considerable.

Chart 5.12. **Percentages of students receiving additional resources over the period of compulsory education in cross-national category B by location**[1, 2]

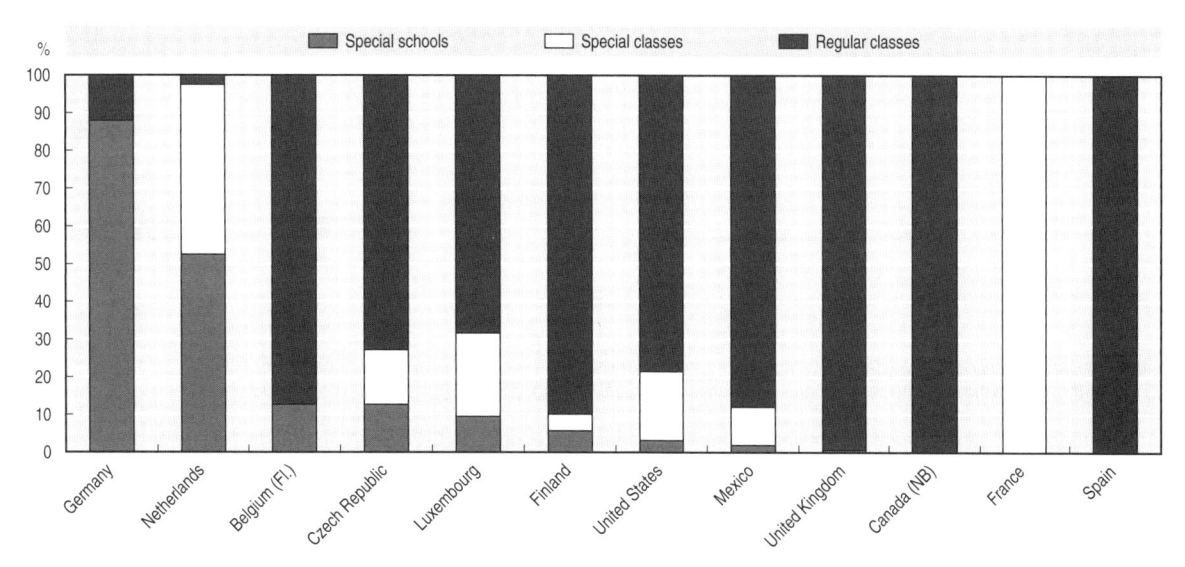

1. In Germany students in special classes are included in special schools.
2. In the United Kingdom students in special classes are included in regular classes.

Chart 5.12 presents data from 12 countries on the location of students receiving additional resources for learning and other difficulties. While again showing major country-to-country variation the typical pattern is for at least two thirds of such students to be educated in regular classes in mainstream schools. This is true for seven of the ten countries where the data enable this to be decided (in the United Kingdom while fewer than 1% are educated in special schools, it is not known how the remaining 99.40% are divided between special classes and regular classes).

An important exception is the Netherlands where only 2.49% of students receiving additional resources because of learning and other difficulties are educated in regular classes, the rest being evenly distributed between special classes and special schools. In Germany 11.9% are in regular classes, but the split of the remainder between special classes and special schools is not available. Apart from the Netherlands (44.83%) the only countries to make major use of special classes are Luxembourg (22.07%), the United States (18.36%), the Czech Republic (14.81%) and, most notably, France where all cross-national category B students are reported as being educated in special classes.

Pre-primary education

Chart 5.13 indicates the number of children receiving additional resources in pre-school education who are considered to fall within cross-national category B for different countries, as a percentage of all children in pre-school education. While fourteen countries are included in the chart, nine of them provide zero values, either because the category is not applicable (*e.g.* no B categories in the national system), or is a known zero figure. Hence the median value for the number of children receiving additional resources because of difficulties is 0%, with an inter-quartile range of 0% to 1.08%.

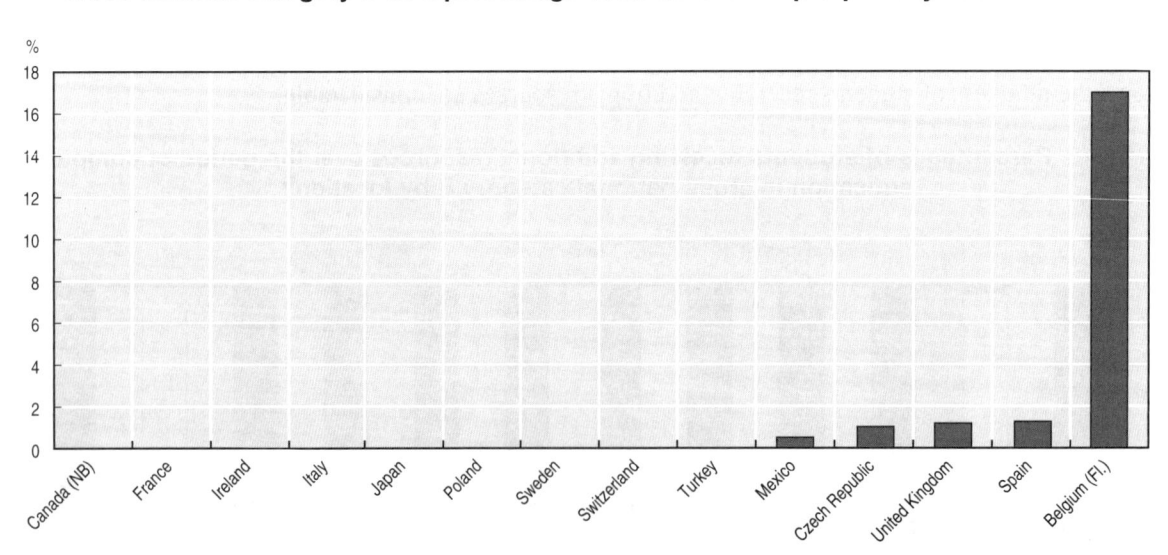

Chart 5.13. **Number of children receiving additional resources in pre-primary education in cross-national category B as a percentage of all children in pre-primary education**[1, 2, 3]

1. In Italy, Japan, Poland and Sweden there no national categories falling within cross-national category B.
2. In Turkey the only national category falling within cross-national category B is "Gifted & talented" which has been excluded from the analysis.
3. Although there are national categories falling within cross-national category B in Canada (NB), France, Ireland and Switzerland no children are in this category in pre-primary education.

However, while it appears that typically countries provide little or no additional resources at pre-school level for these children Belgium (Fl.) (16.96%) provides a notable exception.

As was found above in analysing the data on children with disabilities, these percentages are smaller than the corresponding percentages at primary level (see also Chart 5.15). Table 5.2 gives details for the eight countries where comparisons can be made (excluding countries with no B categories). For all eight countries percentages are greater at primary level giving a statistically significant result (Wilcoxon test n=8 T=0 p<0.05).

Table 5.2. **Comparison of numbers of children with difficulties receiving additional resources in pre-primary and primary education as a percentage of all children in that phase of education**

	BEL (Fl.)	CAN (NB)	FRA	IRE	MEX	CZE	ESP	GBR
Pre-primary	16.96	0	0	0	0.54	1.01	1.30	1.15
Primary	18.44	10.34	0.27	7.86	1.80	5.13	2.65	21.07

Median values for this restricted set are 0.54% at pre-primary and 1.80% at primary level, with the primary percentage exceeding that at pre-primary for all countries. It appears that as with children with disabilities the perceived importance of early intervention for this particular group of children does not currently translate into priority provision for them possibly for diagnostic issues.

Chart 5.14 shows that only five countries can provide data on the location of pre-school education for children with difficulties. The Czech Republic is the only country reporting substantial use of special centres (89.91%). Otherwise the pattern is for almost all children to be placed in regular integrated classes with other children (note again that the split between regular and special classes is not made in UK data returns).

Chart 5.14. **Percentages of children receiving additional resources in pre-primary education in cross-national category B by location**[1]

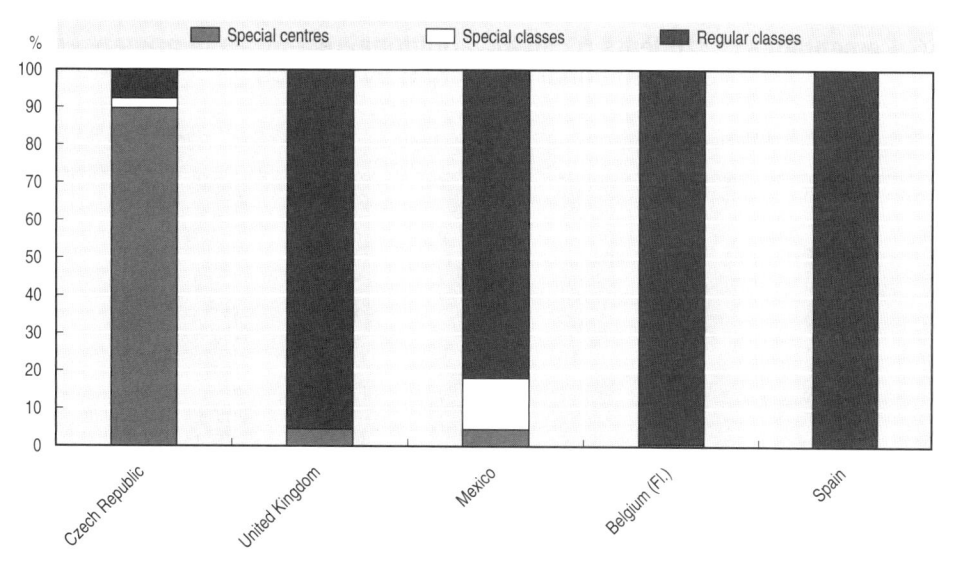

1. In the United Kingdom students in special classes are included in regular classes.

Primary education

Chart 5.15 provides details of the number of students with difficulties receiving additional resources at primary level as a percentage of all students in primary education. The overall median value for the fifteen countries providing data (including five for which zeroes are entered) is 2.65%, with an inter-quartile range of 0% to 10.34%. A notable feature is that for four countries the percentage exceeds 10% – Canada (NB) (10.34%), Belgium (Fl.) (18.44%), United Kingdom (21.07%) and Finland (23.98%).

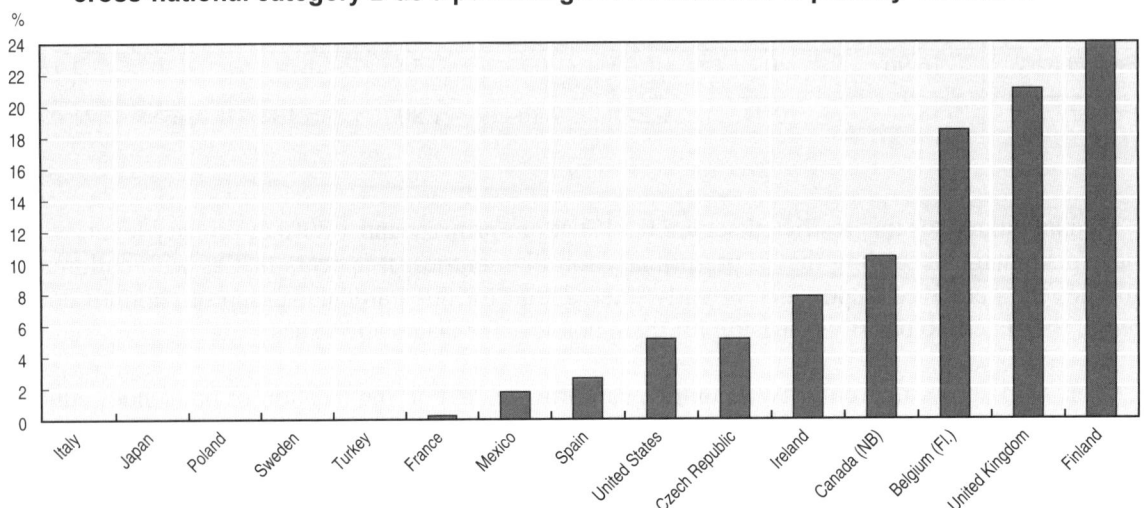

Chart 5.15. **Number of students receiving additional resources in primary education in cross-national category B as a percentage of all students in primary education**[1, 2, 3]

1. In Italy, Japan, Poland and Sweden there are no national categories falling within cross-national category B.
2. In Turkey the only national category falling within cross-national category B is "Gifted & talented" which has been excluded from the analysis.
3. In Finland the vast majority of pupils recognised as having special educational needs in category B receive part-time special education, in which they are given special support, for their minor learning or adjustment problems.

Chart 5.16. **Percentages of students receiving additional resources in primary education in cross-national category B by location**[1]

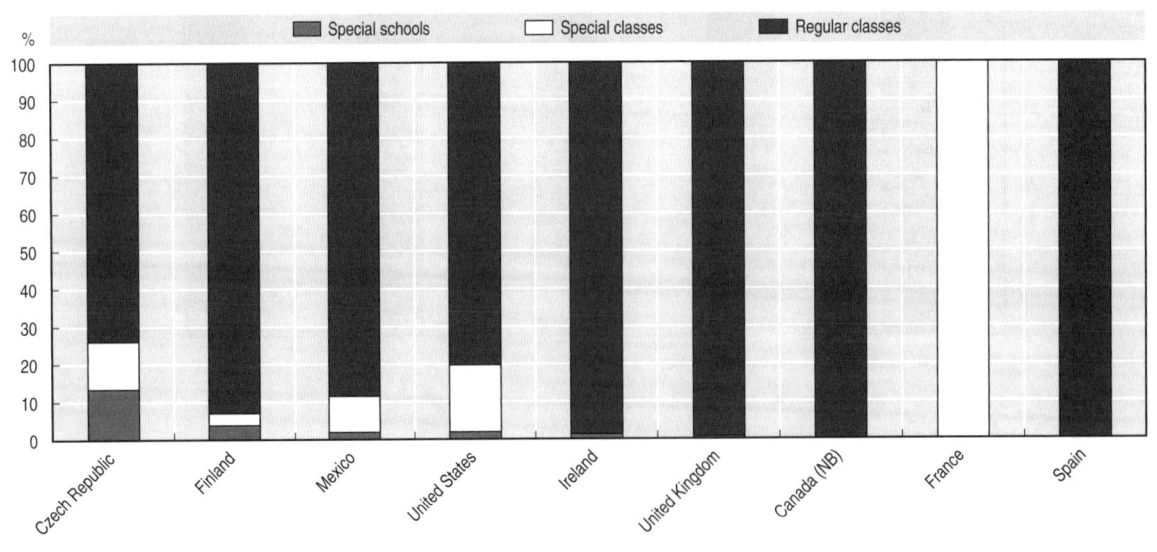

1. In the United Kingdom students in special classes are included in regular classes.

Chart 5.16 reveals that nine countries provided usable data on the location of the education of cross-national category B students at primary level. Typically 80% or more of these students are educated in regular classrooms. The main exception is France where all the provision is in special classes. The United States (17.82%) and Mexico (9.49%) also make use of special classes for students with difficulties, while the Czech Republic has 13.24% in special classes and 13.13% in special schools. As at other phases of education in the United Kingdom while a very small percentage is educated in special schools (0.32%), it is not known how the remaining 99.68% are divided between special classes and regular classes.

Lower secondary education

Chart 5.17 shows the number of students with difficulties receiving additional resources in lower secondary education (again as a percentage of all students at that level). The overall median value for the fifteen countries providing data is 1.02% with the large inter-quartile range of 0% to 12.2%. Four countries have percentages in excess of 10% (Finland, 12.20%, the Netherlands, 13.41%, the United Kingdom, 13.7% and the United States, 14.40%).

Chart 5.17. **Number of students receiving additional resources in lower secondary education in cross-national category B as a percentage of all students in lower secondary education**[1, 2, 3]

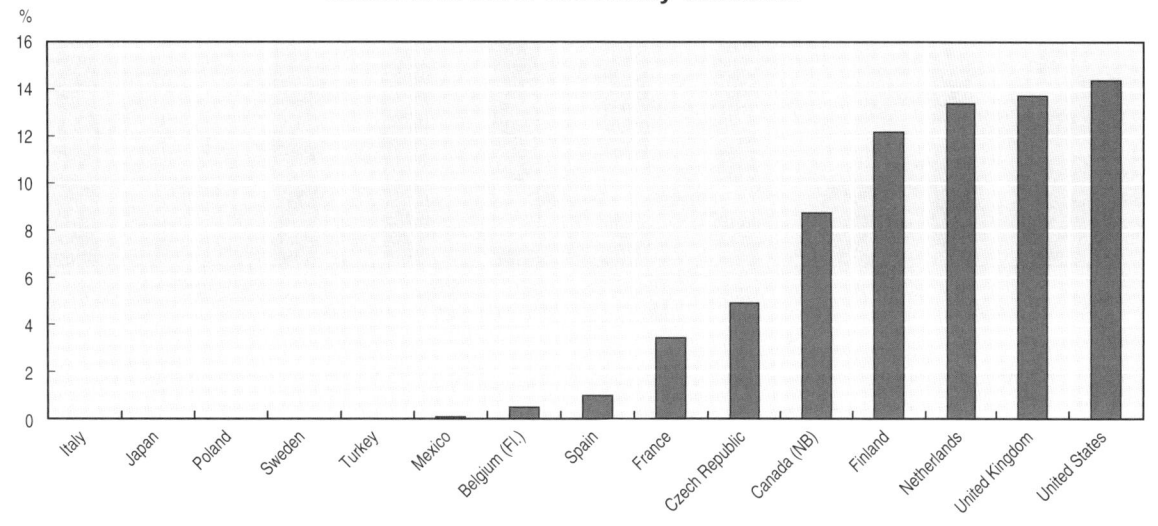

1. In Italy, Japan, Poland and Sweden there are no national categories falling within cross-national category B.
2. In Turkey the only national category falling within cross-national category B is "Gifted & talented" which has been excluded from the analysis.
3. In Finland the vast majority of pupils recognised as having special educational needs in category B receive part-time special education, in which they are given special support, for their minor learning or adjustment problems.

If the analysis is restricted to those countries presenting data at both primary and lower secondary levels (excluding countries with no categories in cross-national category B), the typical pattern for students with difficulties is for a decrease (six decrease and two increase) in the percentage when moving from primary to lower secondary, as illustrated in Table 5.3 (excludes countries with no B categories).

Table 5.3. **Comparison of numbers of students with difficulties receiving additional resources in primary and lower secondary education as a percentage of all students in that phase of education**

	FRA	MEX	ESP	USA	CZE	CAN (NB)	UKM	FIN
Primary	0.27	1.80	2.65	5.09	5.13	10.34	21.07	23.98
Lower secondary	3.44	0.07	1.02	14.40	4.88	8.73	13.70	12.20

However, where there is an increase in percentage from primary to lower secondary it is in both countries substantial (France from 0.27% to 3.44%; the United States from 5.09% to 14.40%) but the difference does not approach statistical significance (Wilcoxon test n=8 T=12 p>0.05).

Data on the location of the education of students with difficulties receiving additional resources is shown in Chart 5.18. It shows a very similar pattern at lower secondary to that at primary level for those countries with data at both phases of education. Belgium (Fl.) and the Netherlands, neither of whom were represented at primary level, are atypical in that over 90% of their provision for students with difficulties at this educational level is in special schools or classes.

Chart 5.18. **Percentages of students receiving additional resources in lower secondary education in cross-national category B by location[1]**

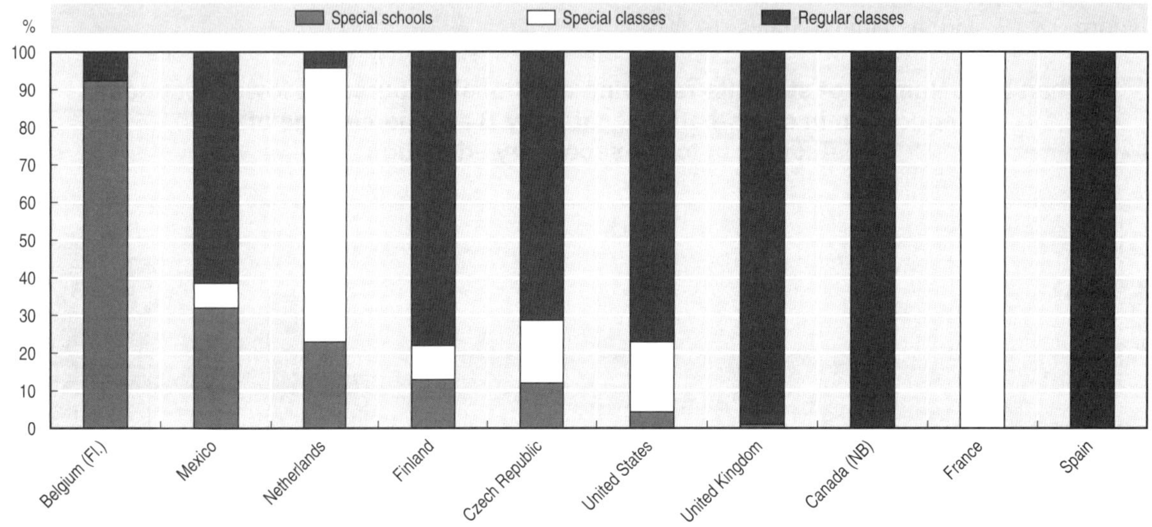

1. In the United Kingdom students in special classes are included in regular classes.

Upper secondary education

Chart 5.19 shows the number of students with difficulties receiving additional resources in upper secondary education (again as a percentage of all students at that level). Typically, no additional resources are made available for students with difficulties at upper secondary level (six of the ten countries where data are available are zero, Spain negligible at 0.05%) – the median value is therefore 0% with an inter-quartile range of 0% to 1.48%. These very low figures may reflect the lack of availability of data at this level – of the ten countries providing non-zero percentages at lower secondary level (Chart 5.17) only four are able to do so at upper secondary. Three of these, Spain, France and Canada (NB), do show substantial decreases from lower to upper secondary. The fourth, the United Kingdom, actually shows an increase from 13.70% to 15.35%.

Data on the location of the education of these students at upper secondary level are only available for four countries (Canada [NB], France, Spain and the United Kingdom). They each show an identical pattern of provision to that at lower secondary level (see Chart 5.18).

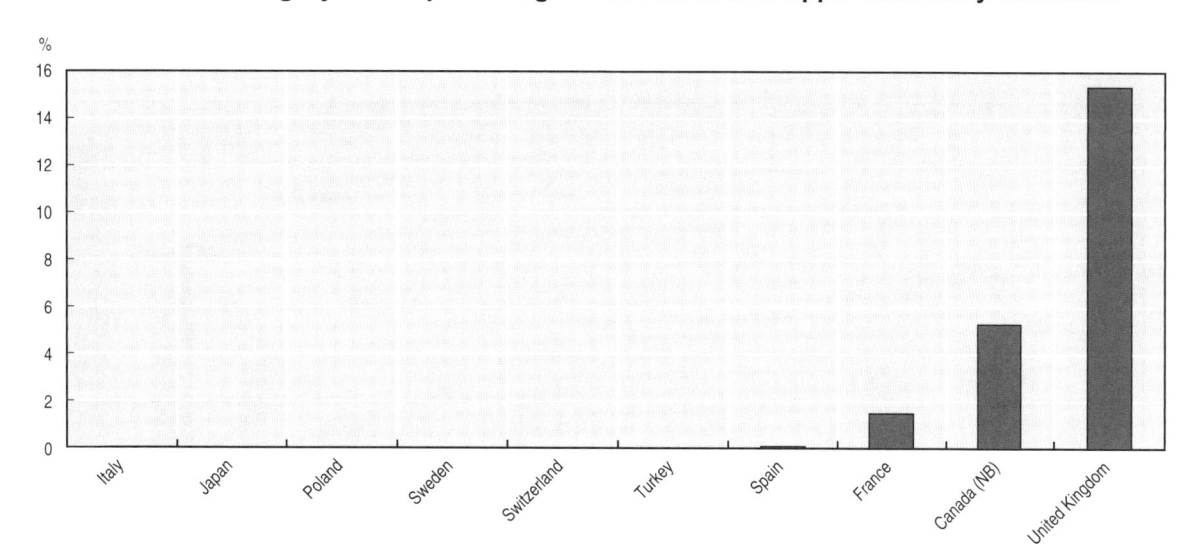

Chart 5.19. **Number of students receiving additional resources in upper secondary education in cross-national category B as a percentage of all students in upper secondary education**[1, 2, 3]

1. In Italy, Japan, Poland and Sweden there are no national categories falling within cross-national category B.
2. In Turkey the only national category falling within cross-national category B is "Gifted & talented" which has been excluded from the analysis.
3. Although there are national categories falling within cross-national category B in Switzerland no children are in this category in upper secondary.

Quantitative data on cross-national category C (students receiving additional resources for disadvantages)

Cross-national category C, as discussed and defined in Chapter 1, covers those national categories referring to students considered to have difficulties accessing the curriculum arising from disadvantages in their socio-economic background. Several countries (Canada [Alb., SK], Turkey and the United Kingdom) had no categories which they placed in cross-national category C, Table 3.2 and Annex 1 give details.

The period of compulsory education

Chart 5.20 shows the number of students receiving additional resources within the period of compulsory education who are considered to fall within cross-national category C for different countries, as a percentage of all students in compulsory education (the period of compulsory education differs from country to country (see Annex 4). Those countries who have no national categories falling within cross-national category C (*i.e.* for whom a zero is entered because the category is not applicable) are, as with cross-national category B charts, included in the chart as this implies that there are no cross-national category C students receiving additional resources. Including these, thirteen countries provide data, the median number of category C students as a percentage of all students in compulsory education being 0.33%. The large inter-quartile range is from 0% to 8.73%.

Chart 5.20. **Number of students receiving additional resources over the period of compulsory education in cross-national category C as a percentage of all students in compulsory education**[1, 2]

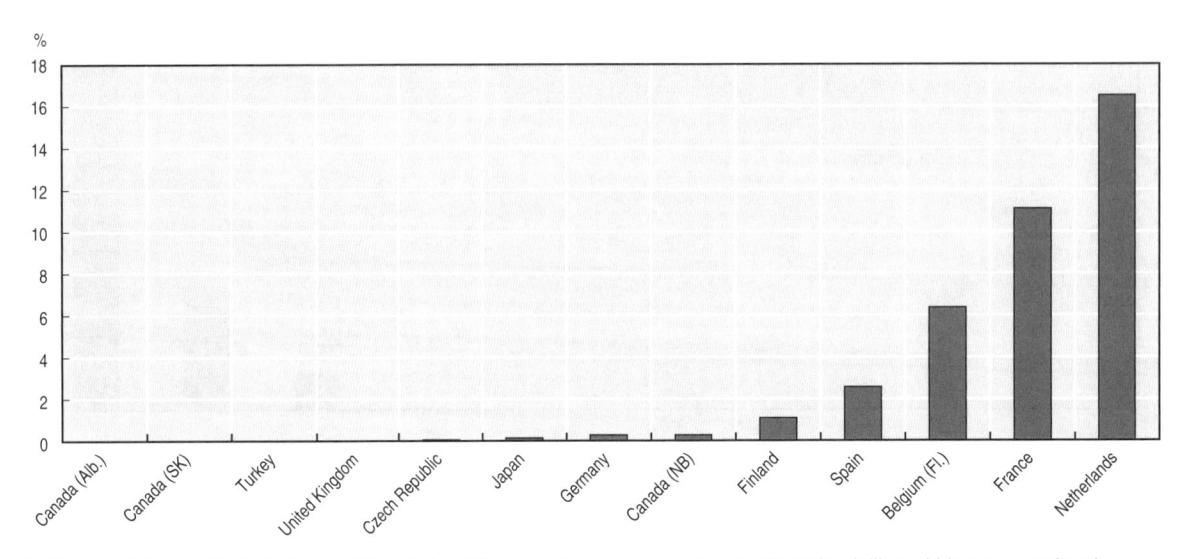

1. In Canada (Alb. and SK), Turkey and the United Kingdom there are no national categories falling within cross-national category C.
2. The value for the Czech Republic is 0.05.

This median percentage for C (0.30%) is lower than that for A and B (2.12% and 1.96% respectively). The inter-quartile range (0% to 4.45%) lies between A (1.61% to 3.07%) and B (0% to 7.45%). These comparisons are, to some extent, vitiated as there are differences in the set of countries providing data for A, B and C. However, if the analysis is restricted to the eight countries (Belgium [Fl.], Canada [NB], Czech Republic, Finland, France, Germany, Spain and the United Kingdom) for which data are available for all cross-national categories, a very similar picture is obtained.

Chart 5.21. **Percentages of students receiving additional resources over the period of compulsory education in cross-national category C by location**

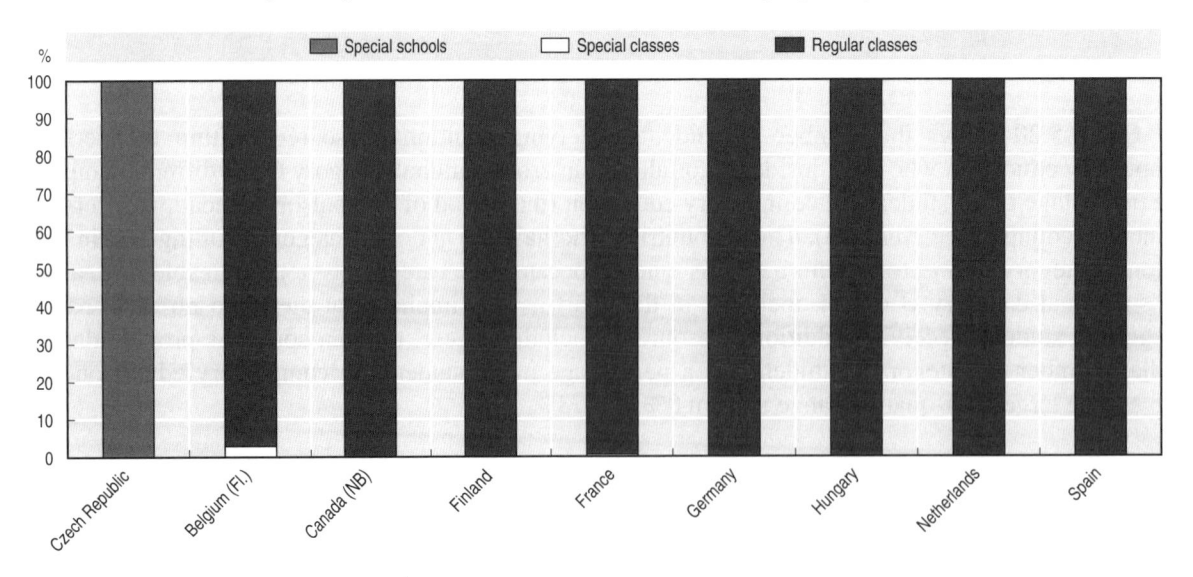

Limiting the analysis to those countries with national categories falling within cross-national category C, data are available from nine countries (median percentage 1.03%; quartiles 0.24% and 8.73%). Taking these figures together with the high values of 11.14% (France) and 16.51% (Netherlands), it appears that *when such categories are recognised in national systems* the numbers of students receiving additional resources can be considerable.

Chart 5.21 presents data from nine countries on the location of students receiving additional resources for disadvantages. In eight of the countries this education is exclusively, or virtually exclusively, in regular mainstream classrooms. The exception is the Czech Republic where category 11 students "socially disadvantaged children: preparatory classes in regular schools" are in fact educated in special schools. Belgium (Fl.) and France both make limited use of special classes.

Pre-primary education

Chart 5.22 indicates the number of children receiving additional resources in pre-primary education who are considered to fall within cross-national category C for different countries, as a percentage of all children in pre-school education. While twelve countries are included in the chart, eight of them provide zero values, either because the category is not applicable (*e.g.* no C categories in the national system), or is a known zero figure. Hence the median value for the number of children receiving additional resources because of difficulties is 0%, with an inter-quartile range of 0% to 0.55%.

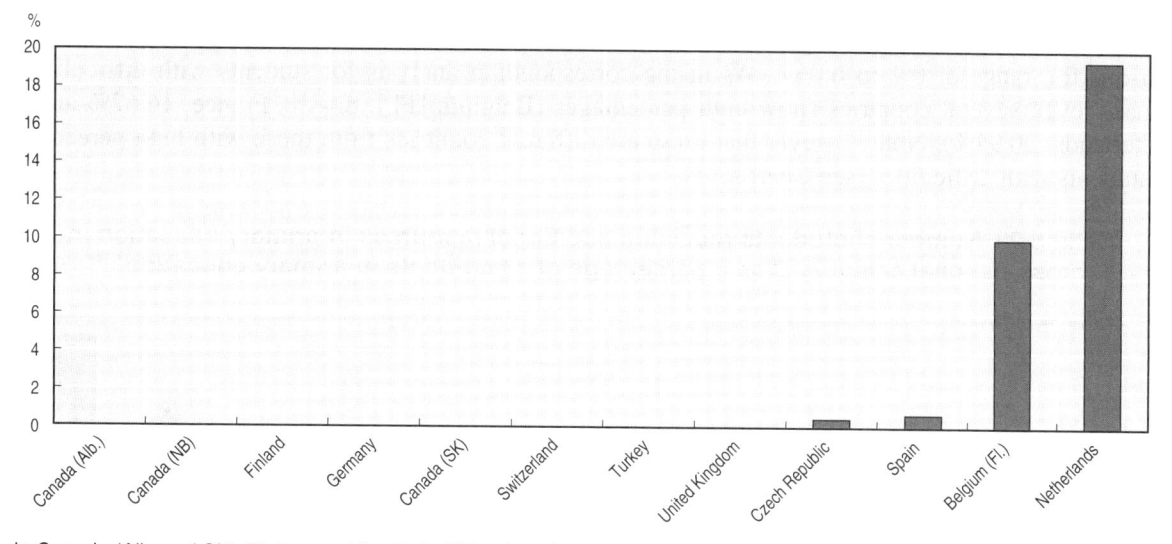

Chart 5.22. **Number of children receiving additional resources in pre-primary education in cross-national category C as a percentage of all children in pre-primary education**[1, 2]

1. In Canada (Alb. and SK), Turkey and the United Kingdom there are no national categories falling within cross-national category C.
2. Although there are national categories falling within cross-national category C in Canada (NB), Finland, Germany and Switzerland no children are in this category in pre-primary education.

However, while it appears that typically countries provide little or no additional resources at pre-primary level for these children, Belgium (Fl.) (9.95%) and the Netherlands (19.44%) are notable exceptions.

As was found above in analysing the data on children with disabilities and with difficulties, most percentages are smaller than the corresponding percentages at primary level but this is not a strong effect here (see also Chart 5.23). Table 5.4 gives details for the seven countries where comparisons can be made (excluding countries with no C categories).

Table 5.4. **Comparison of numbers of children with disadvantages receiving additional resources in pre-primary and primary education as a percentage of all children in that phase of education**

	CAN (NB)	DEU	FIN	CZE	ESP	BEL (Fl.)	NDL
Pre-primary	0	0	0	0.43	0.67	9.95	19.44
Primary	0.39	0	1.21	0.03	3.67	8.24	20.94

Median values for this restricted set are 0.43% at pre-primary and 1.21% at primary level, with the primary percentage exceeding that at pre-primary for four of the six countries for which there is non-statistically significant difference (Wilcoxon test n=6 T=7 p>0.05).

Only four countries can provide data on the location of pre-primary education for children with difficulties. The Czech Republic is the only country reporting segregated provision, two-thirds in special classes and one third in special centres. Otherwise the pattern in Belgium (Fl.), the Netherlands and Spain is for all children to be placed in regular integrated classes with other children.

Primary education

Chart 5.23 provides details of the number of students with disadvantages receiving additional resources at primary level as a percentage of all students in primary education. The overall median value for the twelve countries providing data (including five for which zeroes are entered) is 0.21%, with an inter-quartile range of 0% to 6.06%. As in the corresponding analysis for students with difficulties at primary level, several countries show high percentages (Belgium [Fl.], 8.44%, France, 16.62% and the Netherlands, 20.94%). Note however that these are different countries from those with high percentages for students with difficulties (see Chart 5.15).

Chart 5.23. **Number of students receiving additional resources in primary education in cross-national category C as a percentage of all students in primary education**[1, 2]

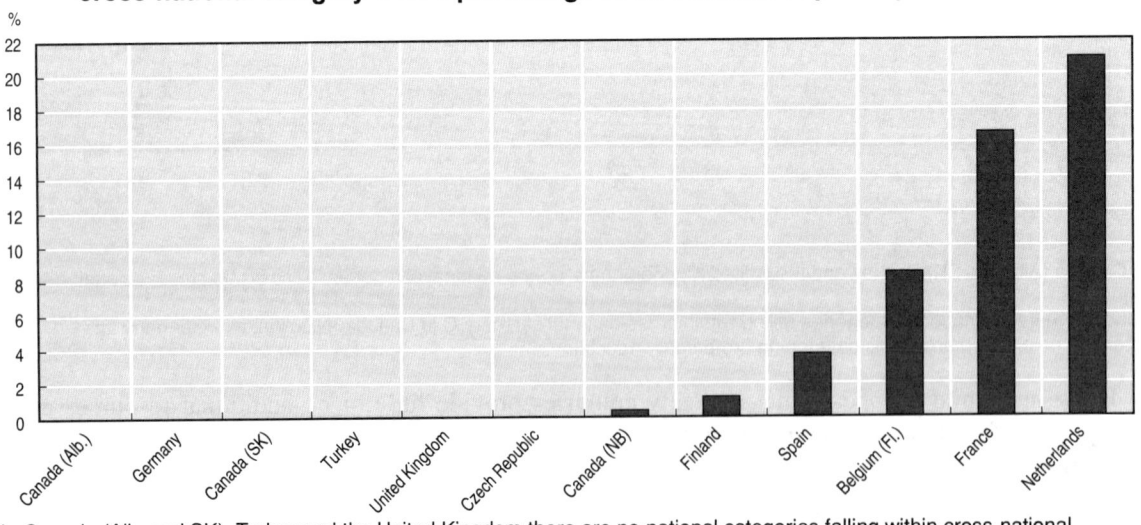

1. In Canada (Alb. and SK), Turkey and the United Kingdom there are no national categories falling within cross-national category C.
2. Although there are national categories falling within cross-national category C in the Czech Republic and Germany no children are in this category in primary education.

The location for the education of these students at primary level is similar to that found in pre-primary education. Seven countries provide data – six (Belgium [Fl.], Canada [NB], Finland, France, the Netherlands and Spain) place them in regular integrated classes. The exception is again the Czech Republic where the provision for socially disadvantaged students is in special preparatory classes in regular schools.

Lower secondary education

Chart 5.24 shows the number of students with disadvantages receiving additional resources in lower secondary education (again as a percentage of all students at that level). The overall median value for the twelve countries providing data is 0.21% with an inter-quartile range of 0% to 2.67%.

Chart 5.24. **Number of students receiving additional resources in lower secondary education in cross-national category C as a percentage of all students in lower secondary education**[1, 2]

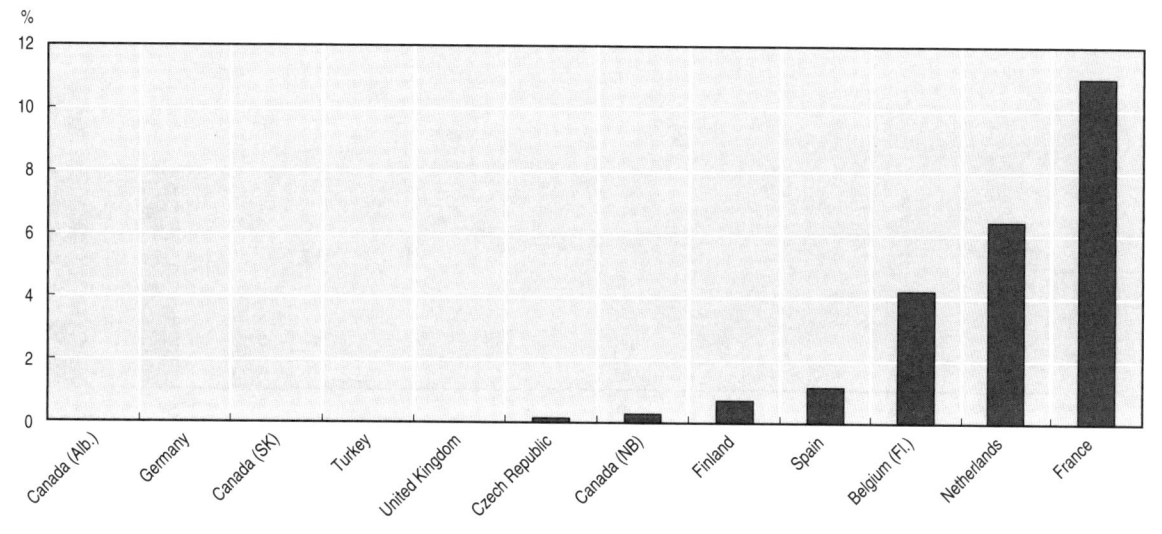

1. In Canada (Alb. and SK), Turkey, United Kingdom there are no national categories falling within cross-national category C.
2. Although there are national categories falling within cross-national category C in Germany no children are in this category in lower secondary education.

If the analysis is restricted to those countries presenting data at both primary and lower secondary levels (excluding countries with no categories in cross-national category C) as Table 5.5 shows, the typical pattern for students with disadvantages is for a decrease (five decrease and one increase) in the percentage when moving from primary to lower secondary. Even though the change is not statistically significant (Wilcoxon test n=6 T=2 p>0.05), the decrease in the Netherlands is quite substantial.

Table 5.5. **Comparison of numbers of children with disadvantages receiving additional resources in primary and lower secondary education as a percentage of all children in that phase of education**

	BEL (Fl).	DEU	CZE	CAN (NB)	FIN	ESP	NDL
Primary	8.44	0	0.03	0.39	1.21	3.67	20.94
Lower secondary	4.22	0	0.14	0.27	0.72	1.11	6.46

Data on the location of the education of students with disadvantages receiving additional resources are similar to that at primary level – the same seven countries giving exactly the same pattern.

Upper secondary education

Chart 5.25 shows the number of students with disadvantages receiving additional resources in upper secondary education (again as a percentage of all students at that level). Typically, no additional resources are made available for students with disadvantages at upper secondary level (eight of the twelve countries where data are available are zero, the Czech Republic is negligible at 0.05%). This gives a median value of 0%, with an inter-quartile range of 0% to 0.72%.

Chart 5.25. **Number of students receiving additional resources in upper secondary education in cross-national category C as a percentage of all students in upper secondary education**[1, 2]

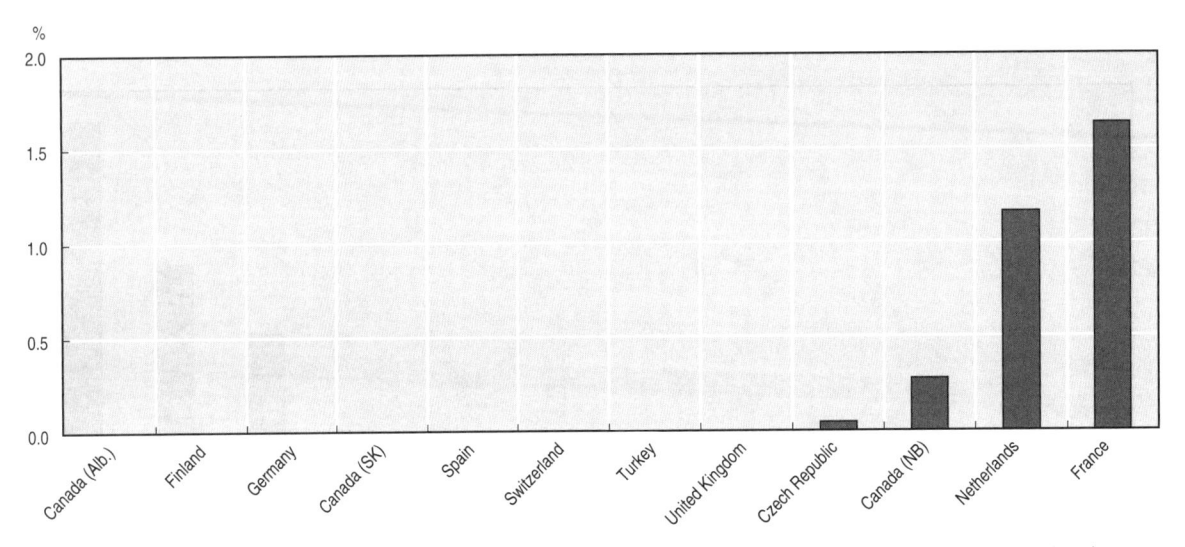

1. In Canada (Alb. and SK), Turkey and the United Kingdom there are no national categories falling within cross-national category C.
2. Although there are national categories falling within cross-national category C in Finland, Germany, Spain and Switzerland no children are in this category in upper secondary education.

Data on the location of the education of these students at upper secondary level are only available for four countries – they repeat the pattern found at primary and lower secondary: Canada (NB), France and the Netherlands place all students receiving additional resources for social disadvantage in regular mainstream classes. The Czech Republic places all such students in special classes.

Overall comparisons across the phases of education for the three cross-national categories

Chart 5.26 compares the average percentage of students receiving additional resources at different levels or phases of education separately for students with disabilities, difficulties and disadvantages. In each case the average is for those countries for which data are available for all phases of education (including those countries where a particular category is not applicable or another known zero). As noted on Chart 5.26 the countries contributing vary from A to B to C. Note also the caution expressed above in making comparisons between data relating to A and B on the one hand and C on the other. However, the main point of interest here is in making comparisons between the relative sizes of percentages through the educational system for A, B and C separately.

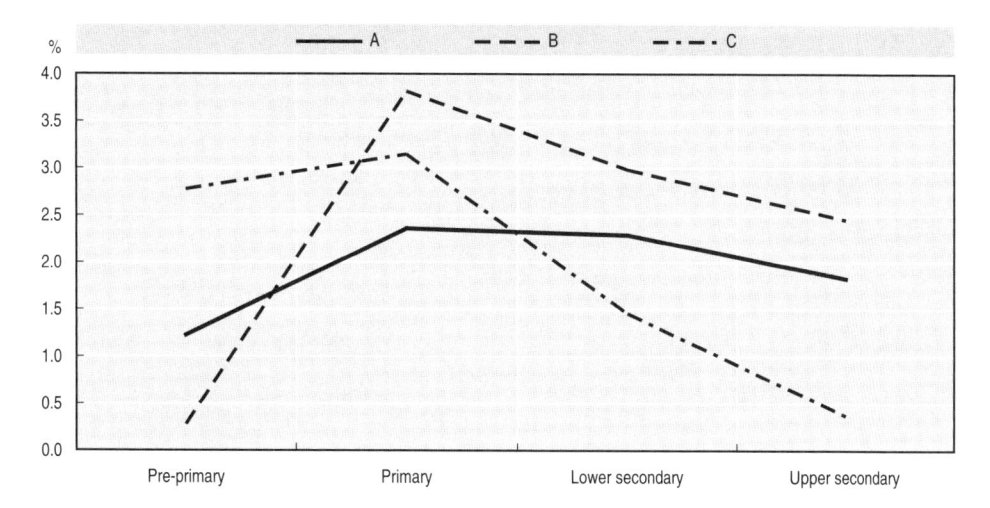

Chart 5.26. **Mean number of students receiving additional resources at different levels of education by cross-national category, as a percentage of all students in that level of education**[1]

1. Based on the countries for which data are available at all levels: for A this is CZE, ESP, FIN, ITA, JPN and GBR; for B this is CAN (NB), ESP, FRA, ITA, JPN, POL, SWE, TUR and GBR; for C this is CAN (Alb.), CAN (NB), CAN (SK), CZE, ESP, FIN, NDL, TUR and GBR. This includes all countries for which the data returns indicate that there are no students within that cross-national category.

Chart 5.26 shows that the proportions of students with disabilities (A) in school are highest at primary and lower secondary levels and they contrast with the data for students with difficulties (B) and disadvantages (C). The last two peak at primary and show substantial reduction in resourcing thereafter. This implies that resourcing remains relatively constant for those with disabilities between primary and lower secondary levels but declines for those with difficulties and disadvantages at a time when they are still in need of additional resources to help them benefit fully from their schooling.

CHAPTER 6
ADDITIONAL ANALYSES OF THE QUANTITATIVE DATA

Introduction

This chapter focuses on what the data tables show about the different physical locations in which students receiving additional resources for disabilities, difficulties, or disadvantages are educated. The simple categorisation, employed in the previous chapter, of special schools, special classes in mainstream schools, and regular classes in mainstream schools, is again used. Several other aspects are also analysed including the gender ratios for these students in different settings and categorisations, student-staff ratios and the age distributions of the students in a number of national systems.

Special schools

The amount of segregated provision in the form of special schools differs widely from country to country. As Table 6.1 shows the number of such institutions expressed as a proportion of the total school population over the period of compulsory education varies from 0 to 82 per 100 000 students, with a median value of 29.4 and quartile[1] values of 11 and 58.4. Where comparative data are available the relative number of special schools typically show an increase from pre-school to primary, and from primary to lower secondary level, with a decrease from lower to upper secondary level. Median values for the six countries for which comparative data are available being 23.5 schools per 100 000 students at pre-primary level; 71.7 at primary, 98.5 at lower secondary level; and 43.9 at upper secondary. Canada (NB) has no special schools, while Italy has a very small number of special schools at all levels, with none exceeding two per 100 000. As noted above, provision is typically low at pre-school levels but two countries, the Netherlands and the Czech Republic show values in excess of 100 schools per 100 000 children (113.4 and 108.4 respectively).

Table 6.2 shows that the average size of special schools over the period of compulsory education varies substantially from country to country. The median value is 64.6 students per school, with quartiles at 34.9 and 70.3. The lowest average size is in Mexico (12.1 students per school), the highest Germany (120.7). Pre-primary centres are very small (median value 14.0), ranging in size from 9.5 (Mexico) to 23.4 (Czech Republic).

Special schools at primary level are somewhat larger (median size 44.3; quartiles at 20.5 and 70.5). For countries where data are available for both pre-primary and primary levels, the latter are all larger. Sizes at lower secondary are somewhat smaller (median 35.7), and are lower in all cases than at primary where comparative data are available. There is some tendency for sizes to increase at upper secondary level (median value 38.6). The 13 Finnish special schools at upper secondary level at an average size of 183.5 students are the largest found at any level.

---

1. See footnote in Chapter 5.

Table 6.1. **Number of special schools by level of education relative to total school population**[1, 2, 3, 4, 5, 6, 7]

	Compulsory education	Pre-primary	Primary	Lower secondary	Upper secondary
BEL (Fl.)	37.0	38.7	45.8	26.5	
CHE	46.2				
CZE	58.4	108.4	99.2	126.4	34.7
DEU	29.4				
ESP	11.0				
FIN	45.3				
FRA	21.9		2.1	2.5	
IRE			26.7		
ITA	1.4	0.7	1.8	0.7	0.3
MEX	82.0				
NDL	50.2	113.4	67	70.6	75.4
POL	15.4				
SWE	62.2		76.4	156.8	78.1
TUR	1.7	13.8	1.7		1.9
GBR	16.3				

1. In France pre-primary data are included in primary; upper secondary data are included in lower secondary.
2. In Ireland pre-primary data are included in primary.
3. In Belgium (Fl.) upper secondary data are included in lower secondary.
4. In Turkey data is for public schools only at upper secondary level.
5. In Spain, the figure in compulsory education includes all levels of education (ISCED 0, 1, 2, 3).
6. Number per 100 000 of total school population at that level.
7. Data are only presented in this table if it is possible to give a non zero value (i.e. it is missing, not applicable, included in other values, or there are no schools at this level).

In most countries the overwhelming proportion of special schools are publicly provided as indicated in Table 6.3 (median value 94.55%, quartiles at 47.14% and 98.13%) over the period of compulsory education. For three (Belgium [Fl.], Spain and Switzerland) over half of the special schools are private. Where data are available for different phases of education, the percentage of private schools is remarkably consistent over phases in a particular country. The sole exception is Finland where the figure drops from 99.32% at primary and 96.67% at lower secondary level, to a majority of private provision (61.54%) at upper secondary level.

The relative proportions of male and female students in special schools are discussed in a separate section below.

Special classes

Data on special classes are sparse compared with those available on special schools. Only five countries provide data which permit the number of special classes per school for students receiving additional resources for disabilities, difficulties, or disadvantages as shown in Table 6.4. Figures for the compulsory education period range from 3.61 in the Czech Republic to fewer than one class per school in France. The most typical figure is an average of one class per school. Average class sizes, also shown in Table 6.4 are, in most cases, small – typically about 10 students per class. The Czech Republic (upper secondary 27.5) is an exception while Italy has very small class sizes at all levels. There are insufficient data to make comparisons between class sizes at different phases of education.

Table 6.2. **Size of special schools by level of education**[1, 2, 3, 4, 5]

	Compulsory education	Pre-primary	Primary	Lower secondary	Upper secondary
BEL (Fl.)	131.6	21.0	127.9	137.8	
CHE	37.0				
CZE	70.3	23.4	42.1	32.4	70.6
DEU	120.7				
ESP	56.6				
FIN	44.8		44.3	38.9	183.5
FRA	64.9		54.3	65.1	
IRE			60.5		
ITA	26.0	17.7	28.6	14.8	46.6
MEX	12.1	9.5	12.4		
NDL	99.0	9.8	93.2	59.4	33.2
POL	71.4		71.4		
SWE	16.9		12.1	8.6	17.5
TUR	67.5	10.3	67.5		38.6
GBR	64.2				

1. In France pre-primary data are included in primary; upper secondary data are included in lower secondary.
2. In Ireland lower secondary and upper secondary data are included in primary.
3. In Belgium (Fl.) upper secondary data are included in lower secondary.
4. In Turkey data are for public schools only at pre-primary and upper secondary levels.
5. In Spain, the figure in compulsory education includes all levels of education (ISCED 0, 1, 2, 3).

Table 6.3. **Percentage of public special schools**[1, 2, 3, 4]

	Compulsory education	Pre-primary	Primary	Lower secondary	Upper secondary
BEL (Fl.)	34.9	36.2	35.0	34.8	
CHE	47.1				
CZE	94.6	92.0	94.5	95.9	92.1
DEU	82.7				
ESP	40.0				
FIN	98.1		99.3	96.7	38.5
FRA			88.0		
IRE			100		
ITA	100	100	100	100	100
MEX	99.7	99.9	99.8		
SWE	96.7				95.1
TUR	95.4		95.4		
GBR	93.8				

1. In France pre-primary data are included in primary.
2. In Ireland lower secondary and upper secondary data are included in primary.
3. In Belgium (Fl.) upper secondary data are included in lower secondary.
4. In Spain, the figure in compulsory education includes all levels of education (ISCED 0, 1, 2, 3).

Table 6.4. **Number and size of special classes**

Average number of special classes per school

	Compulsory education	Pre-primary	Primary	Lower secondary	Upper secondary
CZE	3.6	1.3	2.6	2.7	1.0
FRA	0.8				
GRE	1.0	1.0	1.0	1.0	
IRE		1.0	1.5		
ITA	2.2	1.0	2.0	3.2	

Average size of special classes

	Compulsory education	Pre-primary	Primary	Lower secondary	Upper secondary
CHE	10.1				
CZE	10.0	11.8	8.5	12.1	27.5
IRE		14.0	9.5		
ITA	3.0	4.0	3.1	2.7	
LUX	8.0				
TUR	11.7		11.7		

Gender ratios in special classes are also discussed separately below.

Regular classes

Information about the integrated provision made when students receiving additional resources for disabilities, difficulties, or disadvantages are educated in the same classes as other students is crucial in any assessment of this type of provision. Unfortunately, it appears that this kind of information remains rarely available at national level when statistics are collected. In the current exercise only two countries, Italy and the Canadian province of New Brunswick were able to provide relevant data as given in Table 6.5. These are both jurisdictions with a policy of full inclusion and it is clear that a very substantial number of classes are involved, with multiple classes at all levels. The numbers of classes per school with students receiving additional resources increases markedly at upper secondary level in Canada (NB) possibly linked to the much larger average size of schools at this level.

Gender ratios for students with special educational needs in regular classes are discussed below.

Student/staff ratios

Teaching and other staff are some of the most important resources made available to support the education of students with disabilities, difficulties, and disadvantages. While it was felt to be highly desirable to collect data about support staff of various kinds, the pilot work on the development of the data collection instrument (discussed in the earlier monograph; OECD, 2000b) established that this information was rarely available at national level. It appeared that there was a somewhat greater availability of data on teachers themselves. Table 6.6 gathers together the available data on special schools, special classes and regular classes respectively.

Table 6.5. **Number of regular classes with students receiving additional resources**

Number of classes

	Compulsory education	Pre-primary	Primary	Lower secondary	Upper secondary
CAN (NB)	515	0	257	110	148
ITA	80 431	9 805	46 090	34 341	11 387

Average number of classes per school

	Compulsory education	Pre-primary	Primary	Lower secondary	Upper secondary
CAN (NB)	15.2		10.7	12.2	21.1
ITA	4.1	1.6	3.6	5.0	4.3

The ratios in special schools, ranging from 2.21 to 9.24 for the period of compulsory education (median value 5.78; quartiles 3.06 and 7.34) are clearly highly favourable compared to those in regular education. Directly comparable figures are not available but OECD figures for regular education show ranges from 10.6 to 30.0 at primary level, and ranges from 9.6 to 35.5 at lower secondary level. As figures for the compulsory education period might be expected to fall between those for primary and lower secondary, this strongly suggests that there is no overlap between the distribution of student/staff ratios in special schools and regular education.

Table 6.6. **Student/teacher ratios**

Special schools[1,2]

	Compulsory education	Pre-primary	Primary	Lower secondary	Upper secondary
BEL (Fl.)	4.87	4.89	6.10	3.70	
CZE	7.6	6.6	7.6	7.7	10.5
DEU	6.9				
ESP	4.8				
FIN	6.2		4.2	12.3	5.2
IRE	9.2				
ITA	2.2	1.9	2.3	1.5	1.6
LUX	2.8				
MEX	7.7	8.3	8.8		
POL	3.2		3.2		
SWE	3.9		3.9	3.9	4.1
TUR	7.1		7.1		
GBR	5.4				

1. For Spain, the figure in compulsory education includes all levels of education (ISCED 0, 1, 2, 3).
2. For Belgium (Fl.), upper secondary data are included in lower secondary.

Table 6.6. **Student/teacher ratios** *(cont.)*

Special classes

	Compulsory education	Pre-primary	Primary	Lower secondary	Upper secondary
CZE	8.3	5.9	8.3	8.3	6.8
FIN	6.0		4.9	7.6	
IRE		14.0	9.5		
ITA	1.4	2.0	1.4	1.7	
LUX	6.2				
TUR	11.7		11.7		

Regular classes[1, 2, 3, 4]

	Compulsory education	Pre-primary	Primary	Lower secondary	Upper secondary
BEL (Fl.)	8.8	17.7	13.9		
CZE	14.7	19.5	23.4	16.2	13.1
FIN	13.5	12.3	17.4	10.6	16.6
FRA	12.8	19.3	19.6	12.9	12.7
DEU	15.2	23.7	21.0	16.4	12.4
HUN	10.6	11.8	10.9	10.9	10.3
IRE	14.6	14.7	21.6		
ITA	10.3	13.2	11.3	10.3	10.2
JPN	15.4	19.0	21.2	17.1	14.1
LUX	9.9	16.7	12.5		
MEX	32.2	24.4	27.2	35.5	26.9
NLD	17.7		16.6		
ESP	12.9	17.1	15.4		
SWE	14.5		13.3	13.3	15.5
CHE	12.3	17.8	16.1	12.1	12.6
TUR	16.1	15.3	30.0		16.1
GBR	14.7	16.5	22.5	17.4	12.4
USA	15.6	19.3	16.3	16.8	14.5

1. In Luxembourg and Switzerland data refer to public institutions only.
2. In the United Kingdom data includes only general programmes at upper secondary education.
3. For Belgium (Fl.), Finland, Hungary, Ireland, Italy, Netherlands, Spain and Sweden, see Annex 3 in OECD (2001).
4. Data are only presented in this table if it is possible to give a non zero value.

For the four countries for which comparative primary, lower and upper secondary data are available no consistent pattern emerges. The Czech Republic and Sweden show the highest student/teacher ratios at upper secondary. Finland shows the highest at lower secondary level. Italy has low ratios, typically below two, at all levels.

Student/teacher ratios in special classes are very similar, with a tendency to be slightly higher than in special classes. They range from 1.42 to 11.68 for the period of compulsory education (median value 6.17).

Relative numbers of male and female students receiving additional resources for disabilities, difficulties or disadvantages

A strong and consistent finding reported in the earlier monograph (OECD, 2000b, pp. 91-94) was the preponderance of the number of males over females in a wide range of analyses. Whether done by location (special school, special class, regular class), cross-national or national category, age of student, or stage of education there was a higher percentage of males – typically approximating to a 60/40 split.

Tables 6.7 to 6.9 show gender ratios from the second data collection exercise, focusing on location and cross-national category analyses. The earlier finding is fully replicated, with a small number of isolated exceptions there are more boys than girls receiving additional resources in all three cross-national categories and at all locations at which they receive education.

Table 6.7. **Gender ratios of students receiving additional resources for disabilities (cross-national category A)**

Table values are percentage of males[1]

Special schools	Compulsory education	Pre-primary	Primary	Lower secondary	Upper secondary
BEL (Fl.)	59.8	64.0	59.5	60.1	
CHE	64.6				
CZE	60.0		59.2	59.7	61.1
DEU	62.0				
ESP	60.7	62.9	60.7	62.0	56.9
FIN	65.0	66.6	66.8	61.2	58.9
FRA				73.6	71.7
ITA	63.4	71.3	63.4	62.9	61.0
LUX	60.6				
MEX	59.3	59.1	59.3	59.7	
NDL	68.4	69.3	68.0	69.5	64.7
POL	52.7				
SWE	58.7		58.8	58.7	59.0
TUR	65.1		65.1		
GBR	68.3	64.9	68.0	68.5	65.7

1. In Belgium (Fl.) upper secondary data are included in lower secondary.

Special classes	Compulsory education	Pre-primary	Primary	Lower secondary	Upper secondary
CZE	52.4		46.5	58.7	
FIN	67.1	65.0	68.9	63.0	61.9
FRA				58.9	
ITA	59.5	75.0	60.8	55.8	
LUX	86.7				
MEX	62.8	66.1	61.8	66.4	
TUR	62.0		62.0		

Table 6.7. **Gender ratios of students receiving additional resources for disabilities (cross-national category A)** *(cont.)*

Regular classes	Compulsory education	Pre-primary	Primary	Lower secondary	Upper secondary
CAN(Alb.)	60.9	67.9	61.3	60.0	58.6
CAN(NB)	66.4		63.8	69.2	67.3
CAN(SK)	60.7	63.5	63.7	60.8	58.3
CZE	60.0		60.1	60.7	64.4
ESP	61.8	64.7	62.1	61.0	58.2
FIN	65.6	63.8	65.4	67.1	73.9
LUX	64.7				
MEX	61.1	64.8	61.1	60.7	
SWE	56.0		55.6	56.8	55.5
GBR	68.3	64.4	68.0	68.5	65.7

Table 6.8. **Gender ratios of students receiving additional resources for difficulties (cross-national category B)**

Table values are percentage of males

Special schools	Compulsory education	Pre-primary	Primary	Lower secondary	Upper secondary
BEL (Fl.)	69.1	80.1	67.8	85.5	80.7
CZE	57.0		57.9	55.7	
DEU	64.2				
FIN	66.5	65.0	66.9	66.0	77.2
GRE		71.2	62.3	64.3	
LUX	65.5				
MEX	67.1	60.0	64.3	81.6	
NDL	68.2	68.3	68.1	68.6	63.8
GBR	68.5	64.8	68.0	68.7	65.8

Special classes	Compulsory education	Pre-primary	Primary	Lower secondary	Upper secondary
CHE	61.9				
CZE	65.6		60.5	70.7	74.6
FIN	75.7	68.8	75.8	75.7	76.9
FRA	58.9		60.6	60.3	58.3
LUX	54.6				
MEX	62.2	66.1	61.8	66.4	
NDL	59.1			59.1	

Regular classes	Compulsory education	Pre-primary	Primary	Lower secondary	Upper secondary
CAN (Alb.)	67.1	76.2	67.2	67.2	65.9
CAN (NB)	69.3		70.5	71.7	63.3
CZE	74.2		74.1	74.3	
ESP	58.7	56.8	59.4	56.4	50.2
FIN	64.6		64.0	67.7	
LUX	59.8				
MEX	60.0	66.6	60.0	57.8	
GBR	69.0	64.8	68.0	68.5	65.6

Table 6.9. **Gender ratios of students receiving additional resources for disadvantages (cross-national category C)**

Table values are percentage of males

Special schools	Compulsory education	Pre-primary	Primary	Lower secondary	Upper secondary
CZE	67.7		62.8	73.4	57.1
MEX	51.7	50.1	51.7		
POL					49.9
IRE	52.6				

Special classes	Compulsory education	Pre-primary	Primary	Lower secondary	Upper secondary
BEL (Fl.)				55.9	
CHE	51.2				
FRA	55.6		53.7	56.8	
LUX	57.8				

Regular classes	Compulsory education	Pre-primary	Primary	Lower secondary	Upper secondary
CAN (NB)	57.1		50.0	75.0	58.3
ESP	54.9	52.8	53.9	59.4	
FIN	53.1		52.5	55.2	
NDL	50.6	51.2	50.1	52.3	49.1

Inspection of the data shows that, for disabilities and difficulties, the percentage of males is typically between 60% and 70%, while for disadvantages it is typically between 50% and 60%. Charts 6.1 and 6.2 illustrate this, focusing on the location of their education (for the period of compulsory education for which, as revealed in the tables, more countries are able to provide data than for the phases of education), and the phase of education (across all locations of their education) respectively. The charts have to be viewed with some caution as there is some variation in the countries contributing to the different data points in the charts. Also the number of countries contributing to data points in Chart 6.2 is, in some cases, as low as three.

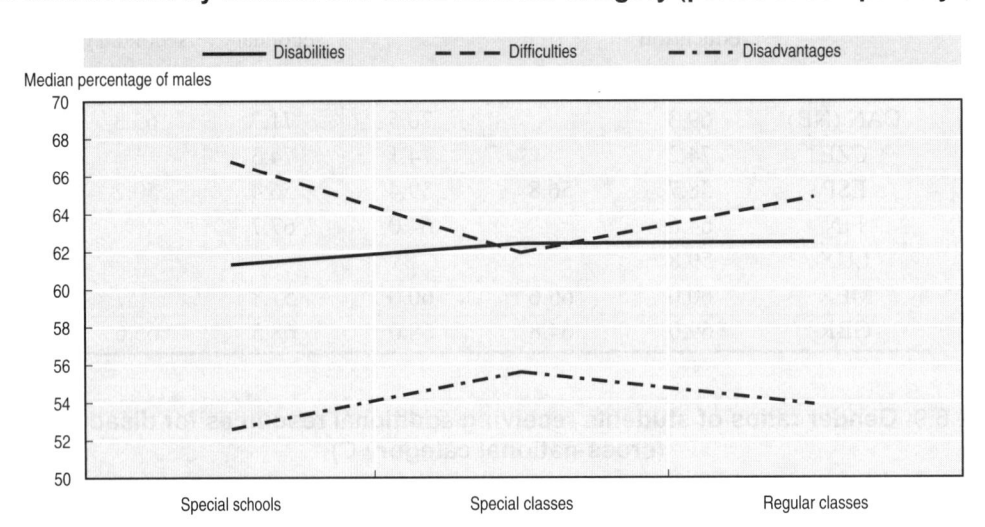

Chart 6.1. **Gender ratio by location and cross-national category (period of compulsory education)**

Chart 6.2. **Gender ratio by phase of education and cross-national category (special schools, special classes and regular classes combined**

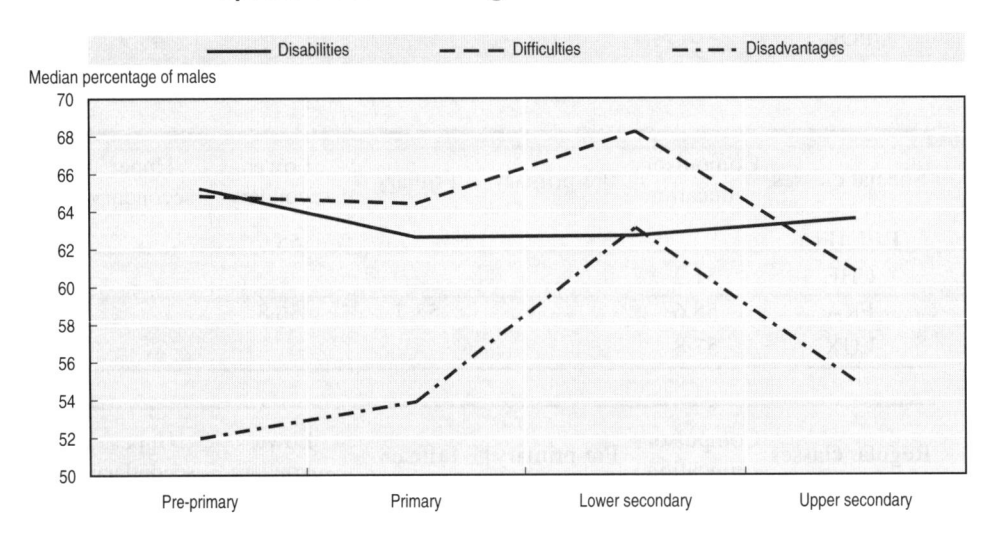

It would clearly be preferable for analyses to be in all cases based on the same set of countries, particularly as inspection of the tables shows considerable country to country variability (*e.g.* in Table 6.7 percentage of males in special schools in Belgium (Fl.), the Czech Republic, Mexico, Spain, and Sweden are relatively low at all phases of education; the Netherlands and the United Kingdom relatively high). Unfortunately the amount of missing data is such that restricting the analysis in this way results in there being too few countries for meaningful comparisons to be made.

An isolated exception occurs when comparing gender ratios in special schools, over the period of compulsory education, for students receiving additional resources for disabilities with those receiving additional resources for difficulties (Tables 6.7 and 6.8). Here data are available, for both categories of student, from eight countries with median values of 61.30 (disabilities) and 66.78 (difficulties), the difference in percentages being statistically significant (Wilcoxon test, $n = 8$, $T=2$, $p<0.05$).

There are tantalising indications of other interesting patterns in the data. It is considered premature to speculate on the interpretation of gender ratios at this time. However it appears highly likely that a more extensive data base will help to understand what lies behind this strong finding of males having greater access to additional resources provided to access the curriculum. The need is to move beyond the overall finding of a broad 60/40 male/female split. Consistent findings of higher and lower ratios, or of variability of ratios, with particular categories, settings, phases of education, or countries, when linked to knowledge about these categories, settings, etc., could provide the key to identifying the mechanisms at work in these contexts in producing this important social and educational phenomenon.

Given the importance of this issue, not least from an equity perspective, there is a strong case for all countries collecting gender information on all students receiving additional resources to access the curriculum.

Age distribution of students receiving additional resources for disabilities, difficulties or disadvantages

The following charts are derived from Table 6 of the data collection exercise which asks for data on students in all categories falling within the resources definition by age. Cohort size is taken into account so that the figures presented are percentages of students in each age group.

Sixteen of the twenty-four returns from twenty-one countries presenting data were able to provide some form of breakdown by age of students with disabilities, difficulties, and disadvantages. Fifteen countries provided data on special schools and eleven on special classes. This is a substantial improvement over the returns for the earlier data collection exercise described in the first monograph (OECD, 2000b, pp. 95-99), when only half of the responding countries were able to supply this type of information. There are, in particular, marked increases in data availability for special classes (up from two countries).

Charts 6.3 and 6.4 illustrate the age distributions for special schools and special classes respectively. Where gender data are available these are incorporated into the charts. It is once again noteworthy that the approximate 60/40 male/female split, discussed above in the section on gender breakdowns, remains strongly in evidence in the age breakdown data. Further discussion on gender is given in Chapter 7.

Distribution of students by age

Charts 6.3 and 6.4 present a breakdown of numbers of students receiving additional resources as a proportion of all students by age in special schools and special classes respectively. For special schools (Chart 6.3) for most countries the charts reveal a steady increase in the proportions of students in special schools from four years of age onwards. The charts rise to a peak and then decline rather sharply. The peak is commonly around 14/15 years of age although there is some variation among countries. There are two notable exceptions; Japan and Mexico. In Japan, the curve stays relatively flat until the age of 14/15 when there is a sharp rise in the proportion of students in special schools. In Mexico, the proportions decline steadily.

The data for special classes (Chart 6.4) reveal more complex patterns. Some countries show proportions rising to a peak and rapidly declining as in the special school data. Japan has a relatively flat curve and yet others, *e.g.* France and Switzerland, show an increase followed by a rapid decline followed by a second increase.

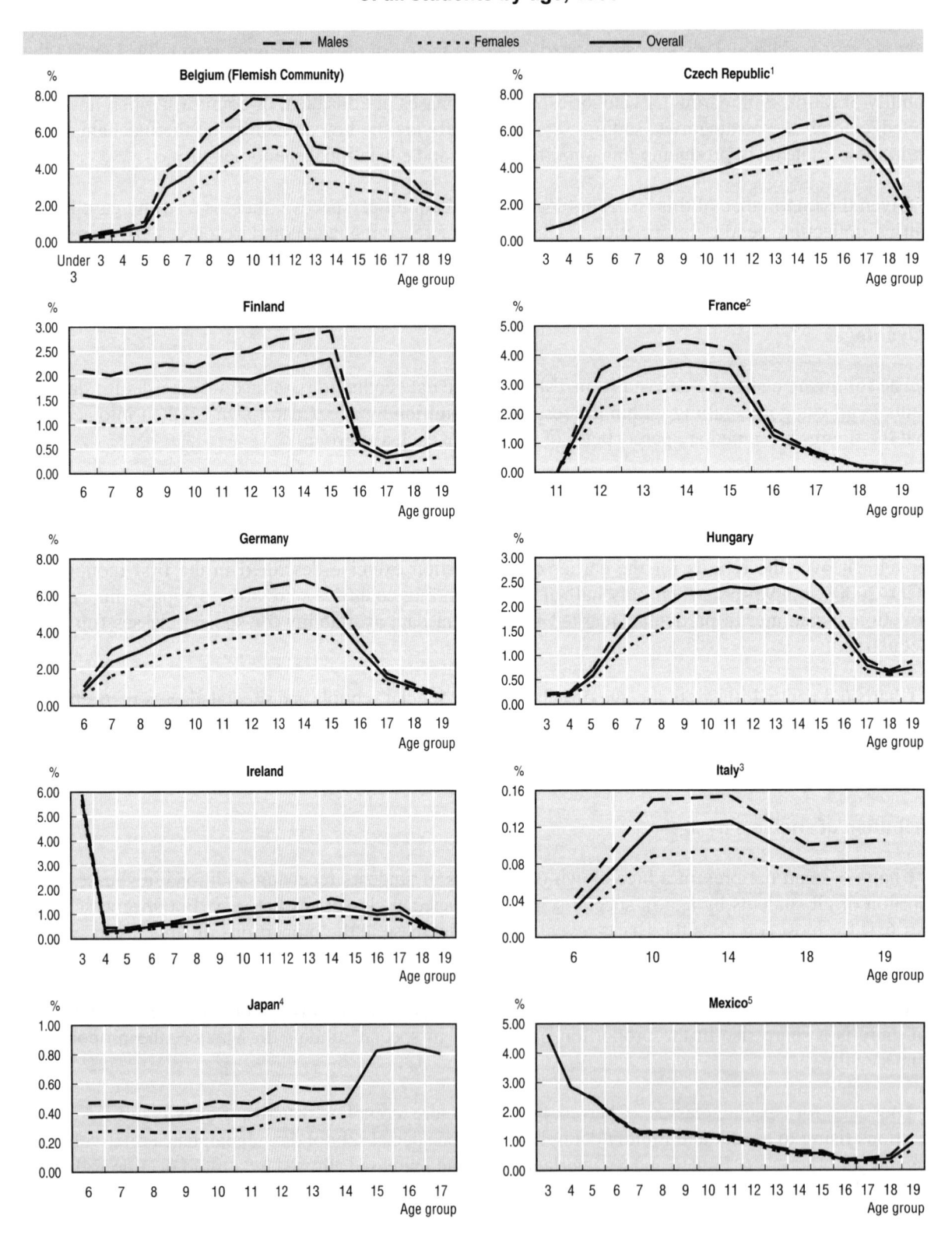

Chart 6.3. **Number of students receiving additional resources in special schools as a proportion of all students by age, 1999**

Chart 6.3. **Number of students receiving additional resources in special schools as a proportion of all students by age, 1999** (continued)

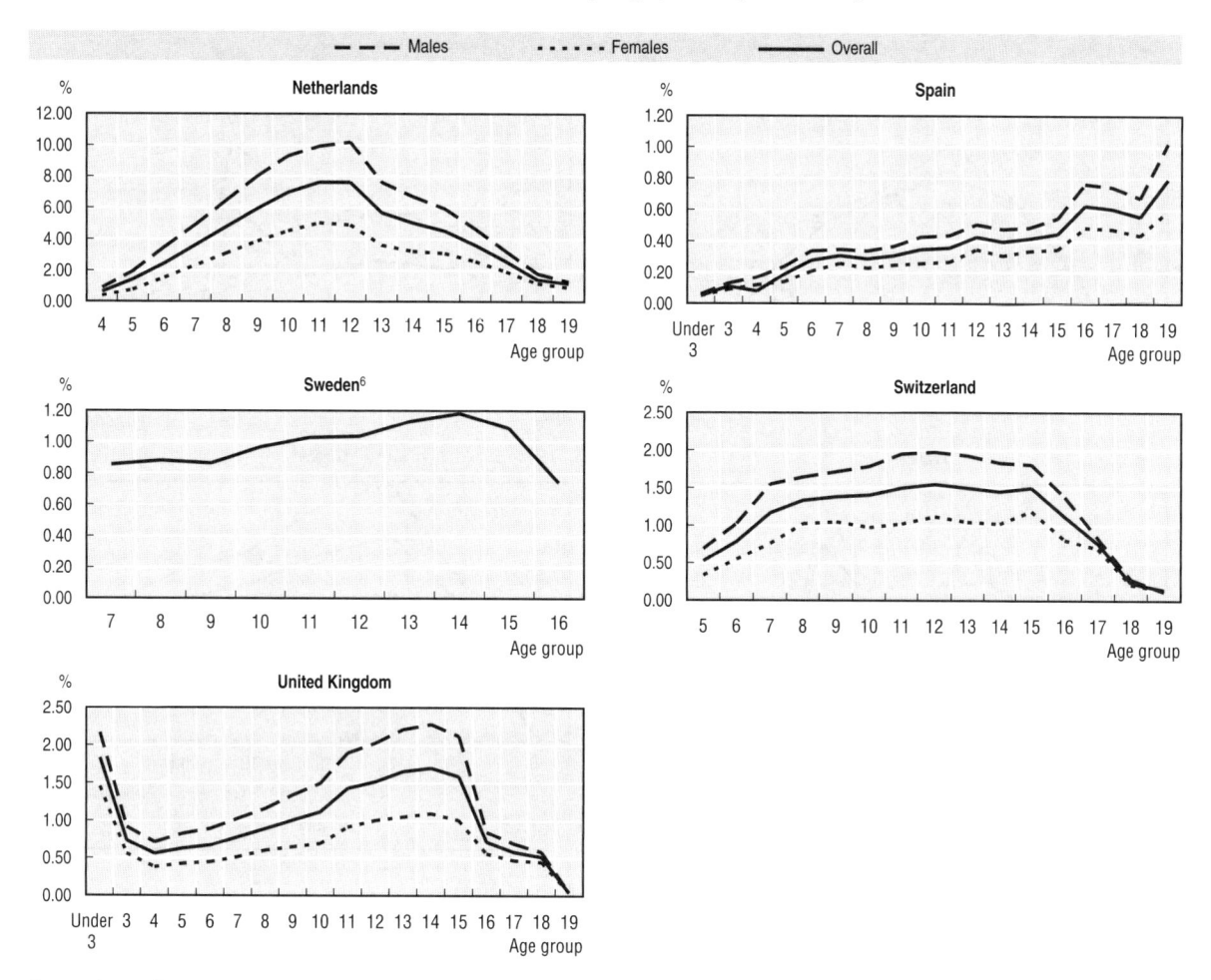

[Charts for Netherlands, Spain, Sweden[6], Switzerland, and United Kingdom showing Males (dashed), Females (dotted), and Overall (solid) lines across age groups]

General note: Data have been supplied by the Ministries of Education and although generally little provision is shown for students of less than 3 years of age, this does not mean that other provision has not been made by *e.g.* Ministries of Health or Social Services.
1. Data not available for children in the age group under 3 years, or separate male-female split below 11 years. It includes students without handicaps.
2. Data type of provision coded as "not applicable" under 9 years, 9-10 years negligible.
3. Children in age groups under 3 years-5 years are included in the 6 years age group, students in the 7-9 years age groups are included in the 10 years age group, students in the 11-13 years age groups are included in the 14 years age group, students in the 15-17 years age groups are included in the 18 years age group.
4. No provision for children in the age group under 3 years; 3 to 5 years data missing; 15-17 years no gender breakdown in the denominator.
5. Data on students in age group 19 years includes 19 years and above.
6. No provision for children in age groups 6 years and under; 17 years and above data not available. Estimations based on assumption that the school year corresponds with the age of students.

Although it is necessary to remain cautious about interpreting those data, a first attempt is made in the following paragraphs.

For those countries showing increases over time, it seems likely that this reflects the way in which countries cope with students who present difficulties of one sort or another to the school, *i.e.* students are progressively referred to special education systems from regular education systems as their needs become more and more difficult to cope with in regular schools. In Mexico it seems likely that as students get older they progressively leave special schools and up to age 8 at least may be transferred to special classes. What happens after that age in that country remains unclear.

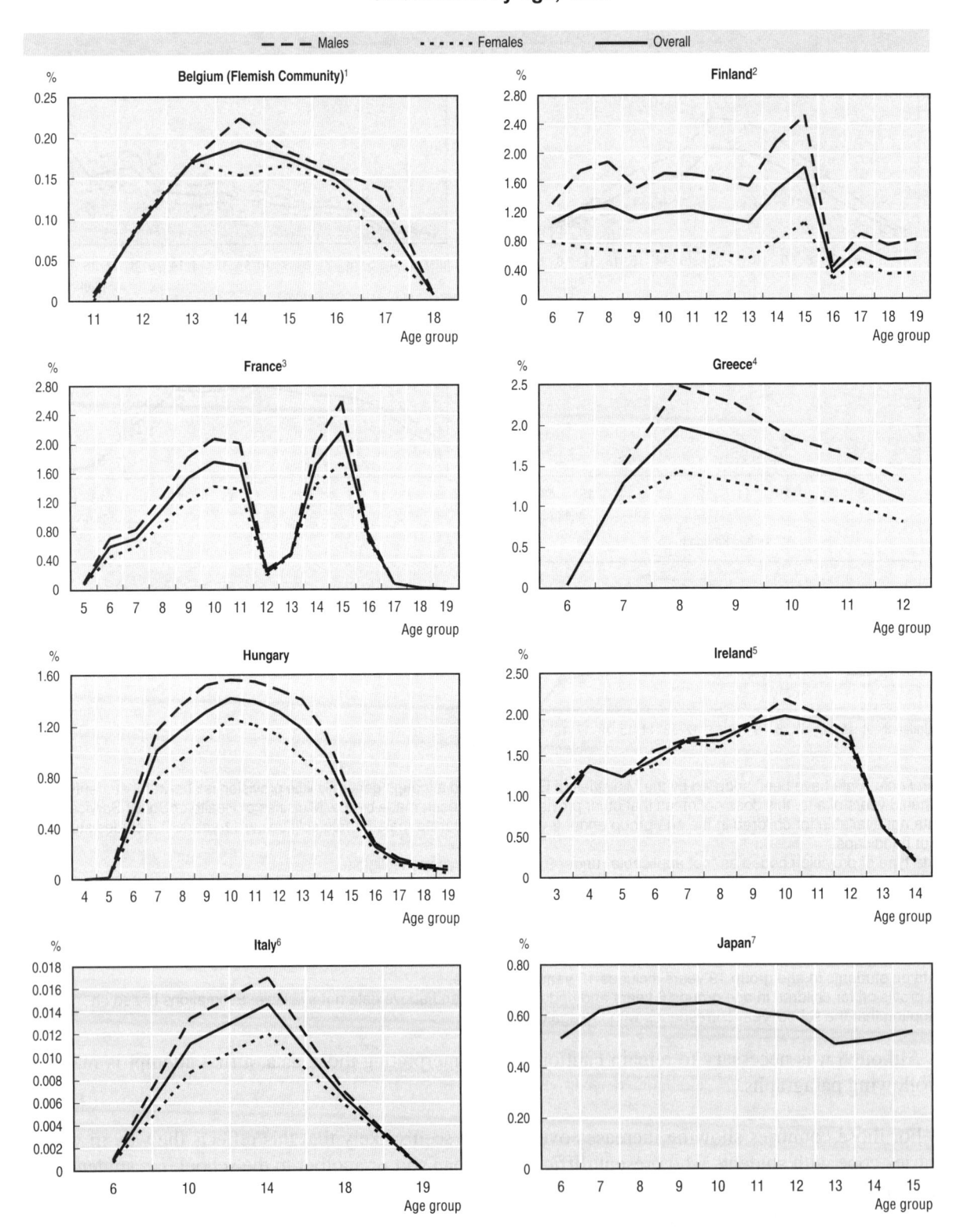

Chart 6.4. Number of students receiving additional resources in special classes as a proportion of all students by age, 1999

Chart 6.4. **Number of students receiving additional resources in special classes as a proportion of all students by age, 1999** *(continued)*

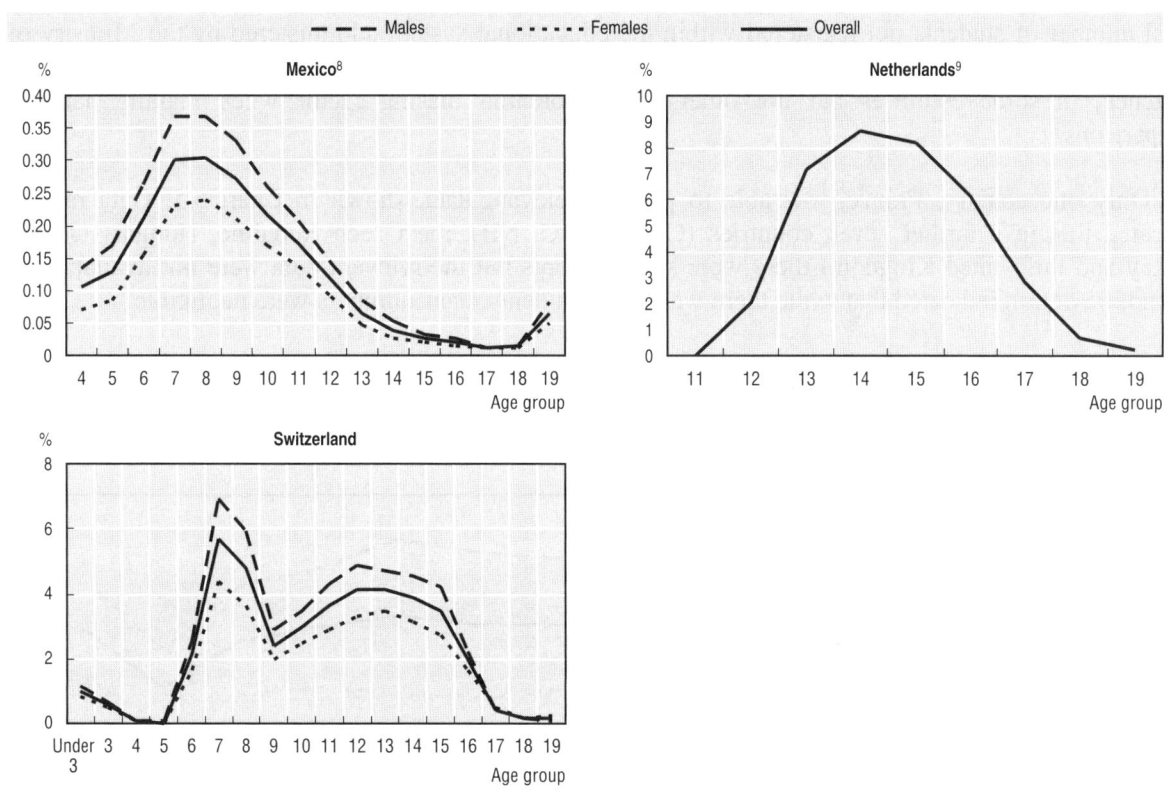

General note: Data have been supplied by the Ministries of Education and although generally little provision is shown for students of less than 3 years of age this does not mean that other provision has not been made by *e.g.* Ministries of Health or Social Services.
1. Age breakdown in special classes is available for secondary education only.
2. No data not available for children under 6 years.
3. This type of provision is "not applicable" under 5 years.
4. No data available for students under 6 years and over 12 years.
5. Under 3 years included in 3 years; data for students over 14 years not available.
6. Children in age groups under 3 years-5 years are included in the 6 years age group, students in the 7-9 years age groups are included in the 10 years age group, students in the 11-13 years age groups are included in the 14 years age group, students in the 15-17 years age groups are included in the 18 years age group.
7. No provision for children in age groups under 6 years. Number of students in age groups above 15 years is zero.
8. Number of children in age groups under 4 years is zero. Data on students in age group 19 years include 19 years and above.
9. Number of students in age groups under 11 years is zero.

A contrast of the special school and special class data for France reveals an interesting story. Within the education system it appears that the majority of A type students are in special classes until the transition to lower secondary school. At this point the proportions in special classes decrease dramatically from 1.70% to 0.24% while at the same time the numbers in special schools increases from 0.01% to 2.86%. Clearly these figures do not account fully for the increase in the special school population which may also be inflated by new students not previously counted within special education. Although in France approximately 0.8% of students are educated outside of the educational system, in this provision the proportions steadily increase over time (see Chart 6.5) and the new numbers in special schools do not match with an equivalent decrease in the non-registered student numbers. On the other hand it does seem likely that the relatively low proportions of students in special schools in the primary years may be linked to the provision made by the health ministry.

Students not registered within the education system

In the data collection exercise reported here an additional question was asked in Table 6 on the "total number of students not registered within the educational system administered by the Ministry of Education". Previous discussions indicated that there were such students in some countries. Their existence, in some countries but not others, is a potential biasing factor when making national comparisons.

Only one country, France, was able to provide relevant data, shown in Chart 6.5. Data returns indicated that in a further seven countries (Canada (BC, NB), the Czech Republic, Hungary, Japan, Turkey and the United Kingdom) there were such students but the relevant data were not available. In Ireland, the return indicated that while there were such students, their numbers were negligible.

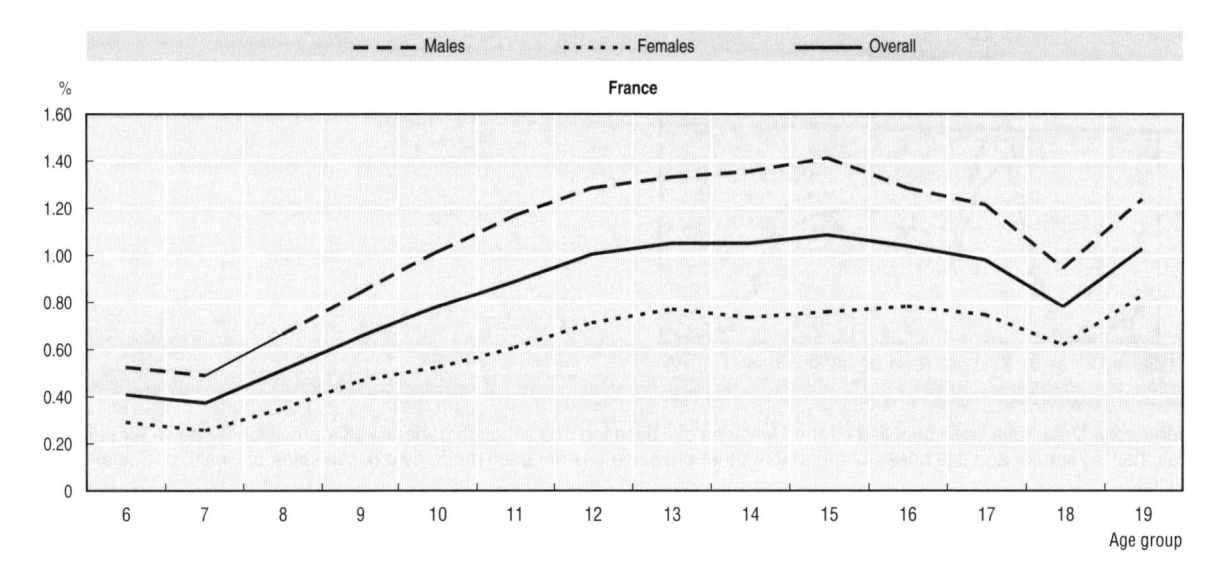

Chart 6.5. **Age distribution of students not registered within the education system**[1]

1. Students not administered by the Ministry of Education.

It is clear that there may be a substantial biasing factor arising from the indication that almost one third of the countries involved in this data collection exercise may be excluding an unknown number of students from the returns made, who in other countries may well be included in their returns. Whereas in some countries all students receiving additional resources for disabilities, difficulties or disadvantages are the responsibility of a ministry or department of education and/or are included in the return made by this ministry, in other countries for organisational or historical reasons some of these students are the responsibility of other ministries and may not be included in the returns made.

Final comments

The chapter provides descriptive information about the amount and nature of the provision in different countries for students receiving additional resources for disabilities, difficulties or disadvantages. As established in the earlier monograph (OECD, 2000b) and confirmed here, there are generally high quality data on aspects of special school systems.

However, although the data coverage is somewhat greater than that found in the previous exercise, few countries are able to provide substantial amounts of data on provision in special classes. Data on the number of regular classes with students receiving additional resources is virtually non-existent, with only two countries out of the more than twenty contributing to the exercise being able to contribute relevant data.

Data on student-staff ratios are also not readily available. Even in special schools few countries can provide these data for different levels of education (three at pre-primary; seven at primary; four at lower and upper secondary), although twelve countries are able to do so for the period of compulsory education.

CHAPTER 7
FURTHER DISCUSSION OF SIGNIFICANT ISSUES

This chapter draws together the main outcomes presented in the monograph. It analyses cross-national categories A, B and C separately and, through consideration of other CERI work, discusses their policy implications. A final section reviews the experience of the last rounds of data collection and in the light of this identifies needed future developments.

It is clear that countries provide substantial additional support for many students in order to help them access the curriculum. The significance of the issue is reflected in the many laws, policies and types of special education provision developed to meet these students' educational needs. Factors repeatedly identified by countries which serve as facilitators for or barriers to equity and inclusion include legal frameworks, funding models, assessment arrangements, school structure, class size, the use of individual teaching programmes, the involvement of additional teachers and aides, teacher training, parental involvement and co-operation with other services. Taken together, these issues present a considerable agenda for reform.

The work also shows the wide variation between countries in the conceptual frameworks that are used to classify these students. The differences are exhibited in Table 3.2 and more fully in Annex 1 where national definitions for each category are laid out. Apart from the inherent interest in the different models used in countries, the tables immediately show the difficulties in making comparisons between countries for these students. Nevertheless, countries welcomed these data displays and analyses and Chapter 4 therefore provides data for those categories where there is most confidence of comparability between countries. Despite their controversial nature these data are included to give a sense of connection with the way in which countries gather their own data. National data sets are published on the Internet, *www.oecd.org/edu/equity/senddd*.

What emerges most strongly from these data presentations are the large between country variations in prevalence rates, and following the resources approach this implies considerable differences in the degree of support given to individual categories of students. The substantial variations at different levels of education and degree of difference in the place of education – special school, special class or regular class are also noteworthy.

Chapter 5 presents the data broken down by cross-national categories A, B and C for students with disabilities, difficulties and disadvantages. This procedure allows for all national variations in the concept of special education and definitions in use to be taken into account. It has the effect of smoothing the data to some extent to improve comparability.

Alternative explanations of these findings are discussed in the next section.

Issues arising from the analyses of the cross-national category A, B and C data

The results of the analyses presented above raise many issues which are discussed below for A, B and C in turn. They are expressed in terms of a set of questions followed by a set of tentative answers and policy action implications. The discussion applies equally to the data presented in Chapter 4, which are used to elaborate answers where relevant. It needs to be emphasised that every effort has been made to ensure that the classification of national data into the cross-national categories of A, B and C is valid and reliable. The classifications provided have been agreed at meetings of national representatives and while the possibility remains that errors exist they are assumed to be minimal.

Cross-national category A – Students receiving additional resources for disabilities

1. Why does the percentage of students receiving additional resources for disabilities differ from country to country?

When the number of students receiving additional resources for disabilities is expressed as a percentage of all students there is considerable country to country variation. The range is from below 1% to above 4% for all phases of education. Suggestions as to possible factors or mechanisms underlying these differences follow, with a commentary. There is, of course, no suggestion that a single factor or mechanism is involved.

- *Differences reflect differential incidence or prevalence of disabilities.* While such a possibility cannot be discounted, it is perhaps best addressed at the level of specific disabilities such as blindness. It is clear that there are large between country variations in prevalences in individual disability categories.

- *Some countries provide additional resources for disabilities which are not so resourced in other countries.* Inspection of Table 3.2 in Chapter 3 and Annex 1 reveal the difficulties involved in assessing this possibility. The number, labelling, and definition of categories of disability vary widely from country to country in a manner which obscures any linkage with overall proportions of students given additional resources.

- *Some countries do not provide additional resources for disabilities at particular phases of education.* Thus Ireland and Switzerland appear not to provide additional resources for disabilities at pre-primary level.

- *Differences reflect policy differences.* Some countries, for instance for reasons of equity, may make the additional resources for students with disabilities an educational priority. Note that this is not a simple question of the relative wealth of countries. The very high United Kingdom percentage at pre-primary and upper secondary (relative both to other countries, and to United Kingdom percentages for the middle years of schooling) may well represent policy considerations.

2. Why do some countries educate virtually all students receiving additional resources for disabilities in regular classes with other students, while other countries educate virtually all of them in special schools?

Inspection of the relevant charts in Chapter 5 shows that, while Italy and Canada (NB) educate virtually all students receiving additional resources for disabilities alongside their non-disabled peers, several other countries educate over 80% of them in segregated special schools. However a majority of countries operate a form of mixed economy involving substantial use of regular classrooms together with special schools and/or special classes.

- *Differences* reflect *policy differences*. It appears highly likely that inclusion or segregation is a matter of national policy in contrast for instance to being a parental decision.

- There are features of mainstream schools and their curriculum, and the attitudes of their teachers, which facilitate or obstruct integration. Study of these features is a priority.

- There are *features* of special schools, and of other segregated provision, which are viewed as desirable by educators and parents. Study of these features is also a priority.

Policy action implications

Given the increased costs of special provision for these groups (at least twice that for non-disabled students, OECD, 1999) countries should carefully review how students become labelled as disabled and how decisions are made about their placement. In addition reviews of the preparation of professionals are called for to serve as a budget neutral preventive mechanism (see OECD, 1999).

Cross-national category B – Students receiving additional resources for difficulties

3. Why do some countries have no national categories falling within cross-national category B (i.e. they appear not to be providing additional resources for students with difficulties)?

All countries providing data in this exercise have national categories falling within cross-national category A. The obvious interpretation is that all countries have within their educational system students who have disabilities, and all countries recognise that such students require additional resources to access the regular curriculum.

However, as made clear in Chapter 1, in 1999 some countries (Italy, Japan, Poland, and Sweden) had no national categories falling within cross-national category B. (Turkey only has students described as "gifted and talented".)[1] The interpretation of this fact is more problematic. Possibilities, of varying degrees of plausibility, include:

- *The curriculum is such that no students (other than those with disabilities or social disadvantages) have difficulty in accessing it.* While this possibility appears close to utopian it would be of great interest if any countries making this claim could explain how their educational system effectively eliminates behaviour, learning and other difficulties affecting access to the regular curriculum.

- *Students have difficulties but additional resources are not provided.* If this explanation is put forward it is reasonable to request a rationale. Note that if there are national categories of difficulties for which no additional resources are provided they are expected to have been declared in the data collection exercise (and further declared as falling outside the resources definition).

- *Students have difficulties and additional resources are provided but relevant data are not available to data providers.* If this is the case the expectation is that appropriate categories falling within B are declared in the data collection exercise and coded as "data not available". This provides a flag that the data are out there somewhere and indicates that a different methodology of data collection (perhaps more locally based) may have to be employed.

---

1. Students considered to be Gifted and Talented are not discussed in this monograph.

Alternatively, the data may be collected by some other agency than that directly responsible for the provision of data, calling for cross-agency liaison.

- *Countries are not prepared to declare national categories falling within B for educational, policy or other reasons.* Such possibilities are recognised and respected. However, the data collection exercise is not dependent on the existence of national categories. If it is accepted that students have difficulties in gaining access to the regular curriculum and additional resources are made available to support such students, it would be expected that some form of classification would be adopted to either allocate, or account for, such resources.

4. Why does the percentage of students receiving additional resources for difficulties differ more widely from country to country than for disabilities?

The range for difficulties is typically from 0% to above 10% for all phases of education (compared to about half this range with disabilities).

- *Some countries which do provide additional resources for difficulties do so for large percentages of students.* When combined with the fact that some countries have no cross-national category B provision this results in large ranges across countries. Factors possibly underlying this are discussed below.

5. Why does the percentage of students receiving additional resources for difficulties differ from country to country?

This is the same question discussed above in section 1 in the context of disabilities (indeed it is a question arising in most aspects of the analysis of the data collected in this exercise – with the exception of gender ratios). Given that issues concerning those countries with no cross-national category B students have been discussed above in section 3, this discussion focuses on differences in percentages between countries with such students.

- *Some countries provide additional resources for difficulties which are not so resourced in other countries.* Inspection of Table 3.2 in Chapter 3 and Annex 1 again illustrates the problems involved in assessing this possibility. The number, labelling, and definition of categories of difficulties vary widely from country to country in a manner which obscures any linkage with overall proportions of students given additional resources.

- *Differences reflect policy differences.* Some countries may make the additional resourcing of students with difficulties an educational priority. The existence of large numbers of students perceived as needing additional resources because of behavioural, emotional or other difficulties in accessing the regular curriculum may be seen positively as indexing sensitivity to such problems, or negatively as a function of a mismatch of curriculum provision and the needs of the student.

- *Some countries' regular systems deal better with individual differences and minimise the need for differentiation.*

6. Why do some countries educate virtually all students receiving additional resources for difficulties in regular classes with other students, while other countries educate virtually all of them in special schools or classes?

Inspection of the relevant charts in Chapter 5 shows that, while Spain and Canada (NB) educate virtually all students receiving additional resources for difficulties in fully integrated settings, several other countries educate virtually all of them in special schools or special classes. While data availability is patchier than for students with disabilities (where most countries operated a mixed economy distributing students with disabilities between special schools, special classes or regular classes), the picture here is more dichotomous with a substantial majority of students at all phases of education being typically either in integrated settings or in special schools or classes.

- *Differences reflect policy differences.* It appears highly likely that integration or segregation is a matter of national policy.

- *There are features of mainstream schools and their curriculum, and the attitudes of their teachers, which facilitate or obstruct integration.* Study of these features is a priority.

- *There are features of special schools and classes, which are viewed as desirable by educators and parents.* Study of these features is also a priority.

Policy action implications

Students who generally fall into category B are those who should be able to receive their education in mainstream schools given relevant changes to the way the regular schools function. The fact that many countries educate these students in special schools or classes also requires review. It is possible that those countries having no "B" students classify them in either A or C. If they fall into A and special school or special class provision is made this is likely to be prejudicial to the students' life chances and hence inequitable.

Countries need to carefully review their decision-making procedures with regard to these students as well as other school based and professional preparation factors. These aspects may well lead unnecessarily to inappropriate and costly labelling. It may also be the case, that there are students who fall into this category who are unidentified and therefore inadequately resourced. Following the resource distribution model, such students would be being treated inequitably.

Cross-national category C – Students receiving additional resources for disadvantages

7. Why do some countries have no national categories falling within cross-national category C (i.e. they appear not to be providing additional resources for students with disadvantages)?

This discussion and analysis mirrors that presented in section 3 above considering cross-national category B.

Some countries (Canada (Alb., SK), Turkey and the United Kingdom) have no national categories falling within cross-national category C. Again interpretation of this fact is problematic, with possibilities including:

- *The curriculum is such that students with social disadvantages have no particular problems in accessing it.*

- *The social system is such that no students are disadvantaged to the extent that they have problems in accessing the regular curriculum.* While these possibilities again appear close to utopian it would be of great interest if any countries making either or both of these claims could explain how their educational and/or social systems effectively eliminate social disadvantage affecting access to the regular curriculum.

- *Students have disadvantages but additional resources are not provided.* If this explanation is put forward it is again reasonable to request a rationale. Note that if there are national categories of disadvantages for which no additional resources are provided they are expected to have been declared in the data collection exercise (and further declared as falling outside the resources definition).

- *Students have disadvantages and additional resources are provided but relevant data are not available to data providers.* If this is the case the expectation is that appropriate categories falling within C are declared in the data collection exercise and coded as "data not available". This provides a flag that the data are out there somewhere and indicates that a different methodology of data collection (perhaps more locally based) may have to be employed. Alternatively, the data may be collected by some other agency than that directly responsible for the provision of data, calling for cross-agency liaison.

- *Countries are not prepared to declare national categories falling within C for educational, political or other reasons.* Such possibilities are again recognised and respected. However, the data collection exercise is not dependent on the existence of national categories. If it is accepted that students have disadvantages in gaining access to the regular curriculum and additional resources are made available to support such students, it would be expected that some form of classification would be adopted to either allocate, or account for, such resources.

8. Why does the percentage of students receiving additional resources for disadvantages differ more widely from country to country than for disabilities?

The range for disadvantages is typically from 0% to above 10% for all phases of education apart from upper secondary (compared to about half this range with disabilities).

- *Some countries which do provide additional resources for disadvantages do so for large percentages of students.* When combined with the fact that some countries have no cross-national category C provision this results in large ranges across countries. Factors possibly underlying this are discussed below.

- *The basis for computing student numbers involved may differ from that in cross-national category A.* As discussed earlier in the chapter, numbers of students receiving additional resources for disabilities (and also for difficulties) are typically based on head-counts. All such students need these resources to access the regular curriculum. Numbers of students with social and other disadvantages may be computed on a group or class basis where the resources are provided for all falling within that classification irrespective of the needs of specific individuals. In these circumstances an inflated figure (compared with that for disabilities or disadvantages) may be produced.

9. Why does the percentage of students receiving additional resources for disadvantages differ from country to country?

This is the same question discussed above in section 1 in the context of disabilities. Given that issues concerning those countries with no cross-national category C students have been discussed above in section 7, this discussion focuses on differences in percentages between countries with such students.

- *Some countries provide additional resources for disadvantages which are not so resourced in other countries.* Inspection of Table 3.2 in Chapter 3 and Annex 1 again illustrates the problems involved in assessing this possibility. The number, labelling, and definition of categories of disadvantages vary widely from country to country in a manner which obscures any linkage with overall proportions of students given additional resources.

- *Differences reflect policy differences.* Some countries may make the additional resourcing of students with disadvantages an educational priority. For instance, for a variety of reasons some countries may have more students living in poverty than others.

- *Numbers of migrants and others requiring additional resources because of linguistic problems differ from country to country.* Second language learning is an important component of the additional resources provided in countries with significant immigration but not for other countries.

10. Why does one country educate all students receiving additional resources for disadvantages in special schools, while all other countries for which data are available educate virtually all of them in regular classes with other students?

Eight of the nine countries providing data for the period of compulsory education, educate students with disadvantages almost exclusively in fully integrated settings. The picture is identical at all phases of education although data are patchy. The Czech Republic provides the exception, educating all such students in special schools.

- *Differences reflect policy differences.* It appears highly likely that integration or segregation is a matter of national policy.

Policy action implications

The education of students from socially disadvantaged backgrounds is clearly a priority in most OECD countries. Increased levels of immigration underline this point. As for A and B, reviews of whether resources are adequate and whether they are being used appropriately for C students are called for. Consideration should be given to school organisation, teaching methods, teacher preparation and identification and outcomes for A, B and C students.

In general terms the effective education of students in A, B and C is predicated on changes in the way the education system functions for them and how education works with other services (*e.g.* OECD, 1995b, 1996, 1998a). Greater attention should be given at a holistic level to the issues identified above.

Gender

11. Why are more males than females receiving additional resources to help them access the curriculum?

The findings reported in the first monograph (OECD, 2000b) concerning gender are fully replicated here. Breakdowns of gender by country, by location and level of education (pre-primary, primary, lower secondary and upper secondary) reveal that except in a few cases more boys than girls are receiving additional resources to access the curriculum. For those with disabilities the median percentage of males is 61.3% and for those with difficulties the median is 66.78%, while for disadvantages the range is typically between 50% and 60%. There is a statistically significant difference between the scores for students with disabilities and those with difficulties.

- *Males are more vulnerable than females.* There is some evidence that males are more vulnerable than females throughout the developmental years to the effects of illness and trauma. Thus they have a greater "natural" need for additional supports in school. This outcome would be seen as equitable since males objectively need more support.

- *The successful education of males is given greater social priority than that of females.* If this is the case then the failure or low performance of males in school is less acceptable than for females and extra resources are made available to lessen the effects and maximise performance. This outcome would be inequitable for females.

- *Males externalize their "feelings" in school more openly than females.* And in so-doing make themselves more likely to be identified and consequently labeled. Recent examples of extreme violence perpetrated by males in schools highlights the point.

- *Schooling is becoming increasingly "feminised".* The greater proportion of female teachers in schools especially during the primary years has been observed (OECD, 2002). Also the increased emphasis on the need for academic learning and the decreased need for standard "working class" skills may be moving schooling away from traditional types of male activity. The significant difference between males with disabilities and those with difficulties noted above may well mirror these issues.

Policy action implications

The fact that in most countries there are substantially more males than females receiving additional resources to help them access the curriculum needs reviewing on three counts.

- First, to establish what aspects of students' identification may bias decisions in favour of males.

- Second, what features of school functioning and decision-making may exacerbate problems thus bringing them to the attention of the "authorities".

- Third, whether the distribution of resources is equitable. That is, should more support be given to females?

Implications of the results of the second data collection exercise for future developments

This exercise was a constructive, rather than an attempted exact, replication of the earlier exercise reported in OECD (2000b). While following the same basic format and approach of the previous exercise, itself modelled closely on that taken in the main UOE data collection exercise to maximise compatibility, attempts were made to broaden its scope (*e.g.* by including pre-primary and upper secondary phases of education), and the mode of administration changed from paper to electronic.

The Electronic Questionnaire

The use of the Electronic Questionnaire (EQ) has been regarded as a considerable improvement by all concerned. By combining this with pre-entry of existing basic data from the previous exercise, completion of the task by data providers has been considerably simplified. It has also substantially reduced the size of the initial data entry task from an analysis perspective. The existence of mistakes, anomalies, miscodings, double entries, etc., continues with electronic entry, and the task of checking and general cleaning of the data set is formidable calling for substantial interaction with data providers. Such problems are inevitable given the complexity of the data entry task and its interpretation in the context of widely differing educational systems. However, increasing familiarity with the EQ in successive data collection exercises, together with further clarification of instructions and, where possible simplification of the data entry task, will be expected to reduce these problems.

Extension including pre-primary and all years of schooling

The extension of the scope of the exercise, beyond the central years of schooling, to pre-primary and upper secondary phases of education, can also be regarded as successful in the sense that it has garnered useful data. The extent of data availability at these levels is, as anticipated, not as great as at primary and lower secondary, but not markedly so. In passing, it is worth pointing out the value of requesting data on the period of compulsory education as a separate category (not a common feature of UOE data collection) as this typically leads to more countries being able to respond with data than for any other phase of education.

Limitations of current methodology

However, while pointing out the utility of extending from pre-primary to the full school range, it should be clearly acknowledged that the majority of countries taking part in this exercise have been unable to provide much of the data requested. The general conclusions of the first data collection exercise in this respect still stand – data availability for students with disabilities in segregated settings (particularly in special schools) is high; data availability for students receiving additional resources in integrated settings is very low. There have been improvements from the first exercise, particularly in relation to the availability of data on cross-national categories B and C (difficulties and disadvantages respectively). And through successive iterations previous anomalies in the allocation of national categories to B and C have been largely removed. However, it appears clear that the current methodology of asking for a central national response on students receiving additional resources in integrated settings (particularly in decentralised national systems) will not work. As discussed in Chapter 5, two countries have data (Canada [NB] and Italy) but for the most part data are either missing or the categories are declared not applicable for all phases of education.

Need for use of EQ at school and/or other sub-national levels

It appears very clear that an alternative methodology is called for. The obvious solution is what has been termed the "School Level Questionnaire"; *i.e.* a version of the EQ where data are collected at school level. This is attractive as it should not be difficult at the level of the individual school to provide data on students receiving additional resources, but it does present other problems (*e.g.* sampling issues; ensuring that local data providers understand the task). It may be that for different countries the optimum solution to the data gathering task is by an exercise based not on individual schools, but on a local administrative area, or a wider region of the country. Trials of this approach have been encouraging and it appears a matter of priority for proposals to be formulated and agreed to, in order to implement this more generally.

Extending collection of data on student gender

The earlier finding of an over-representation of males amongst students receiving additional resources is fully replicated. There are indications of systematic differences in the degree of over-representation, which give considerable promise in the attempt to interpret what lies behind this apparently inequitable distribution of resources.

However, the data coverage is currently insufficient to make trustworthy comparisons. Given the importance of this issue, and the relatively minor changes needed to collect data for males and females separately where total student numbers are currently collected, a clear priority exists for counties to make serious attempts to implement this in the next data collection exercise.

Modifications to the EQ

Need for continuity. It is taken as axiomatic that modifications to the type and form of data collected in the various data collection tables should be minimal. This is in part to avoid complicating and changing the task of data providers with their hard-won experience of completing the present EQ. It is also highly desirable that successive uses of the EQ help to build up comparable longitudinal data so that trends and changes can be examined.

Possible removal of areas with poor data yields. This does not preclude removal of parts of the EQ, particularly where it is clear that the approach of obtaining a central national response leads to poor data yields, as discussed above. However it would appear to be a step backwards to do this without setting in train the use of a different methodology (such as the School level EQ) to provide an alternative route to collecting the required data.

Further efforts to obtain data on resources. A further problematic area with low yields is data on teachers. This is a valuable partial proxy for resources and it appears sensible to continue efforts to obtain these data. This may be another area where a separate exercise is called for, with the aim of extending the call for data to cover other professional and support staff as well as teachers (possibly as part of a wider initiative on the specification of resources).

Inclusion of post-school phase. Possible additions to the EQ include extending the range to include post-school tertiary education. Arguments for and against this are finely balanced. This aspect of education for students with disabilities, difficulties, and disadvantages is of considerable importance. However experience suggests the likely difficulty of getting worthwhile amounts of data using the EQ and it may be that a different, separate exercise is again called for.

Age distribution data. A further possible addition might be to call for separate data on cross-national categories A, B, and C in Table 6 on age distributions. Suggestions that misleading pictures were being presented when data on the three cross-national categories are combined (discussed in Chapter 5) led to their separate presentation in this monograph and it would be consistent to also do this for age distributions.

General terminological points

ABC or DDD? The assignment of national categories to the three cross-national categories was originally carried out by countries themselves. Any apparent anomalies have been the subject of various discussions. Given consensus on the assignment it should be feasible to move beyond the present definition of cross-national category B as a residual category (*i.e.* additional resources provided to access the regular curriculum for students who do not have disabilities or disadvantages) to one descriptive of the set of national categories subsumed under B, which seem in simple terms to be largely captured by the label "difficulties". It may be that for ease of communication there will be advantage in replacing the ABC labelling by the partial synonyms adopted in the monograph of "disabilities", "difficulties", and "disadvantages" respectively (although it is recognised that this, inevitably, does violence to usages in some countries).

Additional resources or special needs. This monograph has deliberately avoided using the terms "special needs" or "special educational needs" when describing the set of students involved. This is because of the different definitions of special needs adopted in different countries (in particular countries with a narrow definition essentially synonymous with disability). Given the use of the resources definition there is an attraction in using the term "students receiving additional resources because of problems they have in accessing the regular curriculum" and stressing that this includes students not only with organic disabilities, but also with various types of difficulties and social disadvantages.

Final comments

The data gathered so far has been determined by what countries have available. Clearly this is an important starting point essential for the development of international comparisons. However, what are also missing are economic data and data on outcomes for students with disabilities, difficulties and disadvantages. This latter element is an important omission and in need of correction. Future data gathering exercises will in addition focus on collecting outcome data. From the academic perspective PISA holds many possibilities. However, for these students other outcome variables are important. These include access to the labour market, entry into further or higher education and keeping away from criminality. Consideration of how to gather this information and other socio-economic indicators is currently underway.

This monograph is a considerable elaboration of that published in 2000. Nevertheless, there are still many significant omissions and there is a need for further development. However, even if exact international comparability has not been attained there are still many substantial differences between country provision that are unlikely to be due to measurement error. These differences (*e.g.* the extent of school inclusion) have potentially large impacts on the futures of individual children and the attainment of equity. They need to be closely addressed to enable the education system to play its full role in increasing social cohesion and contributing even more significantly to national economies.

REFERENCES

Bressoux, P. (1993), *Les performances des écoles et des classes. Le cas des acquisitions en lecture. Éducation et formations*, p. 30.

Brighouse, M.H. (2000), *School Choice and Social Justice,* Oxford University Press, Oxford, UK.

Crahay, M. (2000), *L'école peut-elle être juste et efficace?* De Boeck, Brussels.

Demeuse, M., M. Crahay and C. Monseur (2001), *Efficiency and Equity,* in W. Hutmacher, D. Cochrane and N. Bottani (eds.), *In Pursuit of Equity in Education – Using International Indicators to Compare Equity Policies*, Kluwer Academic Publishers, Dordrecht/Boston/London.

Department of Education (1997), *The Statistical Report of the Department of Education*, Dublin, Ireland.

Department of Education (1999), *The Statistical Report of the Department of Education*, Dublin, Ireland.

EURYDICE (1996), *Information Dossiers on the Structures of the Education Systems in the European Union and the EFTA Countries 1996*: *The Netherlands,* revised edition, December.

Evans, P. (2001), *Equity Indicators based on the Provision of Supplemental Resources for Disabled and Disadvantaged Students,* in W. Hutmacher, D. Cochrane and N. Bottani (eds.), *In Pursuit of Equity in Education – Using International Indicators to Compare Equity Policies*, Kluwer Academic Publishers, Dordrecht/Boston/London.

Hutmacher, W., D. Cochrane and N. Bottani (eds.) (2001), *In Pursuit of Equity in Education – Using International Indicators to Compare Equity Policies,* Kluwer Academic Publishers, Dordrecht/Boston/London.

OECD (1993), "Access, Participation and Equity", OECD, Paris.

OECD (1995a), *Integrating Students with Special Needs into Mainstream Schools,* OECD, Paris.

OECD (1995b), *Our Children at Risk,* OECD, Paris.

OECD (1996), *Successful Services for our Children and Families at Risk,* OECD, Paris.

OECD (1998a), *Coordinating Services for Children and Youth at Risk. A World View,* OECD, Paris.

OECD (1998b), *Education at a Glance – OECD Indicators,* Paris.

OECD (1999), *Inclusive Education at Work: Including Students with Disabilities into Mainstream Schools,* OECD, Paris.

OECD (2000a), *Education at a Glance – OECD Indicators,* OECD, Paris.

OECD (2000b), *Special Needs Education – Statistics and Indicators,* OECD, Paris.

OECD (2002), *Education at a Glance – OECD Indicators,* OECD, Paris.

Rawls, J. (1971), *A Theory of Justice,* Harvard University Press, Cambridge, USA.

UNESCO (1997), *International Standard Classification of Education, ISCED*, UNESCO, Paris.

ANNEX 1
ALLOCATION OF CATEGORIES OF STUDENTS WITH DISABILITIES, DIFFICULTIES, DISADVANTAGES INCLUDED IN THE RESOURCES DEFINITION TO CROSS-NATIONAL CATEGORIES A, B, C

Belgium (Flemish Community)

Cross-National Category A

1. Minor mental handicap – Type 1. Education in type 1 of special education is organised for children with mild mental disabilities: they should be able to acquire basic school knowledge and skills; and to receive vocational training in order to make integration in the regular social and professional environment possible. This type of education is not organised in nursery school (i.e., this type of education is only organised at primary and secondary school level).

2. Moderate or serious mental handicap – Type 2. Education in type 2 of special education is organised for children with moderate to severe mental disabilities. Through social education and special vocational training, children with moderate mental disabilities are prepared for integration in a protected socio-professional environment. The social self-reliance level of children with severe mental disabilities is enhanced by special educational activities. This type of education is organised at pre-primary, primary, and secondary level.

4. Pupils with a physical handicap – Type 4. This category is followed by pupils with a physical handicap. Education in type 4 of special education is organised to fulfil the educational needs of children with physical disabilities, other than those mentioned in types 5, 6, and 7, who are not able to receive education in a standard school because they regularly need medical or paramedical treatments and/or special teaching materials. This type of education is organised at pre-primary, primary, and secondary level.

5. Children suffering from protracted illness – Type 5. This category is followed by pupils suffering from protracted illness. Education in type 5 of special education is organised to fulfil the educational needs of children who suffer from an illness and receive medical treatment in a hospital or in a medical-pedagogical institute organised or accredited by the State. This type of education is organised at pre-primary, primary and secondary level.

6. Visual handicap – Type 6. This category is followed by pupils with a visual handicap. Education in type 6 of special education is organised for blind or visually impaired children who regularly need medical or paramedical treatment and/or special teaching materials. This type of education is organised at pre-primary, primary, and secondary level.

7. Auditory handicap – Type 7. This type of special education is for pupils with an auditory handicap. Education in type 7 of special education is organised for deaf or hearing-impaired children who regularly need medical or paramedical treatment and/or special teaching materials. This type of education is organised at pre-primary, primary, and secondary level.

9. Support at home for children who are temporarily ill. Temporary home-based education applies to both ordinary and special primary education (except for type 5 schools). A child of compulsory school age in primary school (not in nursery education) has the right to receive temporary home-based education when the following conditions are simultaneously satisfied: an absence of over 21 calendar days caused by an illness or an accident; the parents have submitted a written request, accompanied by a medical certificate, to the principal of the school providing home-based education. The medical certificate should show that the child is not able to come to the school but is allowed to be educated; the distance between the school site and the pupil's residence should not exceed 10 km for ordinary education or 20 km for special education. The home-based education is provided from the 22nd calendar day of absence and continues until the child is able to return to its regular school. If the child should suffer from the same illness or accident within three months, the 21-day waiting period does not apply. In order to organise the home-based education, four additional teaching periods per week and per pupil are financed or granted. The travel expenses incurred by the staff member providing the home-based education are repaid according to the value of a first class train ticket. Pupils in permanent home-based education are also included in this category. Pupils at compulsory school age who satisfy the admission requirements for special primary education but for whom it is permanently impossible to be educated in a school due to a handicap, are entitled to permanent home-based education. This does require a recommendation from the Special Education Advisory Committee. Great distance to a school, long transport time, etc., do not qualify as reasons for applying for permanent home-based education. The deciding factor is the seriousness of the handicap which does not allow education in a school, although the child is able to receive education. The school receives four additional teaching periods per week to organise the permanent home-based education. These additional teaching periods are to be performed by a member of the teaching staff and they can never contain any therapeutic treatments.

Cross-National Category B

3. **Serious emotional and/or behavioural problems – Type 3.** This category is followed by pupils with serious emotional and/or behavioural problems. Education in type 3 of special education is organised for children with personality disorders. They suffer from severe structural and/or functional disorders in the affective-dynamic and relational aspect of their personality, which make special educational and psycho-therapist measures necessary. This type of education is organised at pre-primary, primary, and secondary level.

8. **Serious learning disabilities – Type 8.** This type of special education is organised for pupils with serious learning disabilities. Education in type 8 of special education is organised to fulfil the educational needs of children with severe learning disabilities. Although their mental, visual, and hearing abilities are normal, they suffer from disorders in their development of language and skills of speech, reading, writing, and/or arithmetic. This type of education is only organised at primary school level (not for nursery school or secondary education).

10. **Extending care.** For a few years now, the Flemish Government has been developing a program for "*zorgbreedte*" (extending care). It is rather difficult to translate this notion. The idea is linked up with ideas on, for example, "inclusive education". The idea is to organise early attention for those children who might suffer from learning difficulties that may cause problems in the transition between pre-school and primary school. Additional teachers, schools for special education, and the pupil guidance centre (CLB) work closely together with the pre-school teacher. Attention is given to general language proficiency, social skills, prevention, and remediation of learning difficulties, socio-emotional problems, and co-operation with the parents. The target group consists of children who live in less favourable economic and cultural circumstances but who are capable of participating in ordinary education when certain deficits are eliminated.

11. **Remedial teaching.** Remedial teachers in ordinary elementary education. The total of teaching periods in elementary education is conceived in such a way that primary schools have the opportunity to devote special attention and care to children with learning or developmental difficulties. One of the most important goals of giving the schools this autonomy is to make sure that schools are organised so that remediation is possible. In elementary education, pedagogical reform is ensured by working with differentiation elements, carrying out different groupings and taking maximum advantage of remedial teachers. In addition, a lot of attention is paid to consultative conversations between the regular teachers and the remedial teacher, and between the regular teachers, the remedial teacher, the members of the Pupil Guidance Centre, and the school principal. One teaching period for the remedial teacher per group of 20 pupils seems a minimum. It is the remedial teacher's task to help children with learning or developmental difficulties and to detect barriers to learning. The guidance takes place individually or in small groups or assistance within the regular classroom, according to the pupils' needs. The remedial teacher's presence is not based on additional teaching periods or allowances, but is made possible by the flexible allocation of the total number of teaching periods that is assigned to each school based on the total number of pupils. This total package of granted teaching periods is called "*omkadering*".

Cross-National Category C

12. **Educational priority policy.** The languages of the migrant population are not legally recognised as minority languages. Nevertheless, a special policy has been instituted within the education system to provide for adequate learning opportunities, especially for children within compulsory education. This policy is called the "*onderwijsvoorrangsbeleid*" (educational priority policy). This policy is applied at the primary and secondary levels in schools with a significant number of migrant or refugee children. Schools must develop an educational approach with special attention for the quality of the teaching of Dutch intercultural education, the tackling of learning and developmental problems, and co-operation with the immigrant families.

13. **Reception classes for pupils who do not speak Dutch.** Reception education is education for immigrant school entrants who do not speak Dutch and this is to insure their knowledge of Dutch and to facilitate their social integration. After this reception education, the pupils can enrol in regular education (primary or secondary school level). Reception education encourages the active integration of the immigrant school entrant in school life. The focus lies on the relationship with the teachers and the other pupils of his peer group. In elementary education, schools with at least four foreign pupils who do not speak Dutch (*anderstalige nieuwkomers*) and who do not fully understand the language used at school may organise a special language adaptation course for three periods a week. In secondary education, this type of education is organised in 29 selected schools (at least 10 foreign pupils who do not speak Dutch).

14. **Travelling children.** In this category, two specific smaller projects are integrated. The first project concerns the reception of pre-school children of travelling employed population (circus, bargemen, fairmen, showmen, etc.) In the second project, three elementary schools take care of the reception of gypsy children.

15. Children placed in a sheltered home by juvenile court. These children are placed in a sheltered home by juvenile courts and this due to family problems. These children are integrated into regular schools. They are counted as 1.5 (instead of 1) to determine the yearly amount of teaching periods for the school.

16. More favourable teacher/pupil ratio in the schools of the capital region of Brussels. Because of the cultural and linguistic differences of pupils going to school in the Capital region of Brussels (a lot of them do not speak Dutch), a more favourable teacher/pupil ratio is used in comparison to schools in Flanders.

17. Additional resources for schools in some municipalities around the capital region of Brussels and at the linguistic border between the Flemish and the Walloon regions. In six municipalities around the Capital region of Brussels and the linguistic border between the Flemish and the Walloon region, schools can receive additional resources. These additional resources are project-based (based on a work plan for the pupils with cultural and linguistic differences).

Canada (Alberta)

Cross-National Category A

1. Severe mental disability. A student with a severe mental disability (Code 41) is one who: a) has severe delays in all or most areas of development; b) frequently has other disabilities including physical, sensory, medical, and/or behavioural; c) requires constant assistance and/or supervision in all areas of functioning, including daily living skills, and may require assistive technology; d) should have a standardised assessment that indicates functioning in the severe to profound range (standardised score of 30 + or – 5 or less) – functional assessments by a qualified professional will also be considered in cases where the disabilities of the child preclude standard assessments; and/or e) has scores equivalent to the severe to profound levels on an adaptive behaviour scale (*e.g.,* American Association on Mental Deficiency Adaptive Behaviour Scale: Progress Assessment Chart, Vineland).

3. Severe multiple disability. A student (ECS to Grade 12) with a severe multiple disability (Code 43) is one who: a) has two or more non-associated moderate to severe mental and/or physical disabilities that, in combination, result in the student functioning at a severe to profound level; and b) requires special programs, resources, and/or therapeutic services. Students with a severe disability with a second disabling condition should be identified under the category of the primary severe disability. A student with a severe mental disability and another associated disability is not designated under this category, but is designated under severe emotional/behavioural disability. The following mild/moderate disabilities cannot be used in combination with other disabilities to qualify under code 43: a) ADD/HD; b) learning disability; c) emotional behavioural disabilities; and d) speech and language related disabilities.

4. Severe physical or medical disability. (Code 44) A student with a severe physical, medical, or neurological disability (Code 44) is one who has a medical diagnosis of a physical disability, specific neurological disorder, or medical condition that creates a significant impact on the student's ability to function in the school environment (note: some physical or medical disabilities have little or no impact upon the student's ability to function in the school environment) and requires extensive personal assistance and modifications to the learning environment in order to benefit from schooling. A student with severe autism or other severe pervasive developmental disorder is included in this category. A clinical diagnosis by a psychiatrist, clinical psychologist, chartered psychologist, or medical professional specialising in the field of autism is required. A clinical diagnosis of autism is not necessarily sufficient in order to qualify under this category. Eligibility is determined by the functioning level of the student with autism. In order for a diagnosis of autism to be made, the student needs to demonstrate difficulties in three broad areas: 1) social interaction; 2) communication; and 3) stereotyped pattern of behaviour (*i.e.* hand flapping, body rocking, echolalia, insistence on sameness, and resistance to change). A student diagnosed with severe Fetal Alcohol Syndrome (FAS) or Fetal Alcohol Effects (FAE), including Alcohol-Related Neurodevelopmental Disorder (ARND) is included in this category. A clinical diagnosis by a psychiatrist, clinical psychologist with specialised training, or medical professional specialising in developmental disorders is required. A clinical diagnosis of FAS/FAE is not necessarily sufficient to qualify under this category. Eligibility is determined by the functioning level of the student with FAS/FAE. Students with severe FAS/FAE exhibit significant impairment in many of the following areas: a) social functioning; b) life skills; c) behaviour; d) learning; and e) attention and concentration resulting in the need for extensive intervention and support.

5. Deafness. (Code 45) A student with a profound hearing loss (Code 45) is one who: 1) has a hearing loss of 71 decibels (dB) or more unaided in the better ear over the normal speech range (500 and 4000 Hz) that interferes with the use of oral language as the primary form of communication; or 2) has a cochlear implant preceded by a 71 dB hearing loss unaided in the better ear; and 3) requires extensive modifications and specialised educational supports; and 4) has a diagnosis by a clinical or educational audiologists. New approvals require an audiogram within the past three years.

6. Blindness. (Code 46) A student with a severe visual impairment (Code 46) is one who: 1) has corrected vision so limited that it is inadequate for most or all instructional situations, and information must be presented through other means; 2) has a visual acuity ranging from 6/60 (20/200) in the better eye after correction, to having no usable vision or field of vision reduced to an angle of 20 degrees; and 3) has a severe to profound visual impairment that has not changed significantly since the initial approval by Alberta Learning. Documentation from a qualified specialist in the field of vision outlining the severity of the disability and modifications to the learning environment may be sufficient to support eligibility. For those students who may be difficult to assess (*e.g.*, cortical blindness-developmentally delayed), a functional visual assessment by a qualified specialist in the field of vision or a medical professional may be sufficient to support eligibility.

7. Severe communications disorder. (Code 47; ECS only) A child with a severe communication disability (Code 47, ECS children only) has severe difficulty in communication with peers and/or adults because of a severe disability in expressive and/or receptive language and/or total language. This may include little, if any, expressive or receptive communication skills. In order to qualify for severe communication disability funding, the assessment results must be less than or equal to the first percentile. One subset score alone, such as sentence structure or word structure at or below the first percentile, does not qualify as a severe communication disability for funding purposes. If a child has a moderate to severe disability in a non-associated category (in addition to having a moderate to severe communication disability), then the child would be more appropriately identified as Severe Multiple Disability (Code 43). This applies only to eligible ECS children and does not apply for children in Grades 1-12. A severe phonological delay does not necessarily qualify as a severe communication disability. A current speech and language assessment report must be submitted with the application for funding. The speech language report should include a conclusion or summary statement that clearly indicates the level of communication disability (*i.e.*, mild, moderate, severe, or profound). Recommended assessment instruments would be phonological, such as the Hudson, rather than articulation tests. Documentation that clarifies the level of intelligibility and the impact of the speech language disorder on the child's ability to function in an education environment should also be included.

8. Mild mental disability. (Code 51) A student with a mild mental disability (Code 51) is usually delayed in most academic subjects and social behaviours as compared to his or her own same-age peers. Any student designated as having a mild mental disability should have an IQ in the range of 50-75 + or − 5 as measured on an individual intelligence test, have an adaptive behaviour score equivalent to the mildly delayed level on an adaptive behaviour scale (*e.g.*, American Association on Mental Deficiency Adaptive Behaviour Scale; Progress Assessment Chart, Vineland) and exhibit developmental delays in social behaviours.

9. Moderate mental disability. (Code 52) A student with a moderate mental disability (Code 52) requires significant modification to basic curriculum but is able to profit from instruction in living/vocational skills and may require functional literacy and numeracy skills. Any student who is designated as having a moderate mental disability should have an IQ in the range of approximately 30-50 + or − 5 as measured on an individual intelligence test and have an adaptive behaviour score equivalent to the moderately delayed level on an adaptive behaviour scale (*e.g.*, American Association on Mental Deficiency Adaptive Behaviour Scale; Progress Assessment Chart, Vineland).

12. Mild/moderate hearing disability. (Code 55) A student with a mild/moderate hearing disability (Code 55) is one whose hearing condition affects speech and language development and interferes with the ability to learn. A student with a mild (26 to 40 decibels) to moderate (41 to 70 decibels) hearing disability will have an average hearing loss of 26 to 70 decibels unaided in the better ear over the normal range of speech. The normal range of speech is between 500 Hz and 4000 Hz.

13. Mild/Moderate Visual Disability. (Code 56) A student with a mild/moderate visual disability (Code 56) is one whose vision is so limited that it interferes with the student's ability to learn or the student requires modification of the learning environment to be able to learn. A student who is designated as having limited vision should have a visual acuity of less than 20/70 (6/21 metric) in the better eye after correction and/or a reduced field of vision.

14. Mild/moderate communication disability. (Code 57) A student with a mild/moderate communications disability (Code 57) has significant difficulty in communicating with peers and adults because of a disability in expressive and/or receptive language and/or disabilities in speech including articulation, voice, and fluency.

15. Mild/moderate physical/medical disability. (Code 58) A student with a mild to moderate physical or medical disability (Code 58) is one whose physical, neurological, or medical condition interferes with the ability to learn or who requires a modification of the learning environment in order to learn. The existence of a physical disability or medical condition, in and of itself, is not sufficient for the student to be designated under this category; the condition must impact upon the student's schooling.

16. Mild/moderate multiple disability. (Code 59) A student with a mild to moderate multiple disability (Code 59) has two or more non-associated mild/to moderate disabilities that have a significant impact upon his or her ability to learn. Some disabling conditions are closely associated and so would not be designated under this category. For example, students with hearing disabilities frequently have communication disabilities and students with mental disabilities almost always have both academic and communication disabilities.

Cross-National Category B

2. Severe emotional/behavioural disability. A student with a severe emotional/behavioural disorder (Code 42) is one who: a) displays chronic, extreme, and pervasive behaviours that require close and constant adult supervision, high levels of structure, and other intensive support services in order to function in an educational setting – the behaviours significantly interfere with both the learning and safety of the student and other students; b) has a diagnosis of psychosis including schizophrenia, bi-polar disorder, obsessive/compulsive disorders, or severe chronic clinical depression; c) displays self-stimulation, self-abusive or aphasic behaviour; or d) is dangerously aggressive, destructive, and has violent and impulsive behaviours toward self and/or others such as Conduct Disorder. In the most extreme and pervasive instances, severe Oppositional Defiance Disorder may qualify. A clinical diagnosis within the last two years by a psychiatrist, chartered psychologist, or a developmental paediatrician is required in addition to extensive documentation of the nature, frequency, and severity of the disorder by school authorities. The effects of the disability on the student's functioning in an educational setting should be described. An ongoing treatment plan/behavioural plan should be available and efforts be made to ensure that the student has access to appropriate mental health and therapeutic services. A clinical diagnosis of a behavioural disorder is not necessarily sufficient to qualify under this category. Some diagnoses not sufficiently severe enough to qualify include attention deficit/hyperactivity disorder (AD/HD) and attention deficit disorder (ADD).

10. Mild/moderate emotional/behavioural disability. (Code 53) Students with a mild/moderate emotional/behavioural disability (Code 53) exhibit chronic and pervasive behaviours that are so maladaptive that they interfere with the learning and safety of the student and other students. Behaviour disabilities are characterised by a number of observable maladaptive behaviours: 1) an inability to establish or maintain satisfactory relationships with peers or adults; 2) a general mood of unhappiness or depression; 3) continued difficulty in coping with the learning situation in spite of remedial intervention; 4) physical symptoms or fears associated with personal or school problems; 5) difficulties in accepting the realities of personal responsibility and accountability; and 6) physical violence toward other persons and/or physical destructiveness toward the environment.

11. Learning disability. (Code 54) Students with a mild/moderate learning disability (Code 54) usually have average or above average intelligence but have specific learning disabilities that interfere with normal academic learning. Learning disabilities is a generic term that refers to a heterogeneous group of disorders due to identifiable or inferred central nervous system dysfunction. Such disorders may be manifested by delays in early development and/or difficulties in any of the following areas: attention, memory, reasoning, co-ordination, communicating, reading, writing, spelling, calculation, social competence, and emotional maturation. Learning disabilities are intrinsic to the individual and may affect learning and behaviour in any individual, including those with potentially average or above average intelligence. Learning disabilities are not due primarily to visual, hearing, or motor handicaps, to mental retardation, emotional disturbance, or environmental disadvantage, although they may occur concurrently with any of these. Learning disabilities may arise from genetic variations, biochemical factors, events in the pre- to peri-natal period, or any other subsequent events resulting in neurological impairment. Learning disabilities are intrinsic to the individual and may affect learning and behaviour in any individual, including those with potentially average or above average intelligence.

17. Gifted and talented. (Code 80) A student in Grade 1-12 who is gifted and talented (Code 80) is one who, by virtue of outstanding ability, is capable of exceptional performance. This is a student who requires differentiated provisions and/or programs beyond the regular school program to realise his or her contribution to self and society. A student capable of exceptional performance is one who demonstrates achievement and/or potential ability in one of several areas: 1) General intellectual ability. A student possessing general intellectual ability is consistently superior to the other students in the school to the extent that the student needs and can profit from specially planned educational services beyond those normally provided by the regular school program. Usually, this is the student who has a large storehouse of information about a wide variety of topics. The ability to abstract, generalise, and use high level thinking skills is common in this type of student. 2) Specific academic aptitude. A student possessing a specific academic aptitude is the student who, in a specific subject area, is consistently superior to the aptitudes of the other students in the school to the extent that the student needs and can profit from specially planned educational services beyond those normally provided by the regular school program. Generally, this is the student who has an inordinate strength in a specific area, such as mathematical reasoning. 3) Creative or productive thinking. A student who thinks creatively or productively is one who consistently engages in divergent thinking that results in unconventional responses to conventional tasks, to the extent that the student needs and can profit from specially planned educational services beyond those normally provided by the regular school program. Generally, this is the student who is unwilling to accept authoritarian pronouncements without critical examination. 4) Leadership ability. A student possessing leadership ability is one who not only assumes leadership roles, but also is accepted by others as a leader, to the extent that the student needs and can benefit from specially planned educational services beyond those normally provided by the regular school program. Generally, this is the student who can be counted upon to carry out responsibilities and adapts readily to new situations. 5) Visual and performing arts. A student possessing visual and performing arts ability is one who consistently creates outstanding aesthetic productions in graphic areas, sculpture, music, drama, or dance, to the extent that this student needs and can benefit from specially planned educational activities beyond those normally provided in the regular school program. 6) Psychomotor ability. A student possessing psychomotor ability is one who consistently displays mechanical skills or athletic ability so superior to that of other students in the school that the student needs and can profit from specially planned educational services beyond those normally provided by the regular school program. Generally, this is the student with good control of body movement and excellent hand-eye co-ordination.

Canada (British Colombia)

Cross-National Category A

1. Visual impairments. Visual impairment includes the following categories: blind, legally blind, partially sighted, low vision, and cortically visually impaired. A student with visual impairment is one whose visual acuity is not sufficient for the student to participate with ease in everyday activities. The impairment interferes with optimal learning and achievement and can result in a substantial educational disadvantage unless adaptations are made in the methods of presenting learning opportunities, the nature of the materials used and/or the learning environment. It is not intended to include students described as having visual perceptual difficulties unless they also have a vision loss as described below. To be eligible for supplemental funding as a visually impaired student, the following conditions must be met: a current IEP describing a visual acuity of 6/21 (20/70) or less in the better eye after correction; a visual field of 20 degrees or less; any progressive eye disease with a prognosis of becoming one of the above in the next few years; or a visual problem or related visual stamina that is not correctable and that results in the student functioning as if his or her visual acuity is limited to 6/21 (20/70) or less.

3. Deaf/Blindness. A student with deafblindness has a degree of visual and auditory impairment which, when compounded, results in significant difficulties in developing communicative, educational, vocational, avocational, and social skills. To be considered deafblind the student's vision and auditory impairments can range from partial sight to total blindness, and from moderate to profound hearing loss. Students who are identified and assessed as deafblind are eligible for supplemental funding as students with multiple disabilities when the following conditions are met: a current IEP must be in place; and direct, ongoing special education service(s) must be provided. These services should be outlined in the IEP and directly related to the student's identified special need(s). The special education service(s) must be in addition to any services provided under formula funding based on total student enrolment (*e.g.* learning assistance, counselling). Reduction in class size is not by itself a sufficient service to meet the definition.

4. Multiple disabilities. A student with dependent needs is completely dependent on others for meeting all major daily living needs. She/he will require assistance at all times for feeding, dressing, toileting, mobility and personal hygiene. Without such assistance and personal care support, attendance at school would not be possible. Many students may also require health care as defined in the Inter-Ministerial Protocols. The estimated prevalence among school-age students requiring this very intense level of service is 0.07% of the student population. Some students are born with conditions or disabilities that make them dependent, while others acquire conditions or disabilities. For some students, increasing independence as they learn and grow is a reasonable expectation. For other students, decreasing independence may occur due to degenerative conditions or terminal illness (see other multiple disability category: deaf/blind).

5. Hearing impairments. For educational purposes, a student considered to be deaf or hard of hearing is one who has a medically diagnosed hearing loss which results in such a substantial educational difficulty that he/she requires direct services on a regular, frequent and ongoing basis by a qualified teacher of the deaf and hard of hearing. Students with a diagnosis of central auditory processing dysfunction are not traditionally served by teachers of the deaf and hard of hearing unless there is an additional diagnosis of peripheral hearing loss. To be eligible for supplemental funding as a deaf or hard of hearing student, the following conditions must be met: a medical diagnosis of hearing loss has been made; and a current IEP must be in place; and the student must be receiving special education services that are directly related to the student's hearing loss on a regular, frequent and on-going basis from a qualified teacher of the deaf and hard of hearing.

6. Autism. The syndrome of autism is a condition characterised by a marked disorder of communication and a severe disturbance of intellectual, emotional and behavioural development. It is a syndrome defined and diagnosed through the observation of behaviours. The syndrome is caused by an underlying physical dysfunction within the brain or central nervous system, the exact nature of which is, as yet, unknown. The Ministry of Education uses the definition of autism as defined by the American Psychiatric Association: a student with autism exhibits impairment in: reciprocal social interaction; verbal and non-verbal communication; imaginative activity; and restrictive, repetitive and stereotyped patterns of behaviour, interest and activities. To be eligible for supplemental funding, the following conditions must be met: a diagnosis of autism must have been made by appropriately qualified professionals; and a current IEP must be in place; and the student must be receiving additional special education services directly related to the autism on an ongoing and frequent basis. Reduction in class size is not by itself sufficient to meet the definition.

8. Moderate to severe to profound intellectual disabilities. A student is considered to have a moderate to severe/profound intellectual disability if intellectual functioning is greater than three standard deviations below the norm on an individually administered Level C assessment instrument of intellectual functioning, and there is delayed adaptive behaviour and functioning of similar degree. As individuals and as a group, these students have particular learning characteristics. They require support in the development of communication skills, cognitive skills, fine and gross motor skills, self-care, life skills and socialisation skills. Generally, a student with this level of intellectual functioning is also significantly delayed in social-emotional development. There may also be accompanying sensory, physical and health disabilities. Specific instruction is needed for many or all life skills activities.

10. Severe behaviour disorders. Students with severe behaviour disorders who are eligible to be claimed in this funding category are those who exhibit: either antisocial, extremely disruptive behaviour in the school environment and in most other environments, consistently/persistently over time; or severe mental health conditions which manifest themselves in profound withdrawal or other internalising behaviours. These students generally have histories of profound problems, and present as very vulnerable, fragile students who are seriously "at risk" in classroom situations without extensive support. These students must also exhibit behaviours which are serious enough to be known to school and school district personnel and other community agencies and to warrant intensive interventions by other community agencies beyond the school; and a serious risk to themselves or others, and/or with behaviours that significantly interfere with their academic progress and that of other students; and beyond the normal capacity of the school to manage. Students in this category should be recognised as those most in need from a community perspective, and should have access to intensive, co-ordinated school/community intervention. These interventions should be based on co-ordinated, inter-ministerial assessment planning and intervention processes which are required to manage and maintain the students in school and in their community. Students are eligible in this funding category only if the school district can demonstrate that it is incurring extraordinary costs related to delivering the students' educational programs. Reduction in class size is not by itself a sufficient service to meet the definition.

14. Physical disabilities or chronic health impairments. A student is considered to have a physical disability or chronic health impairment based on the need for special educational services due to one or more of the following: nervous system impairment; musculoskeletal condition; and/or chronic health impairment. Medical diagnosis, by itself, does not determine the special educational services required by students with physical disabilities or chronic health impairments. Students are only eligible for funding in this category if their education is adversely affected by their physical disabilities or chronic health impairments. To be eligible for supplemental funding for a student in this category, the following conditions must be met: the student must meet one or more of the above criteria; and a current IEP must be in place; and direct, ongoing special education service(s) must be provided. These services should be outlined in the IEP and directly related to the student's identified special need(s). The special education service(s) must be in addition to any services provided under formula funding based on total student enrolment (*e.g.*, learning assistance, counselling). Reduction in class size is not by itself a sufficient service to meet the definition.

<u>Cross-National Category B</u>
2. Specific learning disabilities. A group of disorders manifested by significant difficulties in the acquisition and use of listening, speaking, reading, writing, reasoning or mathematical abilities, which are intrinsic to the individual, presumed to be due to central nervous system dysfunction, and may occur across the life span. Problems in self-regulatory behaviours, social perception and social interaction may exist with learning disabilities but do not by themselves constitute a learning disability. Although learning disabilities may occur concomitantly with other handicapping conditions (*e.g.* sensory impairment, mental retardation, serious emotional disturbance) or with extrinsic influences (*e.g.* cultural differences, insufficient or inappropriate instruction), they are not the result of those conditions or influences and may include conditions described as dyslexia, dyscalculalia or dysgraphia, and students with Attention Deficit/Hyperactivity Disorder (AD/HD). To be eligible for supplemental funding for Severe Learning Disabilities, a student must also meet the following criteria: Severe difficulties in the acquisition of basic academic skills and/or school performance persist after classroom-based remedial interventions, curricular adaptations and learning assistance support. Persistent difficulties in the acquisition of pre-Academic skills such as recognition of letters and numbers in the early primary years; and/or persistent difficulties in the acquisition of reading, writing and/or arithmetic skills in the later primary years; and/or a discrepancy of two standard deviations between estimated learning potential and academic achievement as measured by norm-referenced instruments in Grades 3-12; and a significant weakness in one or more cognitive processes (*e.g.* perception, memory, attention, receptive or expressive language abilities, visual-spatial abilities) relative to overall intellectual functioning, as measured by norm-referenced assessment instruments, which directly impact learning and school performance.

7. Mild intellectual disabilities. A student is considered to have a mild intellectual disability if intellectual functioning is -2.01 to -3.00 standard deviations below the norm on an individually administered Level C assessment instrument of intellectual functioning, and there is delayed adaptive behaviour and functioning of similar degree. While individual needs will differ, many students with mild intellectual disabilities may require specific instruction for the acquisition of gross and fine motor skills, communication skills, assistance with development of social skills, including personal independence, social responsibility and life skills, as well as with reasoning skills, memory, problem solving and conceptualising skills.

9. Mild to moderate behaviour disorders, including rehabilitation. Students with mild/moderate behavioural difficulties demonstrate one or more of the following: behaviours such as aggression (of a physical, emotional or sexual nature) and/or hyperactivity; negative or undesirable internalised psychological states such as anxiety, stress-related disorders, and depression; behaviours related to social problems such as delinquency, substance abuse, child abuse or neglect; and/or behaviours related to other disabling conditions, such as thought disorders or neurological or physiological conditions; and the frequency or severity of the above behaviours have a very disruptive effect on the classroom learning environment, social relations or personal adjustment; and they demonstrate the above behaviour(s) over an extended period of time, in more than one setting and with more than one person (teachers, peers); and they have not responded to support/interventions provided through usual classroom management strategies. Rehabilitation programs are jointly funded by the Ministry of Social Services and the Ministry of Education. Students can be included in the rehabilitation funding category when, through the assessment process, it has been determined that they meet all of the criteria for students with moderate behaviour disorders, there is funding for the program from the Ministry of Social Services, and a current IEP is in place.

11. Gifted. A student is considered gifted when she/he possesses demonstrated or potential abilities that give evidence of exceptionally high capability with respect to intellect, creativity, or the skills associated with specific disciplines. Students who are gifted often demonstrate outstanding abilities in more than one area. They may demonstrate extraordinary intensity of focus in their particular areas of talent or interest. However, they may also have accompanying disabilities and should not be expected to have strengths in all areas of intellectual functioning. These students must be appropriately identified and be receiving an additional special educational service on a regular and ongoing basis to be eligible for special education funding in this category. Current funding allows for up to 2% of total student enrolment for supplemental funding in this category if supplemental services are provided to identified students on a regular basis, and a current Individual Education Plan is in place. Reduction in class size is not by itself a sufficient service to meet the definition.

12. Learning assistance. Learning assistance services are school-based, non-categorical resource services designed to support classroom teachers and their students who have mild to moderate difficulties in learning and adjustment.

Cross-National Category C

13. English as a second language. Learning another language and new cultural norms, adjusting to a different social and physical setting, or overcoming homesickness or trauma can affect a student's school adjustment and learning. These factors, when combined with a disability or an impairment, can significantly undermine school achievement. Assessing and planning for students with special needs becomes more complex when language, cultural or migration factors are involved. Except for cases of obvious disability (*e.g.* profound intellectual disability, physical or sensory disability), teachers should fully consider cultural, linguistic and/or experiential factors that can affect learning before assuming the presence of a disability or impairment. Consideration should be given to prior educational experience, and the student should be allowed sufficient time for second-language learning and social adjustment. Students may need additional support for language development, and academic upgrading (*e.g.* math), or assistance with social integration, without necessarily presenting a disability.

15. Aboriginal education program. Students who self-report that they are of Aboriginal ancestry are eligible for an Aboriginal Language and Culture Program that leads to knowledge, understanding and fluency in a student's heritage language and culture; including support services to assist such as home-school co-ordination, elder peer community counselling; or aboriginal tutorial assistance. This support is in addition to any special education or learning assistance.

Canada (New Brunswick)

Cross-National Category A

2. Communicational. Students who require support because of deficits in speech/articulation development and language.

3. Intellectual. Students who may require modified or long term intensive special educational programs or services to develop their academic and social potential.

4. Physical. Medical/Health; Physically Handicapped (students who because of physically challenging conditions require mobility assistance or adaptation of physical environment personal care); Hearing Impaired (services received from APSEA); Visually Impaired (services received from APSEA).

5. Perceptual. Students who because of specific learning disabilities continue to experience a wide range of difficulties in coping in the regular classroom environment.
6. Multiple. Students who have combinations of challenging disabilities.

Cross-National Category B
1. Behavioural exceptionalities. Students with severe behavioural challenges that are primarily a result of social, psychological and environmental factors.

Cross-National Category C
7. Immigrant. Students who received tutorial funding to acquire skills in English language.

Canada (Saskatchewan)

Cross-National Category A
1. Intellectual disabilities. Regulation 49c: "Trainable mentally retarded, that is when a pupil has: i) an intelligence quotient below 50 plus 5, as measured by an approved individual test: and ii) a significant deficit in adaptive behaviour, as measured by an approved individual test or confirmed by an observer who is, in the opinion of the minister, competent." Regulation 49 is currently under review and the following definition is under consideration: "A pupil has a mental disability when an individual who is acceptable to the minister and who is qualified to conduct individual psychological assessments certifies that the pupil: a) scored at least three standard deviations below the mean on an individual standardised test of mental ability, and b) demonstrates a deficit in adaptive behaviour, as measured by an individual measure of adaptive behaviour."
2. Visual impairments. Regulation 48a: "Visually impaired, that is when assessment by a certified practitioner acceptable to the minister affirms that visual acuity is 20/200 or less in the pupil's better eye with proper correction or that the pupil's field of vision is so limited that the widest diameter of the visual field subtends to an angle of 20 degrees or less." Regulation 48 is under review and the following definition is under consideration: "A pupil has a visual disability if a duly qualified medical practitioner certifies that the pupil: a) has a measured loss of central visual acuity that may vary from blindness to 20/70 or less in the better eye with correction, or b) has a field of vision no greater than 20 degrees at the widest diameter."
4. Orthopaedic impairments. Regulation 49e: "Orthopaedically disabled, that is when assessment by a duly qualified medical practitioner certifies that the pupil's physical limitations adversely affect his educational performance, seriously restrict his mobility within the school, seriously limit self-help activities or limit his use of conventional transportation to the extent that special education services are required." Regulation 49 is currently under review and the following definition is under consideration: "A pupil has an orthopaedic disability when a duly qualified medical practitioner certifies that the pupil has an identified physical condition that: a) adversely affects the pupil's educational performance, b) seriously restricts the pupil's mobility within the school learning environment, c) seriously limits the pupil's self-help activities, d) limits the pupil's use of conventional transportation, or e) requires specialised technological aids."

5. Chronically ill. Regulation 49f: "Chronically health impaired, that is when assessment by a duly qualified medical practitioner certifies that the pupil's physical health: 1) does not permit school attendance and that hospital or home placement is required for at least three months, or 2) adversely affects his educational performance at school to the extent that ongoing special education services are required." Regulation 49 is currently under review and the following definition is under consideration: "A pupil has a chronic medical condition if, following assessment, a duly qualified practitioner certifies that a) the pupil requires medical procedures, excluding the administration of medication, to ensure the health and safety of the pupil while in school, or b) that the pupil's attendance will be limited due to ongoing medical interventions, or c) that the pupil's school attendance will be limited because the condition adversely affects the pupil's health, or d) the pupil's educational performance will be adversely affected by his/her medical condition."
7. Multiple disabilities. Regulation 49h: "Severely multiply disabled, that is when medical and psychological assessment acceptable to the minister affirms that the pupil has severe concomitant disabilities of the types described in clauses a) to g)." Regulation 49 is under review and the following definition is under consideration: "A pupil has a multiple disability when an assessment by an individual, acceptable to the minister, confirms that the pupil has concomitant recognised disabilities of the types described in this section."

8. Deaf or hard of hearing. Regulation 49b: "Hearing impaired, that is when audiological assessment by a provincial assessment service acceptable to the minister affirms that the pupil's decibel loss in the speech range is greater than 34 decibels in both ears." Regulation 49 is under review and the following is under consideration:" A pupil is deaf or hearing impaired when an audiological assessment by a qualified person acceptable to the minister certifies that the pupil has: a) a hearing loss in which the unaided average of the three most severe of the following frequencies, 250, 500, 1000, 2000, 4000, mH is greater than 34 decibels in the better ear; or b) a unilateral loss in which the unaided difference between the affected and unaffected ear is 50 decibels or more and there is a significant delay in speech or language development."

9. Autism. Students with autism spectrum disorder are typically classified as "severely multiple disabled." However, a current resource published for Saskatchewan teachers presents this definition: [*Teaching Students With Autism: A Guide for Educators* (1999), Saskatchewan Education, Special Education Unit; available at http://www.sasked.gov.sk.ca]. "Autism is a pervasive developmental disorder which is characterised by impairments in communication and social interaction, and restricted, repetitive stereotypic patterns of behaviour, interests and activities (American Psychiatric Association (APA), 1994). It is a complex neurological disorder that affects the functioning of the brain."

10. Traumatic brain injury. Students with acquired brain injury are not classified separately. Depending on the degree of disability, they are accounted for in either "chronically health impaired" or "severely multiple disabled" classifications.

<u>Cross-National Category B</u>
3. Social, emotional or behavioural disorder. Regulation 49g: "Socially, emotionally or behaviourally disabled, that is when a thorough diagnostic study by medical and educational personnel affirms that the pupil exhibits excessive, chronic deviant behaviour which adversely affects educational performance."
6. Learning disabilities. Regulation 49d: "In Division 1 to 4 and is severely learning disabled, that is when assessment by a qualified personnel acceptable to the minister affirms that: 1) the pupil has an intelligence quotient of 85 or higher, as measured by an approved individual test; 2) there is a significant discrepancy, one standard deviation or greater, between aptitude and achievement; and 3) the pupil's average rate of progress in the skills subjects, including reading, is not greater than half that of average pupils as measured by an approved individual test."

Czech Republic

<u>Cross-National Category A</u>
1. Mentally retarded. Students in educational system with mental handicaps (in special schools, special classes, regular schools) that need reduced education or special educational plans. We also include here children that are hardly mentally retarded in auxiliary schools, where they take education in very reduced educational plans.
2. Hearing handicaps. Students with all hearing handicaps – deaf and partially hearing – that need special educational approach (in special schools, special classes, regular schools).
3. Sight handicaps. Students with all sight handicaps – blind and partially sighted – that need special educational approach (in special schools, special classes, regular schools).
4. Speech handicaps. Students with all speech handicaps that need special educational approach (in special schools, special classes, regular schools).
5. Physical handicaps. Students with all physical handicaps that need special educational approach (in special schools, special classes, regular schools).
6. Multiple handicaps. Students with all combinations of handicaps that need special educational approach.
9. Other handicaps. All other handicapped children (that are not defined in the other categories).
10. With weakened health. (Kindergarten only) Children with weakened health in kindergartens that need special educational approach.

<u>Cross-National Category B</u>
7. Students in hospitals. Students in hospitals (and attending schools in hospitals), students in medical institutions.
8. Development, behaviour and learning problems. Students with all development, behaviour and learning problems (including disgraphics, dyslexic children, etc.) that need special educational approach.

<u>Cross-National Category C</u>
11. Socially disadvantaged children, preparatory classes in regular schools. Children in special classes for socially disadvantaged children in regular schools, students from reformatory educational institution for children and youth.

Finland

Cross-National Category A
2. Moderate mental impairment (MOMI). Education for mentally disabled students needing adjustment of curriculum and extensive support (education for students with moderate or severe mental impairment).
3. Most severe mental impairment (SMI). Education for mentally disabled students with a curriculum based on training of everyday activities and with extensive support (education for students with most severe mental impairment).
4. Hearing impairment (HI). Education according to the curriculum for the hearing impaired.
5. Visual impairment (VI). Education according to the curriculum for the visually impaired.
6. Physical and other impairment (POHI). Education according to the curriculum for the disabled (physical disabilities, neurological disabilities, developmental disorders).
8. Other impairments. Education according to other special needs curricula (*e.g.* general education curriculum for hospital teaching).

Cross-National Category B
1. Mild mental impairment (MIMI). Education for children and young persons needing adjustment of curriculum and extra support (education for students with mild mental impairment). Adjustment may concern all or only some subjects.
7. Emotional & social impairment (EI). Education according to the curriculum for the maladjusted.
9. Speech difficulties. Part-time special needs education for students with speech difficulties.
10. Reading and writing difficulties. Part-time special needs education for students with reading and writing difficulties.
11. Speech, reading and writing difficulties. Part-time special needs education aimed at relieving speech, reading and writing difficulties.
12. Learning difficulties in mathematics. Part-time special needs education aiming at relieving learning difficulties in mathematics.
13. Learning difficulties in foreign languages. Part-time special needs education aiming at relieving learning difficulties in foreign languages.
14. General learning difficulties. Part-time special needs education aiming at relieving general learning difficulties.
15. Emotional and social difficulties. Part-time special needs education for the maladjusted.
16. Other special difficulties. Part-time special needs education for other difficulties.
18. Remedial teaching. Temporary teaching usually provided by a general education teacher for students who have temporarily fallen behind in their studies or who need other special support (part-time teaching).

Cross-National Category C
17. Remedial teaching for immigrants. Periodical remedial teaching for students who have moved to Finland from abroad; mother tongue teaching for Sami, Romany and foreign-language speakers; and teaching for Finnish students who have moved back to Finland from abroad in order to maintain the language skills they have acquired abroad (part-time teaching).

France

Cross-National Category A
1. Severe mental handicap. Severe mental handicap (IQ between 20 & 34) concerns persons who can benefit from the systematic learning of simple gestures.
2. Moderate mental handicap. Moderate mental handicap (IQ between 35 & 49) concerns persons able to acquire simple notions of communication, hygiene and elementary safety as well as simple manual skills, but who are incapable of learning how to do arithmetic or reading.
3. Mild mental handicap. This category covers handicaps as regards intelligence, memory and thinking. It concerns persons (IQ between 50 & 70) capable of learning practical skills and how to read, as well as notions of arithmetic thanks to special education, and who can be taught a certain degree of socialisation.
4. Physical handicap. Orthopaedic and motor deficiencies have been broadly interpreted as covering the structure of the body and its visible parts. Such handicaps include mechanical and functional alterations to the face, head, neck, trunk and limbs, as well as limbs which are missing in whole or in part.
5. Metabolic disorders. Metabolic or nutritional disorders include abnormal development and maturation, gluten intolerance, diabetes, malnutrition, and weight loss or gain (but exclude thinness and obesity).

6. Deaf. Disorders in this category concern not only the ear but also its ancillary parts and its functions. The most important sub-division is that of hearing impairment. The term "deaf" should only be applied to persons whose hearing impairment is such that it cannot be helped by any hearing aid. Like blindness, deafness is a serious sensory impairment.

7. Partially hearing. Disorders in this category concern not only the ear but also its ancillary parts and functions. The most important sub-division is that of hearing impairment.

8. Blind. Blindness is a serious sensory impairment. Such impairment may be marked (very poor vision or partial blindness), almost total (severe or almost total blindness) or total (no perception of light). It may affect one eye or both.

9. Partially sighted. Other visual impairments include astigmatism, accommodation deficiency, diplopia (strabismus), amblyopia, and sensitivity to light.

10. Other neuropsychological disorders. Neuropsychological disorders have been defined to include any interference with the basic elements of the mental process. This being so, the functions listed are those which normally involve the presence of basic neuropsychological and psychological mechanisms.

11. Speech and language disorders. Speech disorders or impairment include artificial larynx, severe dysarthria, lack of voice expression, and stuttering; while language disorders or impairment include central impairment of the visual function with inability to communicate (*e.g.* severe dyslexia).

12. Other deficiencies. Other deficiencies are all those not mentioned above.

13. Multiply handicapped. Children or young people in special educational establishments suffer from a main handicap, which is usually the reason they are attending special classes. But they may suffer from other disorders in addition to this main one.

<u>Cross-National Category B</u>

15. Learning difficulties. Special 3rd year classes and 4th year vestibule classes (second level) provide assistance and support to pupils with problems at school and unable to derive benefit from the general and technical instruction normally given. Together with remedial classes, they form part of the system of assistance, support and insertion. SEGPAs (special sections for general or occupational training) are incorporated into public and private secondary schools (usually lower secondary ones). They make it easier for pupils with learning difficulties to pursue their studies.

<u>Cross-National Category C</u>

14. Non-francophone students. Initiation classes (CLINs) have been created in primary schools for non-French speaking pupils of foreign nationality. Reception classes, in 1st to 4th year secondary (but mainly 1st year), are offered to foreign pupils (in principle, non-French speaking, newly arrived in France and whose age corresponds to that of the school).

16. Disadvantaged children – ZEP. "Zones of Education Prioritaires" (ZEP) are geographical surfaces – communes, districts – in which a policy of differentiated education is essential. Two types of criteria governed the delimitation of these underprivileged surfaces: first, school (rate of redoubling, density in vocational schools, classes of reception, etc.); second, socio-economic (low level of study of the parents, poverty, unemployment, discomfort of the dwellings, maladjustment to the language or the culture). "Zones of Education Prioritaires" are also and especially a community project of development centred on the school and aiming at make the children of popular medium enjoy fully their rights to education.

Germany

<u>Cross-National Category A</u>

2. Partially sighted or blind. Students: 1) having a central visual acuity in the better eye or in both eyes of 0,3 or less for the distance despite a correction by glasses but without other aids; or 2) having a visual acuity of 0,3 Nieden V) or less for the proximity regarding a working distance of at least 30 centimetres; or 3) whose faculty of vision is impaired to a similar degree despite better visual acuity; or 4) blind children or youths without visual faculty or whose visual faculty is largely impaired resulting in an inability to act like seeing persons (even after an optical correction, *e.g.* glasses).

3. Partially hearing or deaf. Children or youth who suffer a loss of hearing of more than 90 db in the frequency range above 500 cps or whose ability to hear is affected in such way that even with hearing aids they need special education; or deaf students who, irrespective of their actual deficiency in hearing capacity, are not capable of noticing acoustic signals of their environment and making use of them for acquiring speech, speech hearing and an active or passive phonetic speech competence.

4. Speech impairment. Children or youth whose speech and development of speaking is largely impaired because of 1) Marked underdevelopment of speech with symptoms of multiple or universal stammering and/or dysfunctional grammar; 2) Disorders in trained speech required at an early stage (aphasia, dysphasia); 3) Central handicaps in speech development (audimutisimus, acute agnosia); 4) Morbid changes in the speech organs so that entry into or staying in a regular school with ambulant school-accompanying promotion programs is regarded as insufficient.
5. Physically handicapped. Children or youth with cerebral motor disturbances, myopathia, malformations, paraplegia and other resulting in disorders, retardations, deficits in locomotion and other disabilities which imply the need for special education and further measures and facilities.
6. Mentally handicapped. Children or youth who are severely mentally disabled as a result of damage to the central nervous system before or after birth and who have conspicuous peculiarities in their cognitive and emotional absorption and storage processes, expressive behaviour, motor abilities and their verbal and non-verbal communication.
8. Sick. Children who are being treated in clinics, hospitals or sanatoriums for a longer period of time and who are capable of taking part in lessons; as well as students with chronic illnesses who cannot therefore take part in regular instructions.
9. Multiple handicaps. Children and youth with more than one handicap to be considered in the development of learning.
11. Autism. Children and youth with a severe developmental disability in verbal and non-verbal communication and social interaction with resistance to environmental changes and mostly engaged in repetitive activities and stereotyped movements based on complex impairment of the central nervous system. No statistical data of the large groups available, but programmes are provided.

<u>Cross-National Category B</u>
1. Learning disability. Children or youth needing promotion through special education due to a severe, extensive and long lasting deficiency in learning development, in thinking, remembering, using language, perception, movement, emotion and interaction. The relation between self and environment is lasting difficult. Aims and contents of the mainstream curricula cannot be fulfilled.
7. Behavioural disorders. Children or youth with behavioural and conduct disorders and/or emotional disorders; therefore they need special education to develop the abilities of appropriate experiences and social competences.
10. Unknown, no information, uncategorised. Not available.
12. Remedial instruction. Students in need of support because of particular and limited difficulties in basic skills concerning reading, writing or numeracy. No statistical data of the large groups available, but programmes are provided.

<u>Cross-National Category C</u>
13. Travelling families. Children and youth in need of support because their parents are itinerant workers (circus, fairs, barges). No statistical data of the large groups available, but programmes are provided.
14. German for speakers of other languages. Children and youth in need of support because they don't have appropriate competence in German, so that they cannot follow instructions with adequate effect and success. No statistical data of the large groups available, but programmes are provided.

Greece

<u>Cross-National Category A</u>
1. Visual impairments. We use the term blind for students that cannot read printed materials and acquire knowledge through vision. The term "Blind" refers to students who learn via Braille or other non-visual media. The term "partially sighted" refers to students who require adaptation in lighting or the size of print in order to learn through reading. The Greek Educational system insists that students use their residual vision so that the sensory motor abilities may be reinforced and delays or losses in orientation, mobility, communication, cognitive, and/or social development may be prevented. Blind students attend Special Education schools at the primary level of education and mainstream schools at the secondary level of education. There is no differentiation or special provision for partially sighted students. Blind and partially sighted students follow the common core educational curricula. Flexible curricula are now being prepared for this category so that blind may be integrated in mainstream schools.
2. Hearing impairments. The term "deaf" refers to students who are severely impaired in processing linguistic information through hearing, with or without amplification. The term "hearing impaired" refers to students whose impairment in hearing, whether permanent or fluctuating, adversely affects the educational performance. Thus, deafness prevents an individual from receiving sound in all or most of its forms. In contrast, a child with a hearing

loss can generally respond to auditory stimuli, including speech. The distinction between deaf and hearing impaired is indispensable for diagnosis. The ability to learn oral skills depends in large on the degree of hearing impairment. It also depends on the age at which the student became deaf (especially whether it was before or after acquiring spoken language), the timing of diagnosis of the impairment, the onset of early intervention, the family and the educational system. The new draft law of Special Education stresses the importance of early diagnosis. A team consisting of a primary school teacher, a secondary school teacher, a psychologist, a social worker and an administrative officer will serve at each Centre for Diagnosis, Assessment and Pedagogical Support. Some centres will be additionally staffed with specialists such as a pre-school teacher, a speech therapist and a child specialist. Deaf students follow the common core curricula, which are appropriately adapted to meet their needs with emphasis given on spoken psychologist, an audiologist and a sign language and on articulation. The national educational system provides students with equal opportunities for education and vocational training and promotes social integration. Deaf and partially hearing students attend Special Education Schools (pre-school, primary and secondary) as well as special classes at secondary education.

3. Physical impairment. Motor impaired/orthopaedic disabilities include a heterogeneous grouping of conditions with a wide range of causes. Examples of some of the more common causes are: Nervous system disorders, Traumatic spinal cord injury, Muscular Dystrophy, Cerebral Palsy, Epilepsy, Muscular-skeletal disorders, Cardiovascular disease, Coronary heart disease, Respiratory Disorders, Emphysema, Asthma, Endocrine-metabolic, Diabetes, and Amputation of all types. In Greece, students with motor disabilities attend Special Education schools but the curricula are those of primary and secondary education even though a high percentage of the students is unable to keep up. Furthermore, students spend fewer hours in following curricula, which have not been fully adapted to cover their special education needs, and teachers have not been trained accordingly. Primary school teachers attend a two-year training course. The Ministry of Education and Religious Affairs designed training programs on Special Education for secondary education teachers, which were implemented by universities within the 2nd European Community Support Framework.

4. Mental impairments. The term mental impairments varies considerably. Mental retardation means significantly sub-average general intellectual functioning existing concurrently with deficits in adaptive behaviour and manifested during the developmental period that adversely affects a child's educational performance. Difficulties may occur in communication, in social, academic, vocational, and independent living skills. A child may develop slowly without being mentally retarded or it may be retarded without slow development being present. We can define mental retardation if there are procedures and tests related to the type of retardation and if the genetic conditions and the environmental hazards are in any case examined. According to 603/82 Presidential decrees, an individual is diagnosed and classified as having mental retardation by a qualified team of doctors and educators and by prefectural committees. The team gives one or more standardised (intelligence and adaptive skills) tests, on an individual basis. The test results determine the educational setting that is most appropriate for the student. Students with mental impairments are characterised by the team as able to be educated (I.Q. 50-70) able to be trained and (I.Q. 30-50) profoundly retarded (under 30). According to the diagnosis, the Ministry of Education classifies the students to the appropriate school unit.

5. Autism. Autistic children may present profound or less severe difficulties in behaviour. Development may present unsteadiness unlike mental retardation that can have slower but steadier improvement. The Law 1566/85 for Special Education determines the attitude of the National Educational System in Greece towards children with autism (estimated total number 30 000 of which 6 000 are of school age). According to this law, children with autism are not categorised as handicapped. As a result, the Educational System has no special provision for these students regarding specialised diagnostic committees or personnel (psychologists, speech therapists, social workers) and teachers specialised in this area. The new draft law of April 1994 proposed considerable changes in the framework of special education, one of them being the inclusion of autism as a special educational difficulty. Children with autism are under the supervision of the Ministry of Health and Welfare and are educated at special institutions. More and more children are being admitted in Special Education Schools of the Ministry of Education where there is provision in the form of special educational programmes. This policy signals an effort to prevent children with autism from being institutionalised and include them in primary education. The goals (academic and non-academic) and objectives of the educational programs may include social skills, functional skills (dressing, toilet training, feeding oneself, etc.), communication, and behaviour modification. For the first time during the year 1998-99 within the Operational Plan "Education and Initial Vocational Training" of the 2nd European Community Support Framework, teachers were trained in the special educational needs of autism.

Cross-National Category B
6. Learning difficulties. By learning difficulties, we refer to difficulties due to various reasons and factors: pathological, socio-economic, psychological, unfavourable school environment. This umbrella category shelters several sub-categories of learning difficulties, *e.g.* students with dyslexia (5% in Greece, data of 1994), with behaviour disturbances, communication disorders, emotional disturbance, neurological disorders, solitary behaviour,

rejection due to racial and socio-economic factors, aggressiveness, etc. resulting to social maladjustment and marginalisation. Students follow the common core curriculum but they are provided with special teaching supports in one or more subjects outside the school programme. A special class can be established with the decision of the District Educational Authority, the school advisor of special education and the mainstream school unit of the student, according to the Presidential Decrees 603/83 and 472/83. Teachers are expected to have deep knowledge of the learning difficulty, special training in selecting the appropriate pedagogical approach and accuracy in using the methodology needed.

7. Multiple impairment. This category includes students studying in special schools in some regions of the country. Students happen to present hearing, visual or sensory-motor educational needs but it is not possible for them to follow the special school for their category. This is the case of some regions in remote areas. Students cannot leave their homes and the state educational system establishes a special school unit in which support is provided according to the particular need of the child. Students of category 8 may also be met in this category of special schools in remote areas of the country.

Cross-National Category C
8. Socio-economic/cultural educational difficulties. This category has been included for the needs of this research, and classified in Category C. Students of this category present social disadvantages, which rise from their socio-economic status as well as from their cultural and/or linguistic differentiations. Students of this category do not fall within the framework of the Law of Special Education. (Article 1. (3): "Students whose mother tongue is not Greek, are not considered as students with special educational needs"). They are classified instead in the "Resource definition" as they are provided with extra help and special teaching support. Students of this category follow the common core curricula at primary and secondary level in the regular classes of the mainstream state system of education. Special programmes are planned and implemented by the Ministry of National Education with national and E.U. funds. This category comprises the following populations: 9.7% of students at primary level are of different ethnicity (33 615 Albanians and 24 956 students from countries of Eastern Europe totalling 58 571). Including Muslims (7 065) and Gypsies (8 500), there is a total of 74 136 students or 12.3% of the student population in the general system of education. 3.8% of students at secondary level are of different ethnicity (12 877 Albanians and 14 790 students from countries of Eastern Europe totalling 27 667). Including Muslims (1 912) and Gypsies (1 750), there is a total of 31 329 students or 4.3% of the student population in the general system of education. The percentage of all the above student populations in the general system of State Education is 7.9%. In 1999 the general total of the above populations in State Education was 86 238 whereas in 1996 the general total was 44 093 students.

Hungary

Cross-National Category A
2. Pupils with moderate degree mental retardation. Severe cognitive dysfunction based on impairment of the brain. This group falls into the IQ range 30-50.
3. Pupils with visual disabilities. Blindness or low vision based on impairment of the biological visual organs.
4. Pupils with hearing disabilities. Deafness or hard of hearing based on impairment of the hearing organs.
5. Pupils with motoric disabilities. Various forms of motor dysfunction based on impairment of organs of movement.
6. Pupils with speech disabilities. Various forms of speech disorders based on impairment of the speech organs or based on the slow development of language.
7. Pupils with other disabilities. Various other forms of learning difficulties and/or behavioural problems based on some known or undetected but supposed brain disorder (dyslexia, dysgraphia, autism, etc.)

Cross-National Category B
1. Pupils with mild degree mental retardation. Slight cognitive dysfunction based on impairment of the brain. Definition according to the law. This group belongs to the IQ range 51-70. Many pupils, who were classified as mild mentally retarded, have no brain impairment and therefore could be classified as learning disabled like in many other countries but actually the law of public education does not use the label of learning disability. These are not mentally retarded pupils but learning disabled pupils who would belong to the cross national category B and not category A.

Cross-National Category C
8. Children of minorities. Children of different ethnic minorities and different nationalities.
9. Disadvantaged pupils/Pupils at risk. Disadvantaged pupils/pupils at risk – pupils with behavioural and/or emotional and/or learning problems based on unfavourable environmental conditions according to the law of public education, socially disadvantaged children are not classified as children with special educational needs because they are not disabled. The law however ensures them additional resources, but less than for the children with special educational needs.

Ireland

Cross-National Category A
1. **Visually impaired.** Visually impaired pupils are those who have been formally identified by an ophthalmologist in accordance with agreed criteria.
2. **Hearing impaired.** Hearing impaired pupils are those whose hearing is affected to an extent that renders the understanding of speech through the ear alone, with or without a hearing aid, difficult or impossible.
3. **Mild mental handicap.** Pupils with mild mental handicap have significantly below average intellectual functioning, associated with impairment in adaptive behaviour. Such pupils would lie within the IQ range 50-70.
4. **Moderate mental handicap.** Pupils with moderate mental handicap fall within the I.Q. range 35-50, insofar as an intelligence quotient may be used as an indicator of a general learning disability. Many of these children will have accompanying disabilities.
7. **Physically handicapped.** Pupils with physical handicap have permanent or protracted disabilities arising from conditions such as congenital deformities, spina bifida and/or hydrocephalus, muscular dystrophy, cerebral palsy, brittle bones, haemophilia, cystic fibrosis, asthma or severe accidental injury.
8. **Specific speech and language disorders.** Children with specific speech and language disorders are those whose non-verbal ability is in the average range, or higher, and whose skill in understanding or expressing themselves through the medium of spoken language is severely impaired.
9. **Specific learning disability.** Children with specific learning disability have significant impairments in either reading, writing, spelling or arithmetical notation and it is established that the primary cause of such impairments is not attributable to below average intellectual range, to defective sight/hearing, to emotional factors, to any physical condition or to any extrinsic adverse circumstances.
11. **Severely and profoundly mentally handicapped.** Children in this category are described as having an Intelligence Quotient of 35 or below. (Children with an I.Q. in 35 – 20 range are described as having a "severe" general learning disability. Children with an Intelligence Quotient under 20 are described as having a "profound" general learning disability). Most children in this category will have additional disabilities.
12. **Multiply handicapped.** Children with two or more disabilities are described as having multiple disabilities.

Cross-National Category B
5. **Emotionally disturbed.** This term includes pupils with behavioural and conduct disorders as well as those with emotional disturbance. Emotional disturbance and/or behavioural disorder is defined as an abnormality of behaviour sufficiently marked and prolonged to cause handicap in the pupil and/or serious distress or disturbance in the family, school or community.
6. **Severely emotionally disturbed.** As above (cat. 5) to a more severe level.
15. **Pupils in need of remedial teaching.** Pupils in mainstream schools who have clearly observable difficulties in acquiring basic skills in literacy and/or numeracy or who have some difficulties in learning of a more general nature.

Cross-National Category C
10. **Classes of children of travelling families.** Traveller children are children of families who are identified by themselves and by members of the "settled" community as people with a distinctive lifestyle, traditionally of a nomadic nature even though not now habitually so.
13. **Young offenders.** Children in the age range of 12-16 years who: a) have been convicted of a crime, b) are on remand by the courts, c) are out of control and are under a care order.
14. **Children in schools serving disadvantaged areas.** Educationally disadvantaged areas are those where the quality of the educational environment is low in most of the homes, where the level of education attained by the mother is low in most cases and where there are indicators of relative poverty regarding most homes, *e.g.* living in state housing, having a medical card.
16. **Children of refugees.** Children of parents who have been granted political asylum in Ireland.

Italy

Cross-National Category A
1. **Visual impairment.** Includes blind children and partially sighted children.
2. **Hearing impairment.** Includes deaf children and partially deaf children.

3. **Moderate mental handicap.** This category includes both mild mental retardation and moderate mental retardation It includes therefore those pupils who are classified as "educable" (that is, that can acquire the knowledge in skills demanded of the final year of primary education – age 10- 11) and as "trainable" (that is, that can acquire the knowledge in skills demanded of the second year of primary education – age 7-8). The IQ levels of these pupils range from 70 to 35-40.
4. **Severe mental handicap.** This category includes both the group with serious mental retardation and the group with most serious mental retardation. It includes pupils who can at most acquire a minimum level of communicative language and pupils who at most can acquire very basic self-care and communication skills. The IQ levels of these pupils range from 35-40 to under 20-25.
5. **Mild physical handicap.** Children with a slight motorial impairment and or a manual impairment, that would not prevent from gaining a relative autonomy.
6. **Severe physical handicap.** Children with a profound motorial impairment and or a manual impairment, deeply affecting personal autonomy. These children necessitate adequate and continuous assistance.
7. **Multiple handicap.** Children with two or more of the impairments included in categories from 1 to 6. Residual category.

Cross-National Category C
8. **Students with foreign citizenship.** Approximately 96 000 students with a foreign citizenship attended Italian schools in 1998-99 (20 000 in ISCED0, 44 000 in ISCED1, 21 000 in ISCED2 and 11 000 in ISCED3). Category C – pupils with a foreign citizenship do not directly receive additional resources but benefit rather from the resources allocated to schools to promote and increase activities/projects of inclusion, *e.g.* interculture education, language training, etc.

Japan

Cross-National Category A
1. **Blind and partially sighted.** Those with corrected visual acuity of less than 0.1 for both eyes. Those with corrected visual acuity of over 0.1 but less than 0.3 and who require education through Braille or who will require such as education in the future. Impairment of visual functions other than visual acuity such as contraction of visual field and who require education through Braille or who will require such as education in the future.
2. **Deaf and hard of hearing.** Those with a hearing level of more than 100 decibels for both ears. Those with a hearing level of more than 60 decibels but less than 100 decibels and who find it either impossible or extremely difficult to comprehend normal speech even with a hearing aid.
3. **Intellectual disabilities.** Severe – Moderate – Mild and those who particularly lack social adaptability.
4. **Physically disabled.** Those who find it impossible or extremely difficult to maintain their posture, write, or walk, and those with similar disabilities. Those with milder disabilities and who require medical observation and guidance for more than six months.
5. **Health impaired.** Those with a chronic disease of heart, chest or kidney and who require more than 6 months of medical care or restricted living. Those who are physically weak and require more than 6 months of restricted living.
6. **Speech impaired.** Those with speech impairment other than with speech impairment resulting from deafness, hard of hearing, cerebral palsy, and intellectual disabilities.
7. **Emotionally disturbed.** Those with emotional disturbance other than with emotional disturbance accompanied with intellectual disability or health impairment.

Cross-National Category C
8. **Students who require Japanese instruction**

Luxembourg

Cross-National Category A
1. **Mental characteristic.** Developmental retardation.
2. **Emotionally disturbed children.** Behavioural problems, hyperactivity, aggressiveness.
3. **Sensory characteristic.** Visual impairment, speech impairment.
4. **Motor characteristic.** Cerebral disability.

Cross-National Category B
6. **Learning difficulties.** Dyslexia, dyscalculia.

Cross-National Category C
5. **Social impairment.** Children from socially low established families, children from minorities.

Mexico

Cross-National Category A

1. **Blindness.** Children or youth without visual faculty or whose visual faculty is largely impaired. Optical correction does not improve their visual capacity and they can not function like seeing persons. This is usually a permanent condition. Blind persons require alternative options and/or equipment for curriculum accessibility. They have serious problems of displacement and need special instruction to obtain autonomy for self-care. Blindness does not affect intellectual performance.

2. **Partial visual disability.** It is the diminution of the visual sharpness in both eyes. People with partial visual disability benefit from optical supports such as: magnifying glasses, eyeglasses, binoculars or amplifying screens, but they can not read regular size text or images. They can overcome problems for curriculum accessibility through special equipment or alternative written language supports. They need references to be able to move from one place to another. Regularly they can only see shades or bulks. Visual disability can be progressive until it becomes blindness. This condition does not affect the person's intellectual performance.

3. **Intellectual disability.** This category includes different grades of intellectual disability which, in Mexico, used to be related to I.Q. Since legislation for the adoption of the integration policy, intellectual disability was re-conceptualised. Now it is categorised in relation to the child's performance in his interaction with the environment. It implies significant sub-average general intellectual functioning, learning difficulties and slow development of adaptive behaviour, all of which affect a child's educational performance. In the school context, students with intellectual disability show more difficulties than the rest of his or her peers to understand instructions, abstract concepts and metaphorical or figurative language. As a result, they show dependent conduct and require support to finish any learning activity, especially when it involves a new concept or concept relations. They demand more interactivity with the environment to understand concepts and to have longer periods of attention and concentration. In synthesis, they require full interaction with an enriched learning context for the development of basic learning competence and skills. Children with intellectual disability are also slow in the development of social skills and in the control of their emotional feelings and reactions. Most of these minors can attend basic education in the regular school, with support and curricular adaptations, including flexibility.

4. **Auditory or hearing disability.** The auditory disability is a superficial to moderate loss of hearing. Persons with auditory disability can benefit from the use of a hearing aid to perceive oral language and develop it. Children with auditory disability can develop a great ability for lip-reading as a strategy for better oral language comprehension and thus, better communication skills. This condition does not affect the person's intellectual performance. Some children with mild hearing disability can also learn sign language as a first or second language to communicate with non-oral deaf persons or to act as interpreters.

5. **Deafness or severe auditory disability.** Deafness is a severe sensorial impairment that does not allow hearing and (therefore) the development of oral language. Deaf children use sign language as their mother tongue but can also learn the national oral language after special education intervention. They must learn written language as means of communication with the hearing population and for accessibility to the written learning environment (books, letters, notes, computer information, etc.) They can also develop lip-reading skills to facilitate and enhance their communication with the majority hearing society. Deafness does not affect the person's intellectual performance, but the development of a sign, oral or written language is necessary for the complete development of their intellectual potential and their accessibility to the basic learning curricular competencies.

6. **Motor disability.** This category includes moderate to severe motor disability. Moderate motor disability: when the person's motor condition is determined by peripheral damage. This means that the disability is partial and only affects the movement or the co-ordination of movements of specific parts of the body. Severe Motor Disability: when the person's motor condition is determined by central neurological damage that affects the overall movements (as in cerebral palsy). In both cases but in different degrees, architectonic, physical adaptations of the school environment are required to enhance accessibility, as well as the use of special school furniture and equipment in classrooms. The provision of these adaptations determines success in the integration of children with motor disability to mainstream education. Students with severe motor disability require additional adaptations and supports for fine co-ordination of movements for speech pronunciation, writing, drawing, and other skills related to inputs and outputs of the learning context. Motor disability is generally a permanent condition but does not affect the person's intellectual potential.

7. **Multiple disability.** Students with two or more of the disabilities included in categories from 1 to 6.

Cross-National Category B

8. **Learning difficulties.** Children evidence their difficulties when starting primary school or as soon as they start formal contact with the school curriculum, especially in reading, writing or mathematics. They do not have disabilities and they evidence average or above average intelligence. Normally, their language development is good, although, some of them have associated speech pronunciation problems. These difficulties are not associated with

disadvantages, and have been recently classified as a disruption between the child and the learning context. Learning difficulties are often transitory and can be overcome with transformation of the learning environment, especially through teachers' orientation to significant learning in the classroom in contrast with mechanical, non-significant learning.

9. Outstanding capabilities and skills. These children are described as those who show above average skills in one or several areas of knowledge. Access to curriculum looks easy for them; they show commitment with learning, they are persistent in the fulfilment of tasks and show great creativity in problem solving. Frequently, they show special talents in one or more academic, personal or social areas.

<u>Cross-National Category C</u>
10. Compensatory educational needs. Are those present in all students who attend regular, general or indigenous education services, which have limitations in structure, equipment, stability of the teaching staff and/or low productivity in the school performance indicators. Therefore, additional resources are supplied to the school and/or to the child to assure their access to the school curriculum and the acquisition of basic learning competence with quality and equity.
11. Community educational needs. Students that live in small communities of less than 500 inhabitants, with high marginality, extreme poverty and population dispersion. These communities lack regular basic schooling services and, in general, have linguistic and cultural characteristics of their own, different from those that define behavioural patterns of the national school culture.
12. Indigenous community educational needs. Indigenous education promotes the development of capabilities and skills of those who belong to cultural and linguistic contexts of the indigenous Mexican groups. The educational models are suited to the specific conditions and characteristics of the different cultural and ethnic groups. Largely due to the isolation and population dispersion of the majority of their settlements throughout the national territory, these indigenous people suffer from severe underdevelopment, which reduces their living standards and limits their possibilities for growth. The general aims and objectives of the national curriculum encompass the education provided to indigenous children and grant the necessary adaptations to cater to Mexico's cultural diversity.
13. Migrant educational needs. The Migrant Agricultural Population goes from his/her hometown to another economic region or zone where temporal workforce is required. Sixty per cent belongs to diverse ethnic groups with majority of monolingual or incipiently bilingual members. They live during the harvest in agricultural camps, which they share with migrants from other ethnic groups. The many migratory routes, the diversity of cultures and languages that converge in each camp, and the difficulty to foresee the length of the agricultural cycles have a negative impact in planning and delivery of the educational services targeted to these workers and their families.

Netherlands
<u>Cross-National Category A</u> **1. Deaf children.** **2. Hard of hearing.** **3. Language and communication disabilities.** **4. Visual handicap.** **5. Physically handicapped/motor impairment.** **6. Other health impairments.** (No long hospitalisation) **8. Profound mental handicap/severe learning disabilities.** **9. Deviant behaviour.** **10. Chronic conditions requiring pedagogical institutes.** **11. Multiply handicapped.** <u>Cross-National Category B</u> **7. Learning and behaviour disabilities.** **13. Children in vocational training with learning difficulties.** <u>Cross-National Category C</u> **12. Children from disadvantaged backgrounds.**

Poland

Cross-National Category A
1. **Light mental handicap.** This category covers handicaps as regards intelligence, memory and thinking. It concerns persons (IQ between 51 and 67) capable of learning practical skills and how to read, as well as notions of arithmetic thanks to special education, and who can be taught a certain degree of socialisation.
2. **Multiple and severe mental handicap.** Multiple mental handicap – IQ between 36 and 51, concerns persons able to acquire simple notions of communication, hygiene and elementary safety as well as simple manual skills, but who are incapable of learning how to do arithmetic or read. Severe mental handicap – IQ between 20 and 35, concerns persons who can benefit from the systematic learning of simple gestures.
3. **Profound mental handicap.** Profound mental handicap -IQ between 0 and 19, concerns persons who have many problems with learning of simple gestures.
4. **Blind.** Blind – total lack of sight. Acuity of sight on level 0.00 diopter, or acuity of sight no larger than 0.00 diopter, limited field of vision no longer than 20 degrees, regardless of acuity of sight.
5. **Partially sighted.** Acuity of sight between 0.05 and 0.3 diopter; field of vision limitation to 20 degrees, regardless of acuity of sight (acuity of sight can be better than 0.3 diopter).
6. **Deaf.** Lack perception of sounds or loss of hearing between 80 and 90 dB; the most raised voice can't be heard on various frequencies.
7. **Partially hearing.** Loss of hearing between 40 and 80 dB (students can use an apparatus for test of hearing systematically; students have to use a hearing aid).
8. **Chronically sick.** Refers to students who suffer from various psychosomatic illnesses. It is the reason of long-lasting hospital, health resort or home treatment. Schools are organised in hospitals, health resorts. Organisation and range of classes is adjusted to abilities of sick children.
9. **Motion handicapped.** Refers to students with various forms of motor dysfunction based on impairment of organs of movement. Students have to use: artificial limb, wheelchair, balcony or others.
11. **Autistic.** Refers to students with non-specific developmental disturbance since birth. Autistic students present psychomotor problems, which prevent them from being included in the social environment and the regular educational system. Developmental disability significantly affecting verbal and non-verbal communication and social interaction. Other characteristics often associated with autism are engagement in repetitive activities and stereotyped movements, resistance to environmental change or change in daily routines.

Cross-National Category C
10. **Social disadvantages, behaviour difficulties.** Refers to students who don't accept current social norm. It manifests social negative tendency in behaviour, inability to function in the group, disturbance of emotional process.

Spain

Cross-National Category A
1. **Hearing impaired.** Students with partial or complete hearing loss.
2. **Motor impaired.** Motor system alteration due to a deficient osteo-articular, muscular and/or nervous system activity.
3. **Visual impaired.** Significant or complete vision loss.
4. **Mental handicap.** Intellectual performance significantly below average and substantial limitations in adoptive development, revealed before age 18.
5. **Emotional behavioural problems.** Personality alteration, generally linked with psychosis and autism.
6. **Multiple impairment.** Two or more concurrent disabilities

Cross-National Category B
7. **Highly gifted.** Intellectual capability above average, high degree of devotion to tasks and creativity level.
9. **Programmes addressed to students in hospitals or with health problems.** Addressed to students who have serious health problems and are hospitalised or housebound.
11. **Learning difficulties.** Refers to temporary learning difficulties (dyslexia is included in this category).

Cross-National Category C
8. **Students with compensatory education needs.** Addressed to students with social or cultural problems that are the cause of a delay in the achievement of knowledge.
10. **Problems addressed to itinerant students.** Addressed to students whose parents are itinerant workers (temporary, circus, fairs).

Sweden

Cross-National Category A
1. Pupils with impaired hearing, vision and physical disabilities. Special schools exist for deaf, hard-of-hearing, sight-impaired and speech- or language-impaired children with secondary disabilities. There are eight

special schools in Sweden with approx. 800 students. Most intellectually handicapped children, though, attend compulsory school for those with learning difficulties (cat 2) or are integrated in regular schools (cat 5, 6). Special school is of ten years' duration and has its own syllabus. Term grades are awarded from year 9 and leaving certificates are awarded at the end of year 10. The same rules apply to the assessment of grades as in compulsory school, but the criteria are in respect of year 10 (instead of 9). Suitable parts of those national tests used in compulsory school may be used in special school.
2. Students with mental retardation. Compulsory school and upper secondary school for the mentally retarded has the same curriculum as other compulsory and upper secondary schools but has its own syllabus adapted to this type of schooling and the pupils. Compulsory school for mentally retarded comprises compulsory basic school for the mentally handicapped and training school. It involves nine years of compulsory schooling and in addition to this, pupils are entitled to a tenth, optional school year to supplement their education. Compulsory basic schools for the mentally handicapped are attended by pupils with minor difficulties. They are basically taught the same subjects as pupils in regular compulsory schools. However, the content and scope of the subjects are adapted according to aptitude, with an individual teaching plan for each pupil. Training school pupils have disabilities that prevent them from assimilating instruction in compulsory school for the mentally handicapped. Instead of individual subjects, the training school syllabus has five teaching areas, which together are intended to foster sound, all-round development. Upper secondary school for those with learning difficulties offers vocational education in the same way as regular upper secondary in the form of national, specially designed or individual programmes. All programmes are of four years' duration, apart from individual programmes, and include core subjects and programme-specific subjects. Pupils attending compulsory and upper secondary school for the mentally retarded must be issued a certificate on completion of their studies. A final assessment is also obtainable on request.
3. Students with impaired hearing and physical disabilities. Defined as students in need of special support in their schooling because of their disabilities. Students with impaired hearing and physical disabilities from all over the country can apply to five regular upper secondary schools in Sweden. Almost all deaf students and approx. 20% of the students with impaired hearing or physical disabilities are enrolled in special classes in these schools. Other students in this category attend regular classes.

Cross-National Category C
4. Students receiving tuition in mother tongue (other than Swedish) and/or Swedish as a second language. According to the Education Act and national guidelines all students are entitled to tuition in their mother tongue and tuition in Swedish as a second language if, for example, one or both parents has another mother tongue than Swedish and this language is frequently used at home (for more detailed information on students' rights etc. see the Education Act).
5. Students in need of special support. (Not included in other categories)
Students with special educational needs in inclusive settings, not included in national category 1-4. According to Swedish legislation all students in need of special support are entitled to this. The support is given in various forms in regular schools. We do not currently collect information on this group of students, that can be categorised in CNC C or in CNC B. For students in segregated settings, data is available and presented, but this is a small group relative to all student with special educational need who receive additional resources.

Switzerland

Cross-National Category A
9. Educable mental handicap – Special schools. (See definition category 1). The Swiss Federal Disability Insurance has laid down the following eligibility criteria to receive additional rescues for schooling: * Insured persons with mental retardation, with IQs of 75 and below.
10. Trainable mental handicap – Special schools. (See definition category 1). The Swiss Federal Disability Insurance has laid down the following eligibility criteria to receive additional rescues for schooling: * Insured persons with mental retardation, with IQs of 75 and below.
11. Multiply handicapped – Special schools. (See definition category 1). The Swiss Federal Disability Insurance has laid down the following eligibility criteria to receive additional rescues for schooling: * Insured persons with mental retardation, with IQs of 75 and below.

12. Physical disabilities – Special schools. (See definition category 1). The Swiss Federal Disability Insurance has laid down the following eligibility criteria to receive additional rescues for schooling: * Insured persons with mental retardation, with IQs of 75 and below.
13. Behaviour disorders – Special schools. (See definition category 1). The Swiss Federal Disability Insurance has laid down the following eligibility criteria to receive additional rescues for schooling: * Insured persons with mental retardation, with IQs of 75 and below.
14. Deaf or hard of hearing – Special schools. (See definition category 1). The Swiss Federal Disability Insurance has laid down the following eligibility criteria to receive additional rescues for schooling: * Insured persons with mental retardation, with IQs of 75 and below.
15. Language disability – Special schools. (See definition category 1). The Swiss Federal Disability Insurance has laid down the following eligibility criteria to receive additional rescues for schooling: * Insured persons with mental retardation, with IQs of 75 and below.
16. Visual handicap – Special schools. (See definition category 1). The Swiss Federal Disability Insurance has laid down the following eligibility criteria to receive additional rescues for schooling: * Insured persons with mental retardation, with IQs of 75 and below.
17. Chronic conditions/prolonged hospitalisation – Special schools. (See definition category 1).
18. Multiple disabilities – Special schools. (See definition category 1). The Swiss Federal Disability Insurance has laid down the following eligibility criteria to receive additional rescues for schooling: * Insured persons with mental retardation, with IQs of 75 and below.

<u>Cross-National Category B</u>
1. Learning disabilities/introductory classes – Special classes. The classifications and the assignment of various special schools and classes to categories of special educational needs were established by the Schweizerische Zentralstelle für Heilpädagogik (Swiss Secretariat for Special Education) in co-operation with the cantonal experts. An exact national definition of categories is not available.
2. Learning disabilities/special classes – Special classes. (See definition category 1).
3. Learning disabilities/vocationally oriented classes – Special classes. (See definition category 1).
4. Behavioural difficulties – Special classes. (See definition category 1).
6. Physical disabilities – Special classes. (See definition category 1).
7. Sensory & language impairments – Special classes. (See definition category 1).
8. Students who are ill/hospital classes – Special classes. (See definition category 1).
19. Others of the group "special curriculum" – Special classes. (See definition category 1).

<u>Cross-National Category C</u>
5. Foreign first language. (See definition category 1)

Turkey

<u>Cross-National Category A</u>
1. Visually impaired. (Includes both blind and low vision children) BLIND: The ones whose visual acuity, even after all possible correction, is below 1/10 and who are unable to use their power of vision in their education. LOW VISION: The ones whose visual acuity, even after all possible correction, is between 1/10 and 3/10 and who are unable to use their vision in their education without the use of special materials and methods.
2. Hearing impaired. DEAF: The ones whose loss of hearing, even after all possible correction, is above 70 decibels and who are unable to use their power of hearing in their education. HARD OF HEARING: The ones whose loss of hearing, even after all possible correction is between 25-70 decibels and who are only able to use their power of hearing in their education with the use of hearing aids.
3. Orthopaedically handicapped. The ones who are unable to make use of the educational process satisfactorily because of the defects in their skeleton, nervous system, muscles and joints, even after all possible correction.
4. Educable mentally handicapped. Mentally handicapped whose IQ is between 45-75 as measured by various intelligence scales.
5. Trainable mentally handicapped. Mentally handicapped whose IQ is between 25-45 as measured by various intelligence scales.
6. Speech impairment. The ones who have impairments in the flow, rhythm, and pitch of their speech and in using their voice and articulation effectively.
8. Chronically ill. The ones who need special measures to be taken in their education because of the illnesses which require permanent care and medication.

Cross-National Category B
7. Gifted and talented. The ones whose IQ is 130 or above as measured by various intelligence scales (gifted) and whose IQ is 110 or above as measured by various intelligence scales (talented) who show superior talents in the areas such as fine arts and technical areas as compared to their peers.

United Kingdom

Cross-National Category A
1. Children with statements (records) of special educational needs. The statement (record) of special educational needs is a legal document that sets out the child's needs and all the special help he or she should have, which may include money, staff time and special equipment. It also sets out the responsibility for these resources between the school, local authority and others agencies such as health and social services. The statement (record) will also specify the educational placement of the child – whether in mainstream (regular) school, special school or other form of specialist provision. In England, Wales and Northern Ireland, the vast majority of pupils in special schools will have a statement. In Scotland, a smaller proportion of pupils in special schools will have records.

Cross-National Category B
2. Children with special educational needs without statements (records).

United States

Cross-National Category A
1. Mental retardation. "Mental retardation" means significantly sub-average general intellectual functioning existing concurrently with deficits in adaptive behaviour and manifested during the developmental period that adversely affects a child's educational performance. (34 Code of Federal Regulations §300.7).
2. Speech or language impairment. "Speech or language impairment" means a communication disorder such as stuttering, impaired articulation, language impairment, or a voice impairment that adversely affects a child's educational performance. (34 Code of Federal Regulations §300.7).
3. Visual impairments. "Visual impairment including blindness" means impairment in vision that, even with correction, adversely affects a child's educational performance. The term includes both partial sight and blindness. (34 Code of Federal Regulations §300.7).
5. Orthopaedic impairments. "Orthopaedic impairment" means a severe orthopaedic impairment that adversely affects a child's educational performance. The term includes impairments caused by congenital anomaly (*e.g.* clubfoot, absence of some member, etc.), impairments caused by disease (*e.g.* poliomyelitis, bone tuberculosis, etc.), and impairments from other causes (*e.g.* cerebral palsy, amputations, and fractures or burns that cause contractures). (34 Code of Federal Regulations §300.7).
6. Other health impairments. "Other health impairment" means having limited strength, vitality or alertness, due to chronic or acute health problems such as a heart condition, tuberculosis, rheumatic fever, nephritis, asthma, sickle cell anaemia, haemophilia, epilepsy, lead poisoning, leukaemia, or diabetes that adversely affects a child's educational performance. (34 Code of Federal Regulations §300.7).
8. Deaf/blindness. "Deaf-Blindness" means concomitant hearing and visual impairments, the combination of which causes such severe communication and other developmental and educational problems that they cannot be accommodated in special education programs solely for children with deafness or children with blindness. (34 Code of Federal Regulations §300.7).
9. Multiple disabilities. "Multiple disabilities" means concomitant impairments (such as mental retardation-blindness, mental retardation-orthopaedic impairment, etc.), the combination of which causes such severe educational problems that they cannot be accommodated in special education programs solely for one of the impairments. The term does not include deaf-blindness. (34 Code of Federal Regulations §300.7).
10. Hearing impairments. Hearing Impairment includes deafness and hard of hearing. "Deafness" means a hearing impairment that is so severe that the child is impaired in processing linguistic information through hearing, with or without amplification, that adversely affects a child's educational performance. "Hard of hearing" means impairment in hearing, whether permanent or fluctuating, that adversely affects a child's educational performance but that is not included under the definition of deafness in this section. (34 Code of Federal Regulations §300.7).

11. Autism. "Autism" means a developmental disability significantly affecting verbal and non-verbal communication and social interaction, generally evident before age 3, that adversely affects a child's educational performance. Other characteristics often associated with autism are engagement in repetitive activities and stereotyped movements, resistance to environmental change or change in daily routines, and unusual responses to sensory experiences. The term does not apply if a child's educational performance is adversely affected primarily because the child has a serious emotional disturbance, as defined in paragraph (b)(9) of this section. (34 Code of Federal Regulations §300.7).

12. Traumatic brain injury. "Traumatic brain injury" means an acquired injury to the brain caused by an external physical force, resulting in total or partial functional disability or psychosocial impairment, or both, that adversely affects a child's educational performance. The term applies to open or closed head injuries resulting in impairments in one or more areas, such as cognition; language; memory; attention; reasoning; abstract thinking; judgement; problem-solving; sensory; perceptual and motor abilities; psychosocial behaviour; physical functions; information processing; and speech. The term does not apply to brain injuries that are congenital or degenerative, or brain injuries induced by birth trauma. (34 Code of Federal Regulations §300.7).

13. Developmental delay. "Developmental Delay" means a student "who is experiencing developmental delays, as defined by the State and as measured by appropriate diagnostic instruments and procedures, in one or more of the following areas: physical development, cognitive development, communication development, social or emotional development, or adaptive development and who, by reason thereof, needs special education and related services." (34 Code of Federal Regulations §300.7(b)(1)(2), 300.313(b).)

<u>**Cross-National Category B**</u>
4. Emotional disturbance. "Emotional disturbance" is defined as follows: (i) The term means a condition exhibiting one or more of the following characteristics over a long period of time and to a marked degree that adversely affects a child's educational performance – (A) An inability to learn that cannot be explained by intellectual, sensory, or health factors; (B) An inability to build or maintain satisfactory interpersonal relationships with peers and teachers; (C) Inappropriate types of behaviour or feelings under normal circumstances; (D) A general pervasive mood of unhappiness or depression; or (E) A tendency to develop physical symptoms or fears associated with personal or school problems. (ii) The term includes schizophrenia. The term does not apply to children who are socially maladjusted, unless it is determined that they have a serious emotional disturbance. (34 Code of Federal Regulations §300.7).

7. Specific learning disability. "Specific learning disability" means a disorder in one or more of the basic psychological processes involved in understanding or in using language, spoken or written, that may manifest itself in an imperfect ability to listen, think, speak, read, write, spell, or to do mathematical calculations. The term includes such conditions as perceptual disabilities, brain injury, minimal brain dysfunction, dyslexia, and developmental aphasia. The term does not apply to children who have learning problems that are primarily the result of visual, hearing, or motor disabilities, of mental retardation, of emotional disturbance, or of environmental, cultural, or economic disadvantage. (34 Code of Federal Regulations §300.7).

<u>**Cross-National Category C**</u>
14. Title 1 – Disadvantaged students

ANNEX 2
DISTRIBUTION OF INDIVIDUAL NATIONAL CATEGORIES INTO 22 GENERAL CATEGORIES USED TO DESCRIBE STUDENTS WITH DISABILITIES, DIFFICULTIES AND DISADVANTAGES [1]

	Partially Sighted	Blind	Partially Hearing	Deaf	Emotional and Behavioural Difficulties	Severe Learning Difficulties	Moderate Learning Difficulties	Light Learning Difficulties	Physical Disabilities	Combinatorial Disabilities	Learning Disabilities	Speech and Language Disabilities	Hospital	Other	Autism	Gifted and Talented	Remedial Help	Second Language and Mother tongue teaching	Travelling Children	Disadvantaged Students	Aboriginal and Indigenous	Young offenders
Belgium (Fl.)	6x	6x	7x	7x	3	2x	2x	1	4		8, 11		5	9			10	12x,13,16,17	14	12x		15
Canada (Alb)	13	6	12	5	2,10	1,9	8		4,15	3,16	11	7,14			17							
Canada (BC)	1x	1x	5x	5x	9,10	8	7		14	3,4	2				6	11	12	13			15	
Canada (NB)	4x	4x	4x	4x	1	3x	3x	3x	4x	6	3x,5	2						7				
Canada (SK)	2x	2x	8x	8x	3	1x,10x	1x,10x		4	7	6		5	9								
Czech Rep.	3x	3x	2x	2x	8x	1x	1x		5	6	8x	4	7	9,10						11		
Finland	5x	5x	4x	4x	7,15	3	2	1	6		10,11,12,14	9		8			13,16,18	17				
France	9	8	7	6		1,2	3		4	13	15	11		5,12,10				14		16		
Germany	2x	2x	3x	3x	7	6x	6x		5	9	1	4	8	19				14	13			
Greece	1x	1x	2x	2x	6x	4x	4x	6x	3	7,5x	6x	6x			5x			8x		8x		
Hungary	3x	3x	4x	4x		2	1		5		7x	6		7x				8		9		
Ireland	1x	1x	2x	2x	5,6	11,4	3		7	12	9,15	8						16	10	14		13
Italy	1x	1x	2x	2x		3x,4	3x		5,6	7								8x		8x		
Japan	1x	1x	2x	2x	7	3x	3x	3x	4			6	5					8				
Luxembourg	3x	3x	3x	3x	2	1x	1x	1x	4		6	3x						5x		5x		
Mexico	2	1	4	5		3x	3x	3x	6	7	8				9			11x	13	10,11x	12	
Netherlands	4x	4x	2	1	7x,9	8		13x	5	11	7x,13x	3	10	6				12x		12x		
Poland	5	4	7	6		2,3	1		9			8		11						10		
Spain	3x	3x	1x	1x	5	4x	4x	4x	2	6	11		9			7			10	8		
Sweden	1x	1x	1x,3x	1x		2x	2x		1x,3x				5					4				
Switzerland	16x	16x	14x	14x	13,4	9x,10x	9x,10x		12,6	11,18	1,2,3	7,15	8,17	19				5				
Turkey	1x	1x	2x	2x		5,8x	4		3			6	8x	8x		7						
United States	3x	3x	10x	10x	4	1x,12x	1x,12x	13	5	8,9	7	2		6	11					14		

1. Matrix of 22 national categories covering disabilities, difficulties and disadvantages by country. Since not all countries use all categories there are many empty cells. The number in each cell refers to the number of that category for that particular country as given in Table 3.2. The "x" indicates that the category includes children from one or more of the other 22 categories and therefore on its own makes it non-comparable with a category containing only those children.

ANNEX 3
DATA AVAILABILITY TABLE

	\multicolumn{15}{c}{Cross-national Category A}
	\multicolumn{5}{c}{Special schools}	\multicolumn{5}{c}{Special classes}	\multicolumn{5}{c}{Regular classes}
	Compulsory	Pre-primary	Primary	Lower secondary	Upper secondary	Compulsory	Pre-primary	Primary	Lower secondary	Upper secondary	Compulsory	Pre-primary	Primary	Lower secondary	Upper secondary
BEL (Fl.)	✔	✔	✔	✔	✔	a	a	a	a	a	✔	✔	✔	✔	x
CAN (Alb.)	m	m	m	m	m	a	a	a	a	a	✔	✔	✔	✔	✔
CAN (NB)	a	a	a	a	a	a	a	a	a	a	✔	a	✔	✔	✔
CAN (SK)	m	m	m	m	m	m	m	m	m	m	✔	✔	✔	✔	✔
CHE	✔	a	x	x	a	a	a	a	a	a	m	a	m	m	m
CZE	✔	✔	✔	✔	✔	✔	✔	✔	✔	n	✔	✔	✔	✔	✔
DEU	✔	m	m	m	m	x	x	x	x	x	✔	n	✔	✔	✔
ESP	✔	✔	✔	✔	✔	x	x	x	x	x	✔	✔	✔	✔	✔
FIN	✔	✔	✔	✔	✔	✔	✔	✔	✔	✔	✔	✔	✔	✔	✔
FRA	✔	x	✔	✔	✔	✔	a	✔	✔	a	✔	✔	✔	✔	✔
GRC	✔	m:	✔	m:	m:	✔	✔	✔	✔	x	m	m:	m	m	m
HUN	✔	m:	m:	m:	m	m:	m	m	m	m	m:	m	m	m	m
IRL	✔	a	✔	x	x	m:	a	✔	m:	m:	m	a	✔	m	m
ITA	✔	✔	✔	✔	✔	✔	✔	✔	✔	✔	✔	✔	✔	✔	✔
JPN	✔	✔	✔	✔	✔	✔	a	✔	✔	n	✔	a	✔	✔	a
LUX	✔	x	x	x	x	✔	x	x	x	x	✔	x	x	x	x
MEX	✔	✔	✔	✔	a	✔	✔	✔	✔	m	✔	✔	✔	✔	a
NLD	✔	✔	✔	✔	✔	a	a	a	a	a	✔	a	✔	m:	m
POL	✔	m:	✔	a	m:	m	m	m	m	m	m	m	m	m	m
SWE	✔	a	✔	✔	✔	a	a	a	a	✔	✔	m	✔	✔	✔
TUR	✔	m:	✔	a	m:	✔	a	✔	a	a	m:	m	m:	a	m:
GBR	✔	✔	✔	✔	✔	x	x	x	x	x	✔	✔	✔	✔	✔
USA	✔	a	✔	✔	x	✔	m	✔	✔	x	✔	m	✔	✔	x

	Cross-national Category B														
	Special schools					Special classes					Regular classes				
	Compulsory	Pre-primary	Primary	Lower secondary	Upper secondary	Compulsory	Pre-primary	Primary	Lower secondary	Upper secondary	Compulsory	Pre-primary	Primary	Lower secondary	Upper secondary
BEL (Fl.)	✔	✔	✔	✔	✔	a	a	a	a	a	m:	✔	m:	✔	x
CAN (Alb.)	m	m	m	m	m	a	a	a	a	a	✔	✔	✔	✔	✔
CAN (NB)	a	a	a	a	a	a	a	a	a	a	✔	a	✔	✔	✔
CAN (SK)	m	m	m	m	m	m	m	m	m	m	m	m	m	m	m
CHE	a	a	a	a	a	✔	a	x	x	a	m	a	m	m	a
CZE	✔	✔	✔	✔	a	✔	✔	✔	✔	✔	✔	✔	✔	✔	m
DEU	✔	m:	m	m	m	x	x	x	x	x	✔	n	✔	✔	✔
ESP	a	a	a	a	a	a	a	a	a	a	✔	✔	✔	✔	✔
FIN	✔	✔	✔	✔	✔	✔	✔	✔	✔	✔	✔	m:	✔	✔	m:
FRA	a	a	a	a	a	✔	n	✔	✔	✔	a	a	a	a	a
GRC	m:	✔	✔	✔	x	m:	✔	✔	n	x	m	m	m	m	m
HUN	✔	✔	✔	✔	x	✔	m	✔	x	x	m	m	m	m	m
IRL	x	✔	✔	x	x	m	a	✔	m	m	m	a	✔	m	m
ITA	n	n	n	n	n	n	n	n	n	n	n	n	n	n	n
JPN	n	n	n	n	n	n	n	n	n	n	n	n	n	n	n
LUX	✔	x	x	x	x	✔	x	x	x	x	✔	x	x	x	x
MEX	✔	✔	✔	✔	a	✔	✔	✔	✔	m	✔	✔	✔	✔	a
NLD	✔	✔	✔	✔	✔	✔	a	a	✔	a	✔	n	m	✔	m
POL	n	n	n	n	n	n	n	n	n	n	n	n	n	n	n
SWE	n	n	n	n	n	n	n	n	n	n	n	n	n	n	n
TUR	n	n	n	n	n	n	n	n	n	a	n	n	n	n	n
GBR	✔	✔	✔	✔	✔	x	x	x	x	x	✔	✔	✔	✔	✔
USA	✔	m	✔	✔	x	✔	m	✔	✔	x	✔	m	✔	✔	x

	Cross-national Category C														
	Special schools					Special classes					Regular classes				
	Compulsory	Pre-primary	Primary	Lower secondary	Upper secondary	Compulsory	Pre-primary	Primary	Lower secondary	Upper secondary	Compulsory	Pre-primary	Primary	Lower secondary	Upper secondary
BEL (Fl)	a	a	a	a	a	✔	a	✔	✔	a	✔	✔	✔	✔	✔
CAN (Alb.)	n	n	n	n	n	n	n	n	n	n	n	n	n	n	n
CAN (NB)	n	n	n	n	n	n	n	n	n	n	✔	a	✔	✔	✔
CAN (SK)	n	n	n	n	n	n	n	n	n	n	n	n	n	n	n
CHE	a	a	a	a	a	✔	a	x	x	a	m	a	m	m	a
CZE	✔	✔	✔	✔	✔	n	✔	n	n	n	n	n	n	n	n
DEU	n	n	n	n	n	n	n	n	n	n	n	n	n	n	n
ESP	a	a	a	a	a	a	a	a	a	a	✔	✔	✔	✔	n
FIN	a	a	a	a	a	a	a	a	a	a	✔	a	✔	✔	a
FRA	a	a	a	a	a	✔	n	✔	✔	n	✔	m	✔	✔	✔
GRC	m	m	m	m	m	m	m	m	m	m	✔	✔	✔	✔	✔
HUN	a	a	a	a	x	a	a	a	a	a	✔	m	m	m	m
IRL	✔	a	✔	x	x	a	✔	a	a	a	m	m:	m:	m	m
ITA	a	a	a	a	a	a	a	a	a	a	n	n	n	n	n
JPN	m	m	m	m	m	m	m	m	m	m	✔	a	✔	✔	✔
LUX	n	x	x	x	x	✔	x	x	x	x	m	x	x	x	x
MEX	✔	✔	✔	m	a	m	m	m	m	m	m:	✔	m:	m	a
NLD	a	a	a	a	a	a	a	a	a	a	✔	✔	✔	✔	✔
POL	✔	✔	✔	a	✔	m	n	m	m	m	m	m	m	m	m
SWE	a	a	a	a	a	m	a	m	m	m	m:	m:	m:	m:	m
TUR	n	n	n	n	n	n	n	n	n	n	n	n	n	n	n
GBR	n	n	n	n	n	n	n	n	n	n	n	n	n	n	n
USA	m	m	m	m	m	m	m	m	m	m	✔	m	✔	✔	m

Note: The table indicates the availability of data referring to the total of male and female students in public and private schools combined.
✔ indicates that data are available. Other codes in the table indicate that data are missing (**a** signifies "not applicable"; **m** – "not available"; **m:** – "data available for some national categories within the cross-national category, but not available for others"; **n** – "nil"; **x** – "included in other cells").

ANNEX 4
COMPULSORY SCHOOL EDUCATION[1]

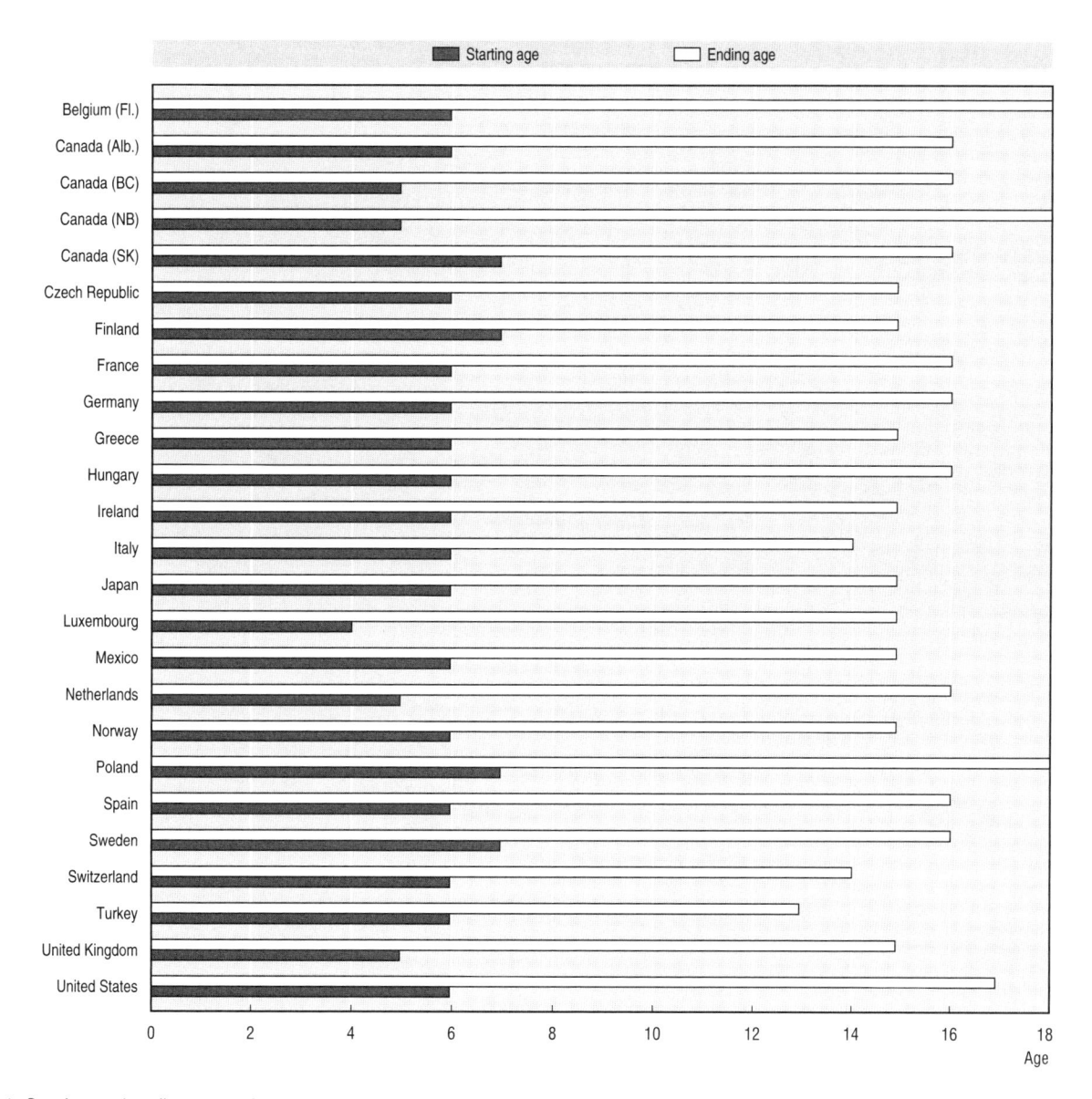

Country	Starting age	Ending age
Belgium (Fl.)	6	18
Canada (Alb.)	6	16
Canada (BC)	5	16
Canada (NB)	5	18
Canada (SK)	7	16
Czech Republic	6	15
Finland	7	15
France	6	16
Germany	6	16
Greece	6	15
Hungary	6	16
Ireland	6	15
Italy	6	14
Japan	6	15
Luxembourg	4	15
Mexico	6	15
Netherlands	5	16
Norway	6	15
Poland	7	18
Spain	6	16
Sweden	7	16
Switzerland	6	14
Turkey	6	13
United Kingdom	5	15
United States	6	17

1. Starting and ending ages of compulsory school education as reported in Table 1 of the electronic questionnaire.

OECD PUBLICATIONS, 2, rue André-Pascal, 75775 PARIS CEDEX 16
PRINTED IN FRANCE
(96 2004 05 1 P) ISBN 92-64-10368-6 – No. 53117 2004